THE
WIDOW'S
GUIDE

THE WIDOW'S GUIDE

*Practical advice on how to deal with grief,
stress, health, children and family, money,
work, and finally, getting back into the world*

ISABELLA TAVES

SCHOCKEN BOOKS · NEW YORK

First published by Schocken Books 1981

10 9 8 7 6 5 4 3 2 1   81 82 83 84

Library of Congress Cataloging in Publication Data

Taves, Isabella.
    The widow's guide.

    1. Widows—United States—Life skills guides.
I. Title.
HQ1058.5.U5T38   646.7   80–6219

Designed by Nancy Dale Muldoon
Manufactured in the United States of America

ISBN 0–8052–3769–0

ACKNOWLEDGMENTS

GRATEFUL acknowledgment is made to the following authors and publishers for permission to reprint copyrighted material:

from Erna Furman, *A Child's Parent Dies*, copyright © 1974 by Erna Furman, reprinted by permission of Yale University Press;

from T. H. Holmes and R. H. Rahe, "Social Readjustment Rating Scale," from *Journal of Psychosomatic Research*, 11:213–218, copyright © 1967 by T. H. Holmes and R. H. Rahe, reprinted by permission of Pergamon Press, Inc.;

from Joshua Loth Liebman, *Peace of Mind*, copyright © 1946 by Joshua Loth Liebman, renewed © 1973 by Fran Liebman, reprinted by permission of Simon & Schuster, Inc.;

from Anne Morrow Lindbergh, *War Within and Without*, copyright © 1980 by Anne Morrow Lindbergh, reprinted by permission of Harcourt Brace Jovanovich, Inc.

from Dave Lindorff, "Advice to the Job-Lorn," from the *Soho News*, 1980, reprinted by permission of Dave Lindorff;

from Jack Riemer, ed., *Jewish Reflections on Death*, copyright © 1974 by Schocken Books Inc., reprinted by permission of Schocken Books;

from Marguerita Rudolph, *Should the Children Know?*, copyright © 1978 by Schocken Books Inc., reprinted by permission of Schocken Books;

from May Sarton, *Journal of a Solitude*, copyright © 1973 by May Sarton, reprinted by permission of W. W. Norton & Company, Inc.

With special thanks to

EDWARD F. BAUMER
Financial Consultants, Los Angeles, California

DORIS LYNCH

MADELEINE KROEPLIN

EDWARD J. MADARA
Consultation and Education Department
St. Clare's Hospital, Denville, New Jersey

LILLY SINGER
Jewish Community Services, Inc., White Plains, New York

BETTY STONE
clinical social worker and child psychotherapist

JUNE WIMPIE
Cancer Care

CONTENTS

A PERSONAL NOTE
TO THE NEW WIDOW

On a blustery winter night, bedded down with a temperature of 103° and shaking with chills, I had a call from old friends, Leon and Paula, inviting me to one of their wonderful Sunday night United Nations suppers.

"I can't," I croaked. "I have the flu."

"Bother the flu," said Leon. "Somebody brought us a whole smoked salmon from England and we've just baked bread. I have some Japanese artists coming and a mysterious Egyptian and Paula has one of her Rhodes Scholar Indians."

"My doctor would kill me."

"Doctors are for the birds. The last time I let a doctor look at me, a dozen years ago, I challenged him to find something wrong. He kept clucking about overweight and working too hard, but he couldn't find a damned thing wrong. I haven't been in a doctor's office since. Come over, we'll cure you."

I couldn't, much as I hated missing one of their parties. And on Sunday night, surrounded by fascinating friends and good food, Leon—loved by so many—dropped dead of a massive heart attack.

Six months later Paula still mourns, "If I had only persuaded him to go to a doctor."

Last Thanksgiving Eve, as I was working my way through a new gourmet recipe for turkey stuffing, I had a call from a dear friend in California. Her voice sounded dead and far away, just as it had a few years earlier when she'd telephoned to say her oldest boy, fifteen, had drowned in a boating accident. Now she said, "I just lost Don. He dropped dead on the tennis court."

Her husband Don was fifty-two. Five years earlier, he had undergone open heart surgery. He had been a championship tennis player, and afterward his doctors encouraged him to keep on playing. Kate, who developed diabetes after the shock of her son's death, now repeats, "I shouldn't have let Don play singles. I knew singles were too hard on him. But I've been such a drag lately, I hated to act like a spoilsport."

And there is Sherry, beautiful, talented Sherry, who last year was on top of the world with a wonderful job and a delightful photographer husband. He went into the hospital with what was diagnosed as jaundice; then they discovered it was cancer. Now he lies in the bedroon day and night, because the hospital could no longer keep him and she could not bear to put him in a nursing home. She goes on working because they need the money. A practical nurse takes care of him by day, and at night Sherry takes over. She is frantic, exhausted, and at times irritated, for a sick man, like a frightened child, can be so irrationally demanding. And she is alone—terribly alone. Her isolation of grief began even before she was a widow, since few outsiders have the courage to pay painful visits to the household of a dying man who sometimes knows them and sometimes doesn't.

Death—whether it comes suddenly or after a long illness—brings shock with it. It is the same whether you are Paula or Sherry, a young career woman or a seasoned diplomat, a wife of many years or the mother of young babies. At first there is a cushion of numbness that protects you from the agony. And then the flood of despair, the regrets and guilt. The fruitless thought that "if only" you had done this or that, you could have saved him, made him happier those last days, prolonged his life. And so often there is denial, whether you recognize it or not, the hoping—dreaming—that you will wake up and find the nightmare is over.

Friends can help. Friends want to help. Letters pour in, the telephone rings, gifts of food appear on the doorstep with notes of sympathy from neighbors. Important people stop in the course of their busy lives to send wires or call, make personal visits to say how much they admired your husband, how he will be missed.

You walk through all this like a zombie. Everybody is being "wonderful," and so are you. You do not cry at the funeral or the memorial service. You stand dry-eyed, shoulders back. An old friend presses your hand and says, "Your husband would have been proud of you."

Then suddenly it all falls apart. Other people remember they have their own problems, their own lives. Just when the numbness is wearing off and you need people, the support disappears. You weep alone, behind locked doors. The subtle sense of isolation makes you feel there is a pane of glass between you and the rest of the world—old friends, family, even children. Gradually there comes bitterness, the resentment because other people still have what you have lost, and because none of the relationships seem strong enought to survive your emotional shifting of gears.

So there you are, with your problems, your regrets, your hurts, and your questions. How are you fixed for money? Will you have to sell the house? Can you afford to send the children to college now? That chest pain—is it a heart attack? And why go to a doctor? Wouldn't a heart attack and oblivion solve everything? What are you going to do about his clothes, hanging there in the clost, reminders of happiness that is lost forever? Have them sent to a thrift shop for strangers to paw over? And what about probate? And taxes? And the insurance papers you can't seem to find? And the children who refuse to go to the cemetery with you, and the friends who complain you go too often?

The reason I wanted—needed—to write this book was not to tell you how sorry I am, even though my heart does indeed bleed for you, but to offer you a practical guide out of the morass, to show you that what you are feeling, strange and agonizing as it may be, is not crazy or self-indulgent or socially inacceptable, but normal and inevitable. To explain to you, as best I can, where to go for help, what to do about money, jobs, lawyers, probate, your children's grief (or seeming lack of it), and sex. Yes, even sex, when the stirrings start again because you are a human being. There are some answers that are easy, some shortcuts that will help. But there are high hurdles and tough obstacles, and you should know about them, too, so that you won't batter your head bloody in the attempt to find quick solutions.

As I see it, there is only one real danger facing you and every other new widow. That is, simply, the danger of becoming a perpetual widow, the sort of woman your friends describe as "hopeless—he has been dead three years and she still can't get over it." I might add that these same friends are undoubtedly part of a modern society that does its best to obstruct the normal channels of grief. The way to avoid perpetual mourning is, as the kids say, to let it all hang out. Only when you have wept, only when you have pounded your pillow and expressed your anger and guilt, will you be able to lose the fear and the void and emerge as a whole person ready for a new life. A better and wiser person, more caring and more worthy of love and friendship, even, I dare suggest, a person more successful in the job market.

I am addressing this book both to the widow and to the woman who is facing her husband's impending death, trying to share his agony along with her own dread of the future. I've included practical advice about costs of funerals and cremation, of lawyers and accountants, because in these days of inflation, money matters are too important to be ignored or solved casually. I have told about husbands—not your own—who move in on the new widow, figuring she will be vulnerable. And the so-called friends who take advantage of your early confusion and try to borrow money. Six major categories are covered: the grieving process, health, money, children, and finally, recovery, the re-building of your life. For I promise you, the healing comes when you have discharged your grief, when you are ready. Underneath all the agony and depression, each of us carries the sustaining spark, the secret little flame of hope. Don't, by denying your grief, let it be smothered.

1

GRIEF IS THE PRICE WE PAY
FOR LOVE

WILLIAM Faulkner once said that between feeling grief and nothing he would choose grief.

Wise words. Reassuring words. To go through life like a zombie without attaching yourself to other human beings is to be a failed person. Virginia Barckley, a public health nurse with the American Cancer Society, wrote in an Ohio health journal:

> All grief must not be thought of as dreary and destructive. The world would be worse without it, if no man's life were significant enough to cause weeping, if birth and death were unmarked, if the measure of our years on earth were nothing, we might be house flies rather than human beings, made in God's image. Profound grief is preceded by deep love which gives life meaning. In the deepest sense, our days would be empty and futile if we never grieved or never, dying, left emotional chaos behind us.

A divorcée, watching her father's grief after the death of her mother, told me, "To have loved someone so much is a blessing not given to many of us. Watching him, I wondered if I would ever care enough for someone to mourn as he did."

Yet it is difficult, when we are suffering so terribly, to be thankful that we have earned the privilege of grief. And it is doubly hard when the outside world seems to lose patience with the widow who can't stop crying.

Psychiatrist Eric Lindemann did a classic study of grief in the

1

early forties after the Boston Coconut Grove nightclub fire. Working with the survivors, he concluded that grief symptoms should be treated like those of a disease that can be cured in time. Modern authorities differ. June Wimpie, senior social worker at the nonprofit New York organization called Cancer Care, says, "Grief isn't like a disease, for you have to get worse before you get better." And Dr. Phyllis Silverman of Harvard says that the widow who is going through a perfectly normal period of grief doesn't need psychiatric treatment but instead "some assurance about the typicalness of what she is feeling."

There is no right way to grieve, nor can anyone supply a timetable for what Lindemann imaginatively called the "reconstruction of identity." We are all different; each one of us must find her own way at her own speed, although it helps to know that our grief symptoms are normal, that others have felt and feel the same way.

In older cultures, there were patterns to follow. In early India, the greatest service a woman could perform for her dead husband was to throw herself on his funeral pyre so she could attend him in afterlife. But this was a privilege of the upper classes; in middle- and lower-caste families, the household could not afford the loss of two workers. Other communities on this subcontinent then forbade the remarriage of widows. They took away their ornaments, shaved their heads, and forced them to live in seclusion, dressed in ugly distinctive costumes. Made thus unattractive, they would not be sexual targets for men outside the family, and so would avoid any danger of bearing children not of the family line.

Patriarchal societies, however, wanted their women to bear children as long as possible. Some of these forced a widow to marry a brother or other male relative of her husband's—usually a younger one—as his first or later wife. An alternative to polygymy was the system known as levirate marriage, whereby a male relative "entered the hut" of the widow to "raise up the seed" of the dead man so that the children she bore as a consequence could be considered as belonging to her dead husband. In Africa there were so-called ghost marriages, where another man married the widow in the name of her dead husband, continued to function as her husband had, caring for the stock, and performed his sexual duties so that the dead man would have at least one son to bear his name. The traditional Jewish practice of the unmarried brother marrying his dead brother's widow is an extension of the same desire to give the dead man a son and continue his seed. In this case the dead man had to have been the first and only husband, and there had to have been no children from the marriage.

None of these customs was designed to benefit the widow, but they did assure her continued membership in the family unit. And bearing children, expecially sons, guaranteed her continued acceptance in the community. In fact, in places like China and India, the widowed mother of grown sons wielded great power over the family, controlling not only her sons and daughters, but her daughters-in-law and grandchildren.

The Victorians of the mid-nineteenth century locked women back into the home with their children, and widows were given the example of Queen Victoria, the perpetual and chronic mourner who promoted her Albert to instant sainthood and turned her life into a shrine for him. In those days—unless a woman was a member of a pioneer society and was needed to help out as an extra hand as well as a producer of children—the widow was turned into an instant old woman, relegated to the kitchen and back parlors of life with the other widows, dressed in black, helping out with the grandchildren. Even in recent years, the widow in Western society not only lost her protector and the father of her children, she forfeited her status in the community. Remarriage, even to an undesirable man, became the only way she could regain her place in a society of couples.

Although the women's rights issue in America began as far back as the 1840s, it has only been in the last decade that the liberation movement has grown roots and flowered. The effect has been felt on women of all ages. Young wives and mothers, born in the fertile forties and fifties of the baby boom, have routinely been part of the labor force. If they dropped out to have children, their interest in business and careers did not lag. Even women born in the twenties and thirties who stayed home after they married— because either they or their husbands wanted it that way—have been far from insulated. Their volunteer work, directing community and charitable projects, has contributed service beyond price to society. Whether she had a previous career or a non-paying job, the widow of today is not helpless. Far from it. Her skills and interests have not rusted. She may not be qualified to get a paying job immediately, or step back into an office and pick up where she left off, but she is far from ready or willing to retreat into the world of past generations, the world where widows played bridge and lunched and cared for grandchildren.

The result is that today's widow faces a dilemma far different from the one her widowed mother or grandmother encountered. When she loses her husband, she loses more than a protector or breadwinner. Her loss is more poignant and cuts deeper. As the result of being very much her own person, the relationship between her and her husband has deepened; otherwise, given the ease of divorce in today's society, one of them would have cut out. Understanding has been strengthened. Mental as well as emotional intimacy has brought them very close. Thus, when her husband dies, she is confronted by the loss not only of a lover, but also of a close companion and friend, someone who knew almost as much about her as she did about herself.

In addition, the widow of today, for all her gains, suffers a serious deprivation. Funerals have become empty rites; weeping and shows of emotion are considered not only unacceptable but embarrassing. So she is not encouraged to express honest feeling, and has no patterns of emotional outlet to follow.

The traditional ways of mourning—the Jewish shivah, the seven days of mourning, the Irish wake—have always had their psychological reasons. They provided necessary emotional outlets for the widow and gave friends and neighbors a way of helping her. Even the often ridiculed casserole brigade of neighbors is seen less and less in our sophisticated urban society. (When my husband died, only one neighbor rang my bell with a bunch of flowers, out-of-season anemones. The rest kept their distance, not out of indifference, I am sure, but from fear of intruding.) And the funeral service, or the memorial, seldom gives her a chance to release her emotions.

The widow also tends to repress emotion because she is numb, in shock. Whether the husband has died suddenly or after a long illness, the confusion and demands of the moment leave her in a fog. I have been told by funeral directors that even when a widow does produce a show of emotion, breaks down, or tries to throw herself into the open grave, she usually is enacting a mourning tradition, doing what her culture expects of her. The man in charge of one of the biggest funeral homes in New York, where the rich and famous dead are sent off to their rewards, confided that his staff has orders not to restrain a widow who tries to plunge into the grave, since "if you don't try to stop her, she draws back."

The bad times come when the initial cushion of shock has worn off, when the widow realizes she is alone. Then comes the craziness, the helplessness, disorientation, the sleeplessness, the guilt, the anger—and the tears that will not stop. And the friends and relatives who had praised us for being "wonderful" begin to wonder how long they have to put up with self-pity. So we cry alone.

The advertising manager of a chain of stores told me, "I manage to function at work. But when I get in my car to drive to my office, I start crying. I weep all the way there and all the way home." An insurance executive said, "I never shed a tear in front of anybody, even my sons. But at night, when I came home from my office, I would lock myself in my apartment and cry until I was exhausted enought to sleep for a few hours." In a pamphlet on widowhood published by the American Association of Retired Persons (AARP), actress Helen Hayes is quoted as saying: "For two years I was just as crazy as you can be and still be at large. I didn't have any normal minutes during those two years. It wasn't just grief. It was total confusion. I was nutty and that's the truth. How did I come out of it? I don't know because I didn't know I was in it."

To those in its grip, grief is a terrifying emotion, akin to fear. And it only adds to our isolation to realize that friends, relatives, even children are embarrassed by us. When a widow tries to talk over what happened, relive her husband's final hours, or day-dream back to happier days, she is met with impatience; life must go on, life is for the living. So she hides away. Or in her anger and frustration, she lashes out at those closest to her, alienating them further.

So she is more alone than ever. The telephone rings less frequently; who wants to talk to a whiner? The mailbox overflows with bills and statements demanding attention, but few personal letters. And although old friends, couples who had been close when her husband was alive, continue to include her in their plans, she begins to feel like an outsider. She is now the odd woman out, a "fifth wheel," the extra woman. And every wife knows that extra women are a nuisance and a social burden.

It is difficult enough for a hostess to find an extra dinner partner for a bright, talented single woman who has something to contribute to a gathering. But a widow, a grieving widow, is a dead weight—and an ugly reminder that this, too, might happen to other wives. Even more ego-damaging is the realization that the bright single women whom we've admired when we were in the couple society, don't have time for us now. They have their plans, their well-filled lives, their routines. One, more honest than the rest, told me, "I need another woman friend like I need a hole in the head."

Before I was widowed, I watched my aunt, then my mother, go through their grief at losing their husbands. I was sorry, I grieved, too. But I had a husband and a career and a busy life. I learned nothing watching them suffer. I was "nice" to the wife of a colleague of my husband's who died of cancer; but I learned nothing from her grief, either; I was too busy doing the correct thing and then vanishing. When I was in my teens, my widowed grandmother came to live with us. We all loved her. But we were all busy. I remember she spent most of her time in the kitchen, cooking. On Sundays, when my father and mother went for their traditional ride through the Chicago park system, they sat in front and she was in the back seat.

Shortly after my husband died, a couple we'd known well invited me for the weekend. They called for me in their car. The wife sat in the front with her husband. I hopped in the back seat, feeling like my own grandmother.

But not long after that, I discovered I wasn't invited very often even to sit alone in the back seat. Old friends began to go on with their own lives. This happens to all widows, but knowing there is nothing personal in the neglect doesn't help. There are certain words which turn people off and among them are *death, cancer,* and *widow*. When someone is dying of cancer, the family finds itself alone. After a husband dies, the widow sometimes feels she has some deadly disease that other people are afraid of catching if they come too close. And even the traditional sources of comfort, the church and the medical profession, fail us. Ministers and priests and rabbis become just as embarrassed as friends when a widow cannot control her grief. As for doctors, unless you find one in a million, don't expect sympathy. They don't have time.

A widow who went to a doctor for a checkup shortly after her husband's death told me, "He acted as though he was afraid to be alone with me. He kept calling in the nurse. Did he think I was going to try to rape him?" I suppose that some men doctors have had unpleasant experiences with emotionally upset widows who just wanted comforting. Sex is not uppermost in the minds of most recent widows, however. Far from it. Depression inhibits sexual interest; therapists consider it a sign of improvement when a widow mentions sex. But we live in a world of quick-in and quick-out medical treatment. When a widow starts to say how depressed and miserable she feels, the doctor reaches for a prescription pad and gives her tranquilizers or antidepressant drugs.

Drugs are not the answer. All they do is cloak the symptoms. That may make a widow more socially acceptable, but until she can express and explore her grief, she is not ready to face the world alone.

Long before Freud, a doctor named Karl Abraham had already discovered the "talking cure for grief," which is as valid today as it was then. The only way to get over grief, to work your way out of the denial and the depth of your depression is to cry, feel sorry for yourself, talk about your guilt, vent your anger. A Johns Hopkins study of thirty-five women with advanced breast cancer found that the patients who were angry and hostile, who did not hesitate to make their distress known, had a much higher survival rate than those who suffered in silence. After further research with other diseases, the researchers at the medical center suggested that a person's emotional reactions may in turn influence hormonal and immunological functions that speed recovery.

My friend Sarah Morris, a psychologist and a widow herself, who has written two books on grief, compares recovery from grief to recovery from a wound. A cut heals well only if the healing is

gradual and the final scar covers good healthy tissue. But sometimes if a wound does not heal properly, it is because there is an
underlying infection. In Morris's opinion, the "infection" of grief
is made up of unresolved feelings that emerge later in the form of
emotional or physical problems.

Yet how can we vent our agony? Where can we weep and not
be made to feel ashamed? It is a cliché among widows that the
people who are most supportive are not the ones we would expect
to help, but casual acquaintances, even strangers, people who
understand because they have grieved themselves.

The two women who helped me most were widows. One I had
known casually because she had worked with my husband. Her
husband had died about two years before, and she had remarried.
She was the one who telephoned regularly, who told me what my
reactions were going to be, who invited me to dinner even though
I made an awkward number at the table. The other was a stranger,
a neighbor. She had been a widow for about six months. One
night she stopped me on the street and suggested we go to a
movie. Afterward we went back to her apartment and I talked.
Poured it all out. And wept. I saw her regularly after that. And
made a mess of myself, unashamedly. Not long ago she told me
affectionately, "The first year I knew you, you always had a red
nose from crying."

Today, the new widow is not isolated, unless she chooses that
route deliberately. All over this country, in Canada, and in
England, there are bereavement groups, widow seminars, and
widows' and widowers' clubs, large and small, organized and
impromptu, where she can go, get help, discover that what she is
going through is normal, and make new friends. Sometimes, in
small groups such as the bereavement group at Cancer Care in
New York, where there are both men and women, a family-type
atmosphere develops. June Wimpie, the senior social worker in
charge, encourages this. They argue, scold each other, make
suggestions and helpful comments. After the meeting they have
dinner in a local restaurant without the social worker. A group I
was invited to observe was planning to share a holiday dinner at
the home of one of the members. Sometimes romances result and,
occasionally, marriages. That is natural, too, although it is not the

purpose. In fact, in the larger organized clubs, the widowers who attend are deliberately looking for both companionship and sex, along with other kinds of help.

But the major point of these groups—indeed, the point of all self-help groups—is to help men and women cope with their emotional reactions by sharing them with others. Sometimes just the chance to air a problem means release: the "talking cure." Sometimes listening to others talk about their troubles, the opportunity to offer suggestions, even a moment in which the sufferer can laugh at herself or himself a little, gives the widow or widower a sense of restored value.

The first widows' club, so far as I've been able to discover, was founded in 1957 in Chicago by NAIM, a Catholic group for the widowed. This served as a model for the "Widow to Widow" program established in Boston ten years later by Dr. Phyllis Silverman of Harvard. Five widow volunteers were trained as aides and sent out to visit new widows whose names were obtained from the obituary pages. In addition, the new widows were also invited to social and discussion groups of widows organized by the aides. Out of that program came a national organization sponsored by the American Association of Retired Persons (AARP) called the Widowed Persons Service, which includes widowers as well as widows. It is staffed by volunteers, men and women, who find therapy for themselves in sharing their experiences with the newly bereaved. Now there is hardly a community that does not offer some kind of service for the widowed—whether sponsored by private individuals or by religious and community groups, mental health services, and hospitals. One young social worker, who discovered that some newly widowed people were reluctant to return to the hospital where they had lost a mate, persuaded a local funeral director to sponsor such a group.

In Appendix B (see p. 257) I have included lists of national and regional organizations, and information about where to write to ask about an organization near you. However, many of the most effective are the so-called "splinter" groups that have sprung up locally, started by widows and widowers themselves. Sometimes these little clubs meet in churches or community halls. Once in a while a business organization will let them use a board room. Often local restaurants are meeting places, where the members come on a Dutch treat basis. Local newspapers—expecially the small dailies or weeklies—list these meetings. Sometimes the phone book includes a few names of groups, and often church bulletins and community health centers have listings. Once you start inquiring, word of mouth will lead you to a group you will find congenial.

Don't consider yourself above seeking out help like this. A friend whose rather important husband died recently was shocked when I suggested that she attend one of these meetings. An independent soul, a free-lance photographer who had worked in the theater, she resented the idea of having to ask strangers to help her. It wasn't until later, after many talks with a priest who realized she needed some kind of therapy, that she swallowed her pride and went to a widows' group meeting in a small community near her. It was the entry into a new life. She telephoned me to say, "Why, they are women just like me. And they are so understanding. I had the flu last winter and missed a meeting. The next day I had calls from several members asking if I was okay. And one of them insisted on driving over and picking me up the next week so I wouldn't have to drive. I made a whole group of new friends."

Whenever we go through any traumatic experience—an incapacitating physical loss, a divorce, or the loss of the most beloved person in our lives—there has to be a period of mourning, a time during which the full impact of loss gradually becomes real. And it helps if you know that this period has recognized symptoms that psychiatrists and psychologists write books about. Individual therapy sometimes is necessary. But more and more, experts have decided that these widow and widower groups, which include people in all stages of grief, can often do more than one-to-one treatment. For one thing, they are far less expensive. Membership charges, if any, are nominal, as such groups are either self-sponsored or backed by nonprofit organizations. They are not limited as to time. A widow can attend as long as she feels the need, although occasionally a therapist who senses that a participant has become too dependent may suggest a break, a "vacation." And they supply that necessary ingredient that every widow needs: sympathetic new friends who know what she is going through because they have been there themselves.

The most important single thing that these mutual-help groups can offer, according to Dr. Roy Menninger, president of the famous Menninger Foundation in Topeka, Kansas, is to offer those who feel isolated from society the "constant interaction with people, the caring" that can restore to them their confidence. Or to quote from the concluding statement of a booklet describing mutual help, published by the Department of Health, Education, and Welfare, "The basic dignity of man is expressed in his capacity to be involved in reciprocal helping relationships."

A good therapist leading these group sessions does two things. She encourages you to help yourself, and to learn by listening to other members of the group. Only occasionally does she insert her own opinion. For example, therapist Lilly Singer is the only paid member of a group called Young Widows and Widowers of Westchester. (Actually, despite the title, some of the members looked to me nearer to sixty than twenty.) Volunteers she has trained lead the discussion groups, but Mrs. Singer herself takes charge of those who attend because they are newly bereaved. One evening a woman in Mrs. Singer's group said she had come because her second husband had just died of a heart attack. Her first husband, father of her children, had died of cancer. She told the group, "I never grieved for my first husband because the doctors warned me that intense emotion can bring on cancer. But now I can't stop crying. I feel it's the end of my life. I would never marry again. I don't know what to do."

Singer's comment: "You have every right to cry. You are not only mourning two husbands, you are mourning a way of life. Your unresolved grief for your first husband makes this especially painful."

Margaret Barbeau, a clinical social worker in Southern California who has worked with the survivors of natural disasters and airplane crashes, says that even the obsessive thinking and re-thinking of the death scene can be helpful. "It's a good thing if the person is trying to put it all back together again—it's an effort at mastering the experience. It becomes a negative process only if somebody uses it as an excuse to drop out of life to treasure this one experience."

June Wimpie at Cancer Care gives the impression of not interfering, but once in a while she interrupts casually to make a comment. A widower told the group, "I'm so afraid. I'd like to start seeing some nice woman, but I'm afraid to remarry. I could never go through again what I did with my wife. I gave her pills three times a night, then four times as she got worse. When she went back into the hospital, I would stay all night with her. It went on for months and months. I never could face that again."

For once, the group was speechless. Then Wimpie, in a quiet voice, remarked, "Louie, I think you must be proud of yourself for the devotion with which you cared for your wife. I know your children are proud. You not only did a fine job, you have become a better person because of what you did." The group relaxed. One pretty young widow smiled and said, only half in jest, "I'd like to cook dinner for that better person some night." Later Wimpie told me, "Actually, when someone makes the kind of a remark that Louie did—and I hear it often—what he is showing us is a picture of anger and self-pity, both acceptable emotions at a time of grief. He isn't ready to hear that yet. But he will be able to accept it eventually."

When strong emotional reactions are suppressed, when the widow has no one to help her talk out her fears and grief and anger and guilt, she can escape, or try to, into drugs or alcohol. But alcohol is a depressant and exaggerates unhappiness. Drugs postpone the inevitable. So she runs away or tries to kill herself. Running away, either through suicide or an attempt to change a life style, never works. If you choose the first, you escape permanently—but that is no solution. If you try the other, you create a different focus and delay the recovery process. Only a trip through the valley of despair will heal you.

To help you, there are other advances in hospital care made in recent years. Death is no longer the last taboo, and the dying in hospitals are no longer placed in rooms most remote from the nursing station. Death courses are taught in universities and high schools and given by social workers in hospitals. Many large teaching hospitals today feature the "hospice concept," whereby patients and relatives receive help from trained staff and social workers, and are encouraged to talk about their grief and their feelings about dying.

If a woman facing the death of her husband is able to attend lectures or classes on death, she may find doors opened for her. A friend whose husband had terminal cancer, a courageous, intellectual woman, enrolled in a university course on dying given by a brilliant Oriental teacher. She was able to attend two classes before her husband died.

She told me, "I learned I was hanging on to my husband, willing him to stay alive. I kept making new deadlines. He had to stay alive until our son came from Washington, then I begged him not to die at Christmas, not to let me go through the holidays alone. The lectures I heard made me realize it was time to let go, to allow him to die in peace and end his suffering." Later, after her husband died, she reentered the class and was able to benefit not only from it but from the support of other class members who knew of her experience.

While my husband was terminally ill, I read books by psychiatrists, psychologists, trying to get a handle on what I knew was going to happen even though I could not accept it emotionally. My husband was fighting so hard to stay alive; the few talks we had had about my future were always set in the context of "if" he should die. It might have been better for me had I been able to accept the fact that he was dying before the day he lay in his final coma and an angry young resident who saw how I was hiding behind my delusion ran down the hospital corridor after me to say, "Lady, don't you know that man is dying?"

A woman in Honolulu made all the plans for the funeral and memorial service in advance, consulting her husband as to his wishes. To friends, she sent out photocopies of bulletins. I saved one that said, "The cancer has spread so that not one, but four neck discs are involved. A shade more would have to be the area with the nerves controlling his breathing. In the past two weeks the lung cancer has appeared on the X-rays. No one says how much time is left. I keep busy making the arrangements for his death, burial, service, etc., and I hope this is a healthy way to handle my grief."

It is, and the name for it, in clinical terms, is anticipatory grief. However, not all people are able to face reality with such courage. And some people—doctors tell me this is particularly true of men—cannot or will not talk about their own death. A well-known doctor who knew his leukemia was terminal (his twin had died of the same thing two years before) was able to carry on, with medication and treatments, as usual until the last six months. When he was bedridden, his youngest daughter, who had taken the course on death that her high school offered, wanted to talk to her father about his dying. He told her to go about her business. Later he asked his wife, "Please explain to Janie that I wasn't angry with her, it is just that talking about dying is something I can't cope with right now."

You cannot force a dying man or woman to accept that fact. My feeling is that there is nothing the relatives and family can do except enter into the game of make-believe. A friend I'd always admired, the vice-president of a large advertising agency, took six months off from her job to spend with her terminally ill husband. She told me, "I never left his side, day or night. We had nurses, housekeepers, the works. David had cancer. I think he knew it— after all, he was no dope, he was a brilliant corporation lawyer— but we never said the word. Until the last few hours, when I finally had to take him back to the hospital in an ambulance. Then he asked me, 'Is it cancer?' And I looked him in the eye and said no. Maybe I was wrong. But I knew my husband, and I think I handled it the right way."

2

THE SUBMERGED SYMPTOMS
OF GRIEF

THERE is a healing that takes place when you are able to recognize that certain emotions that you have submerged, feelings of guilt and anger, should be released, because only then can you get on with your own life. According to Thomas Scheff, a sociology professor at the University of California, Santa Barbara, a large part of mourning is an emotional shifting of gears, a breaking down and permitting involuntary reflexes to take over. There is nothing to be ashamed about if you weep like a baby, he says, because "for an infant, separation is not acceptable, and there is an infant in all of us. We have to deal with that infant in us when we lose something important." And don't be alarmed if your reaction, instead of tears, is anger.

Sometimes it is directed at the person who died because "he left me with all these problems." Or, "he didn't take care of himself, wouldn't go to the doctor." Or it is the "Why me?" kind of anger, directed at God or society for letting this happen. One widower I met kept asking himself and anyone else who would listen, "Why doesn't somebody prepare you for widowhood?" I remember feeling anger at a doctor who refused to face what was wrong with my husband; I still feel I was right, but perhaps nothing would have helped, perhaps his "neglect" was benign. I was also irrationally annoyed with friends because they didn't appreciate their husbands. Now I realize I was really mad because they had husbands and I didn't.

A not uncommon anger is directed at the dead man who was unfaithful. While the philandering husband was alive, the wife either did not know or perhaps didn't want to know. Once the husband is no longer there, the widow vents her bottled anger. The widow of a famous doctor, a woman who had always lived in his shadow, unlocked one of his desk drawers after he died to find packages of love letters from a patient. Her grown children were angry because she told everyone about the affair, hurting their father's image. Gradually they discovered that her anger was making her into a more positive person. She went back to school, took her master's degree and now is teaching.

Lois Gould, author of *Such Good Friends*, wrote the novel (her first) after her husband died in a freak accident. During "minor" surgery, he had a fatal reaction to the anesthesia. Her anger at the hospital and doctors was not surprising. But it also included her mother and her husband. In white heat she wrote it all out in the book, which became a best-seller and was made into a movie. The plot deals with a widow who discovers a little black book her husband kept, listing the names of the women with whom he'd had affairs—all such good friends of hers. Gould's anger and her ability to write it out launched her on a career as one of the important feminist authors.

The danger of anger is that if it goes on, ultimately it no longer represents healthy rebellion but becomes a resentment of everyone and everything. Then it is debilitating. Then all the different problems snowball into one huge tight ball of anger, so that it is hard to find out exactly what the trouble is. Here is where professional assistance may be needed. Let your anger out and say what you are thinking. It is the buried anger that tends to become long term.

Denial of death may serve as a cushion so the widow can function through the funeral and afterward without really experiencing the loss. Psychiatrists say that a widow when in this state frequently exhibits "exaggerated personality traits" and point out Jacqueline Kennedy as an example. I knew a twenty-nine-year-old woman whose husband was killed in a commercial airline disaster. Flown out to the site of the crash, she stood dry-eyed and straight as his body, charred beyond recognition, was buried.

Home again, clutching her eleven-month-old baby in her arms, she said, "I don't believe it. I expect him to walk in the door any minute and tell me it isn't true." For a long time she continued to dream of finding him again, living in some remote area. If the telephone rang after she was asleep she would immediately think it was Lloyd, asking her to come to the airport to pick him up, as he had done so many times in the past.

A man whose wife was drowned during a visit to her parents in Maine said, "Nothing was real, not the funeral, not the people who were standing beside me crying. When I was packing my bag to go back to our apartment, I kept thinking she was in the next room packing hers." A widower who lost his wife through cancer often thought he saw her on the street. One day he got off a bus and followed a woman who was wearing a red coat like his wife's. When he caught up with her, a surprised stranger thought he was a mugger.

A widow who had taken over her husband's real-estate business often talked to his picture at night, asking his advice. A woman whose husband had died of a sudden heart attack when he was lying beside her in bed did not change the sheets for months. When things were particularly bad, she would rush up to her bedroom and cradle his pillow in her arms. She said when she did that she could actually "feel" him near her. One day she looked down and saw how soiled the pillow was. "I grabbed the case and the sheets and put them down the laundry chute. I guess that told me he was dead."

A teacher whose husband had died kept his clothes hanging in one of their bedroom closets for almost a year after he died. Finally she asked her married son to help her get rid of them; she couldn't do it alone. The wife of a well-known illustrator kept his studio, attached to the house, just as it was the day he died. She didn't even throw out the butts in his ashtray, although he had died of emphysema and was not supposed to smoke. Not until she sold the house was his studio opened again.

Guilt is something a lot of us carry around with us, an unnecessary and cumbersome burden. When you have really harmed someone by words or actions, you *should* feel guilt, and if possible, do something to make up for your mistake. But unnecessary guilt such as a widow feels is not only needless, it can be actually harmful. Yet few of us are spared that kind of guilt. In the sessions of widows' clubs and bereavement workshops, guilt is one of the most common problems expressed by the participants. When a leader asks, "How many of you feel guilty?" hands shoot up all over the room. Yet to any outsider the reasons given for guilt seem irrational in most cases. Sometimes just the fact that a widow is alive and her husband isn't is enough to make her feel guilty. A widow carrying a package told me, "I was feeling so happy, I found this blouse at a bargain counter. Suddenly I felt guilty. Why should I be happy when Ron is dead?"

A fifty-two-year-old widow blamed herself, after her husband's death, for not having shown him more affection. When a friend, who knew how reserved the husband had been, asked if he had ever shown affection, she said, "No, not really. But maybe he was waiting for me." One of the most devoted wives I have ever known, a busy Chicago career woman who dropped everything when her invalid husband called her at the office—as he did several times a day because he was lonely—said after he died, "Ralph loved orange juice. I used to buy him the big containers of concentrate. But maybe if I had taken the time to squeeze him fresh orange juice, he would have lived longer."

The little things—the fresh orange juice you didn't squeeze, the cushion for his chair you didn't buy—are small nitpicking nags. But what do you do when you are faced with real guilt?

A therapist of a bereavement group told me that there was a widow in one of her groups who would never talk about herself, although she was frequently hostile when other members repeated tales of how their husbands and wives had died. Then, for two weeks in a row, she was absent. The therapist called to ask if she were ill. The widow said, "No. I'm just tired of hearing other people do their deathbed scenes." After a minute, the therapist suggested that she had never mentioned her own husband's death. The widow hung up. The therapist did not expect her at the next meeting. But she came and started the conversation by saying, "I killed my husband. He had been in a coma for ten days. He was all hitched up to tubes. When the doctor told me it might go on and on—costing thousands of dollars when I had so little left—I told him to do what they call 'pull the plug.' For a few thousand dollars, I killed my husband."

In the silence that followed, another widow said, "Isn't that what he would have wanted you to do?"

At what was billed as a "drop-in" session for widows on Saturday morning at the YWCA, a widow who looked to be in her mid-forties told an even more painful tale of guilt. Her husband had been an alcoholic. But he was "recovered" until something upset him badly. He warned her that if he ever did start drinking again, she was to keep away from him because he could become violent and be dangerous. She did not believe him until one night when, in a rage over the financial demands of his ex-wife, he sent out for a bottle and finished it, growing angrier all the time.

"He tried to kill me," she said. "I ran into the bedroom, locked the door, and called the police." They came just as he was breaking down the bedroom door. They kept him overnight. The minute he got out, he headed for the nearest bar and got drunk again. He came and pounded on their front door. She'd had the locks changed so he could not get in.

He telephoned from the corner, calling her terrible names. She reminded him that when he was sober he had warned her to stay away from him when he was drinking. Then she hung up. The telephone kept ringing. She went into the bedroom and stretched out on the bed, trying to calm herself. After a long time it stopped. She was just thinking that maybe he had come to his senses when she saw his face at the bedroom window. He had gone up on the roof and climbed down the fire escape. Luckily, the window was locked. He pounded on it, yelling at her. She pulled down the shade. Finally the pounding stopped. She sat on the bed, shivering, for a long time. Then she went to the window and lifted the shade. He was gone. But as she stood there, something fell past the window. She thought she heard a scream. She learned later that he had apparently climbed back to the roof and swung himself down on the television cable, planning to kick in the window. But the cable had broken. He fell fourteen storeys to the ground.

She said, and it was obviously not the first time she had told the story, "I cannot tell you what agony it was to know I had killed my husband. I could see his face at the window, hear his voice begging me to let him in. It took months of therapy before I realized that he would have wanted me to do what I did, because he might have killed me. And my death on his hands would have haunted him all his life."

Confession is not only good for the soul. It is good for the ego and one of the most proven, traditional ways of absolving guilt. In every widows' group there are the ones who want to talk all the time and the others who hang back and listen. If you have been clutching your guilty feelings to your tortured bosom, just one visit to a widows' group, a one-time venting of your feelings, may not cure, but it will go a long way toward helping. You must learn that what is past is past and if you have done something wrong—if you took your husband back to the hospital to die, as one woman confessed, when you had promised him you would never put him in there again—you did it, it is past, nothing can undo that wrong, that broken promise, and you must get on with your life. (Besides, wasn't it selfish of him to make you promise? Did he ever think of the impossible burdens of nonstop nursing and sleepless nights?)

At this point in your life, you are doing no one a favor by feeling guilty—not your dead husband, not yourself, not your children, or relatives or friends. You are burying yourself in the past when you should be getting on with the business of your own life. Guilt may even be a way of postponing that dreaded reentry. So get rid of it. Other symptoms of grief may have to wear out their time, but you can do something about guilt.

Another destructive emotion is idealization of the dead man, the Queen Victoria syndrome. Few marriages are perfect. Mine was good, most of the time. But it entailed compromises and the compromises, in order to keep the marriage good, were made mostly by me. It had to be that way because he was that kind of man—demanding, assertive, fascinating, and terribly, terribly critical of anything less than perfection. I knew he was far from perfect, but after he died I was still so much under his spell—I call it that for want of a better word—that I found myself refusing to go out with men I felt he wouldn't have thought top drawer. I remember when the last and final specialist came, as a favor to another doctor, to our apartment, Dan remarked afterward, "He was wearing brown shoes with a blue suit." Well, little things like that—silly, unimportant things—would put me off men until finally, at long last, I came to my senses. Dan wasn't always right or even always just in his critiques. So why should I go on perpetuating what really had been a flaw in his nature?

The best marriages are, I believe, a mixture of fun and communication and mutual respect. A widow I rode home with from a club meeting one night gave me the best description of a happy marriage I've heard in a long time: "Milton was such fun to live with. He made even a trip to the grocery store an adventure."

The quality of a marriage, however, has little to do with some widow's memories. I am suspicious when a dead husband is promoted to instant knighthood, and I am turned off when a widow tells me, "He was a saint, a living saint. I used to say to him, how come I ever had the luck to get you?" When I hear comments like that, and have never met the now revered husband, I begin to wonder if the sainted husband didn't pass on just to get rid of such a ridiculous wife.

One old friend who used to complain (with reason) about her eccentric husband, can't stop talking about his good qualities now that he is dead. I think it is fine that she has pleasant memories of what must have been a difficult marriage, but I have to admit I get tired of hearing her go on and on about Charlie. She told me the other day that even her grandson, four years old, says, "Things aren't as much fun without Grandpop." I'm glad the child has nice memories. But I'm not surprised that her three unmarried sons get bored when Mom suggests they spend an afternoon looking through an album of photographs of their father.

Ann Kliman, director of a situational crisis center in White Plains, New York, wrote a brilliant book entitled *Crisis*, in which she deals with family grief. "It is crucial," Kliman says, "that all types of memories of the dead person be shared with the living. Not just the loving ones, but also those that were characterized by sadness, disappointment and hurt. . . . Unless we do that, we are running the risk of devaluing, even rejecting, our relationship with the living."

The healthy, normal widow doesn't cherish her grief. She relishes any sign of progress, whether it is pleasure in a sunset or hunger for a meal. The chronic mourner, on the other hand, refuses to forget anything about her dead husband, so that she turns her life into a shrine for him. This may seem admirable, but therapists are convinced that the perpetual widow hangs on to her grief not because of her undying love for her husband, but because she is afraid of becoming part of the world outside. Grief is a cocoon in which she hides.

A widow may try to keep her husband alive by following his hobbies—stamp collecting, music, foreign languages. Society applauds this, particularly if the hobby was an important cause or charity. But it can be a mistake if she lacks the enthusiasm that propelled him. Then she is merely following in his footsteps; if she attains a certain amount of success or recognition, she will feel dissatisfaction because the goal was not hers.

In order to break the tenacious bonds of habit that tie her to a life that is past and a husband who is gone, she must find her own goals. A Nebraska widow told me, "My husband was an intellectual. He never had that much schooling, so he was always learning, teaching himself. I admired him for it. But after he died, I went to adult education school and took every silly course I could find, from belly dancing to karate. I never would have done it when he was alive, he would have been shocked. But I guess I needed to express myself."

These are minor things, of course, but no widow can remake her life in one giant step. The small successes and triumphs all help to build her confidence, show her that she is making progress. Everyone grieves at his own pace, and your tiny triumphs may not seem astonishing to others. But they are steps on the way to recovery. And you do forget pain eventually. Meanwhile, relish the progress. Going alone to a restaurant where you used to eat together, watching a television show you always enjoyed together can be difficult. But facing these things alone is part of the recovery process.

You will have setbacks. Expect them. The shock and the denial, the disorientation, and even the crazy impulses give way eventually to plain depression, with its handmaidens insomnia, restlessness, lack of interest in yourself and the things you used to do. And depression comes when you know you are alone, that he isn't coming back. Then you hit bottom.

Depression, however, is just another stage of grief. Dr. Frederic Flach, who wrote the intelligent and encouraging book *The Secret Strength of Depression*, says, "I worry when a widow isn't depressed. That in itself is abnormal. The capacity to be depressed is characteristic of a healthy personality."

Depression may seem endless. Beds are left unmade, dust gathers. There seems no point in doing anything. Food has no taste. Sometimes an inability to swallow makes even the sight of food repulsive. You feed the children pizzas, hot dogs, TV dinners. No matter how interested you used to be in cooking and nutrition, you can't bring yourself to fix a balanced meal. You think there is no end in sight.

But there is. The curtain lifts, sometimes for just a few minutes, then for longer periods. And when you can look back at the horror and bleakness, you recognize that in spite of everything, depression had its uses.

May Sarton writes in *Journal of a Solitude*:

> The value of solitude—one of its values—is, of course, that there is nothing to cushion against attacks from within, nothing to help balance at times of particular stress or depression. A few moments of desultory conversation . . . may calm an inner storm. But the storm, painful as it is, may have some truth in it. So sometimes one has to endure a period of depression for what it may hold of illumination if one lives through it, attentive to what it exposes or demands . . . . There is nothing to do but go ahead with life moment by moment and hour by hour—put out the birdseed, tidy the room, try to create peace and order around me even if I cannot achieve it inside . . . . With the return of cheerfulness, I feel a sense of loss . . . . I am "normal" again, no longer the fountain of tears and intense feeling I have been for months. Balance is achieved. But at what price?

Depression can be a period of creativity, of growth, of knowledge of one's self. A young widow with two children was away over Christmas visiting her parents. When she returned, she found the house had been burglarized. "I expected to fall apart. My husband had always been the big protector, the one who took care of everything, shielded me from worry. But somehow, I coped. I called the police, the insurance people, had the locks changed. That night when I went to bed exhausted, I suddently thought, 'Maybe I'm not a weak person after all. Maybe I am stronger than anybody ever knew.' "

Dr. Arthur Carr, of the Foundation of Thanatology at Columbia Presbyterian Medical Center, makes the point that change itself, even change for the worse, may stimulate unsuspected areas of growth in a person. Your own ability to cope with situations such as the one described by the widow above, may surprise you. And the discovery that you can cope may enable you to reach out to others and help them channel their own grief creatively.

But on the whole, although others may help and you should use all the help you can get, in the end you must be your own doctor and psychologist. The widows' group will help, especially in making new contacts. When you are ready for social outlets, groups like Parents Without Partners will guide you to other single people. But there will come a time when you will have outgrown them.

In a medical manual, I read the following: "The customary support of family and friends does not appear to be very effective in reducing immobility of maladjustment in widows."

True, too true. In the old days of big families, the widow was absorbed and kept busy. There were always people around, hungry mouths to feed. She could cry, then get up and bake a pie, then cry again. But today when we are all isolated, it is difficult for friends and relatives to know what to do for a widow. At first, expecially in neighborhoods not urban, there are the dishes of food, the hams, the cakes. But later, it is so hard to know what to do. Sympathy makes her cry. Attempts to be practical, to suggest what she should do, are often resented. At first, friends and relatives are tolerant. But before long human nature asserts itself. Consciously or unconsciously, people go about their own business and forget her.

And a widow, in her own severe reaction to the loss of her husband, may discount her need for friends and relatives. (To quote Dr. Roy Menninger, "If we only took as good care of our relations to people as we do of our cars.") She may feel they deserted her when she was in trouble. And she may be right. Some people hate hospitals. Others do not know what to say or do when they visit someone who is very ill. So, out of shyness, they stay away. So when these people attend the funeral and attempt to reconcile with the widow, she may reject them angrily. Anything can happen at a time when emotions are unstable—quarrels, old grievances brought up and aired, new ones plucked out of the air. The widow may be unreasonable; fatigue, worry about money and decisions, all take their nagging toll.

In need of friends, she may resent those who try to tell her how sad they are. She may be hurt because her children, hurting themselves, can't talk to her about their father. Or she may be ashamed to ask them for help, because her role has always been to care for them. A widow made a trip to her daughter's college a few months after her husband died. The brief kiss they exchanged brought tears to the eyes of both. When the widow left, she gave her daughter a pat on the arm and ran to the plane. Back home, weeping, knowing the meeting hadn't been a success, the mother called the girl. "I wanted to hug you when I left. I didn't dare. I was afraid of breaking down." The daughter responded, "I thought you were so tied up grieving for Dad the rest of us didn't matter anymore."

In her relations with in-laws, the new widow may also make mistakes. When her grief is so fresh, it may be hard for her to realize that her husband's parents have lost a child. While she is asking them for help, they may be needing her sympathy. In fact, being human, it is possible that they may be secretly wondering why their son had to die while his wife lives on. Or they may fear that the widow will remarry and take away their grandchildren, the only links left with their son.

Relations with in-laws require patience and tolerance. There may be anger and resentment on both sides. But a widow must try to remember that in the weeks and months and years ahead, you can support each other. Children need grandparents; they must never be cut off from them. And in many cases where restraint and good judgment was exercised by everyone, widows have become closer to their in-laws than they ever were before.

In my capacity as a veteran, I must warn the new widow about one unhappy transition, her shift from a role as wife of a celebrity or important corporate official, to the role of his widow. Everyone will be attentive right after his death; the officers of the company or the board of directors may attend the funeral in a body. So may the mayor, the governor, the famous and near-famous. But their attention span is brief. His work will be taken over by someone else, and you—and eventually he—will be forgotten except by a very special few.

There is nothing you can do about this. You have to accept it. The widow of a doctor who was head of staff at a large teaching and research foundation found herself excluded not only from staff functions, where wives were invited, but also from wives-only groups. The wife of the rabbi who wrote one of the best-sellers on peace of mind, with a chapter on death, found herself virtually isolated from many of his old friends and admirers. My husband was an important and respected editor. He died at Thanksgiving. At Christmas I did not even get the usual engraved card from his boss and wife. I knew some secretary had removed our names from the company list. But still . . . .

Margaret Barbeau, in her work with survivors of airplane crashes, discovered that "in a crisis there's often a sense of needing to do something, to make decisions. But abrupt decisions create a different focus and delay the recovery process. I usually suggest waiting a few weeks until the thinking is clearer before going through with any abrupt decisions."

Where widows are concerned, the waiting period suggested by experts in all fields is a year. You are going to see the point made several times in this book, simply because it is so important. Out of panic and anxiety, a need to turn herself into another person who doesn't have all these problems, a woman can turn her life around and do a lot of things that are absolutely wrong for her. Sometimes she just feels she has to do something or she will go crazy. Panic has its place in the widow experience. It's a familiar feeling. Sitting in the movies with friends, you feel that you have to get away or you will scream. At a family dinner, surrounded by people who wish you well, you are overcome by the sensation that you can't take this another minute. Don't worry about this panic. It will pass. When you have to fly, when you have to return to your bed as to the security of the womb, do it and don't make too much of it afterward.

But do not make any major changes in your life unless there is no possible way that they can be avoided. Sometimes friends and family will push you. Don't listen to them. Wait until whatever move you make seems to be so right and inevitable that it is not an escape, but a step forward. I knew a widow in Minneapolis who walked out of her home in which she'd lived for twenty years, leaving everything, even her clothes, and moved into a new apartment that she furnished in a style entirely different from her old house. She let her kids sell the house, the furniture, even her clothes. Six months later, she went into such a decline she couldn't leave her bed.

A seventy-year-old widow gave up her house and sold her furniture and moved in with a divorced niece to take care of the niece's two-year-old baby while the mother worked. A friend reported, "She ran around the park after the kid, she wore herself out. She just couldn't take it. But she hung on because she had no place else to go. Then what happened? The niece remarried, and her new husband wanted no part of an aged aunt in his household. She had to go into a retirement home, which was just one step away from the grave."

The mistake the new widow—as opposed to the older one—makes is to invite an older relative to live with her, particularly her own widowed mother. It is even worse for her to move back to the house where she lived as a girl, with her parents, because there she becomes an instant child again. If you have young children, and want to work, this may be a temptation. But don't make any long-term commitments for a year. (Then, if the benefits outweigh the disadvantages, you may have to do this; see the section on children and grief.) Meanwhile, if you need someone to live in, choose a student (they tend to be mobile and ready for changes). Or a housekeeper you can fire.

You and your children are better off with your panics and depressions in a familiar environment; change only adds stress. A Cincinnati widow first moved to Arizona with her kids. They were miserable. Six months later she left the children and went to Europe. Then she came back to Florida, where her parents had the kids, and found she couldn't bear living with her parents, so many thousands of dollars poorer, she went back to Cincinnati and rented an apartment a block from her old house. Another widow I met told me she had moved from her old house into a condominium, thinking this would give her children lots of new friends when she went back to work. She was wrong. A widow wasn't accepted as part of the couple clan in the building, nor were her children.

It usually takes a year to settle an estate. Try to use this period to let you get through your grieving process, to learn your responsibilities to yourself as a woman alone. Don't make mistakes that it will be difficult to correct. If you have not worked at a full-time job since before the children were born, it may be hard on all of you if you throw yourself into a job that is demanding of both your time and limited energy. If you have been working, and the children have someone familiar taking care of them, falling back into a routine takes your mind off your grief and can be a relief to the children. But stepping immediately into the stressful situation of a new job may not only be bad for them, but could condemn you to failure because you aren't ready for challenges. (More about this in chapter 9.) But you can do things like going back to school at night, or retraining yourself while the children are at school. Or you can take what some widows refer to as a Band-Aid job, temporary work which is less demanding but gets you out into a different world.

Remarriage has to be in every new widow's mind, even as she mourns her husband. There is nothing unnatural about this. Soon after Dorothy Parker's husband died, a sympathetic friend asked her that inane question every widow hears: "What can I do for you, darling?"

Parker, who was no darling, promptly answered through her tears, "Get me another husband."

To anyone who has liked being married, the immediate reaction is to rush out and find a replacement. And here is where the crazies are apt to set in. You are in no shape to make any decision like that; it is far more serious than throwing all your money away on trips or even moving to a strange city. Helena Znaniecki Lopata, in her scholarly book *Women as Widows*, reports that the most unhappy widows she met were those whose remarriages had not worked. Even when remarriage occurs after a widow is once again back in her right mind, there often are shocks and adjustments she didn't expect. A too-fast remarriage is almost invariably doomed. Fortunately, she is often prevented from taking this foolish and harmful step by the simple fact that there are a lot more widows than widowers. And the fact that widowers, if they can, will often marry younger women, women much younger than their dead wives, and are put off by young children.

According to recent statistics, there are ten million widows in the United States and less than two million widowers. A widower, if he is in reasonably good health and not in financial difficulties, can usually remarry if he wants to. Most of them do. They are used to being married. No matter how handy a man is, how accustomed to helping around the house and with the children, the routine is in his wife's hands. She plans the meals, does most of the cooking. If the children are grown, she keeps in touch with them and their children. The social life revolves around her planning. She makes the household wheels go around. He can learn to do this alone. But as any widower can tell you, it isn't that much fun.

So, unless he needs a nurse, not a wife, he can confidently look forward to remarrying "when he finds the right woman." Right women seem to be a dime a dozen. A widower wrote plaintively in *Modern Maturity* (a magazine published by the AARP) about his mystification at the attention he had from women shortly after his wife died—invitations, telephone calls, some inviting him for dinner, others going so far as to hint they would take him to bed.

A man I worked with was widowed after nursing his wife through a long illness. He told me during that time, "I hate to lose her, but she is in such pain sometimes I wish it were over." He lived in a suburb, where there must have been plenty of widows ready to help her—and him—during her illness, for he remarried less than six months after she died. Even before his remarriage, when he turned up late for a meeting he apologized by saying, "It takes a bachelor longer to get going in the morning." A seventy-seven-year-old widower lives in an attractive retirement village where, as one might expect, there are many widows. A friend visited him and found him up in the attic, rereading love letters he had written to his wife many years ago. He'd found them in a trunk. "He was crying. But meanwhile, the telephone kept ringing with invitations not only from widows, but from married women."

A widower has his own problems with grief. They are different from those of a widow, and he usually recovers faster because society offers him more help. He is not only in demand among single women and divorcées and widows, he is useful in social gatherings given by married women. Though he no longer has a wife, he has his career or job, around which his life has always centered in any case. If he has to, he can learn to do the cooking and even cleaning; these are chores that do not require deep concentration.

But his loss can be devastating for one important reason: He has lost his mother all over again. Any baby has his first emotional tie with his mother or a mother substitute, a woman. With a boy, this is his first love, and his relationship with his wife in a marriage can take on maternal aspects. She calls him "Dad" and he calls her "Mother." (The woman has a similar tie to her father, but the relationship is not quite as close, as the father was her second object of attraction.)

A widower with children living at home has additional problems. Because he, by tradition, is supposed to be strong, he seldom allows himself the indulgence of tears. He goes back to work right away. And if circumstances force him to have to take time off (for example, if he has to take the children to the doctor for shots so that they can go to summer camp) he often finds his employer difficult. A woman in the same situation gets more consideration. And he has to find help, perhaps live-in help, to take care of the house and children. Full-time housekeepers come high. Single or widowed female relatives, brought in as a temporary measure, can become household tyrants, managing not only the house and children, but also the widower's life. It is no wonder he needs another wife—and fast.

The older widower does not have such an easy time. He can find life more difficult than an older widow. If the couple has been retired, she has fixed meals, busied herself with household chores. He feels helpless. (A widower who tried to plan a Thanksgiving dinner for his married children and grandchildren gave up when he found out he couldn't even find the good silver; his wife had it locked up someplace.) He can become desperately lonely, particularly if he has ailments. And the prospect of moving in with his married sons or daughters, or being sent to an institution, can be disheartening.

It is not surprising that during the first fifteen months of bereavement, three times as many widowers as widows kill themselves. Most of these, of course, are older men.

Widows of retirement age are invariably better able to cope with life alone. Their health may be better because women watch their weight and take better care of themselves. They are also less apt to see themselves as old. And they will find a greater number of their peers who are willing to help them make the adjustment and supply a social life—different from the ones they had with their husband, but often livelier and broader. A widow who has stayed in the small Kentucky town where she lived with her husband for many years wrote me, "I've had a couple of offers— one illegitimate by an old fool who makes passes at anything he bumps into, and one legitimate by a creature who thinks I am rich because I live in the big old house—but I can tell you this. I wouldn't dream of marrying a man who would have me."

Meanwhile, one of the first real shocks a widow has is how many husbands, some of them belonging to your best friends, are ready to step in and take you to bed. Their attitude is sometimes cavalier, even patronizing. They are doing you a favor.

I didn't realize this about myself at the time—you are in such a state that you can't—but there is a poignant vulnerability about new widows. They are appealing, especially to husbands with lecherous instincts. And I suppose it is the old story: they must have a certain number of successes or they wouldn't be so confident that you are eager and willing.

But if you have been out of circulation for a time, happily married and concentrating on keeping things that way instead of going the divorce route, you may be taken aback. Some of the tales told by widows in the mutual-help groups are enough to make your hair stand on end, even in this time of liberated women. I'm going to add my own, a funny one. I went out from Manhattan to attend a social gathering of the Young Widows and Widowers of Westchester. It's a lively, sophisticated group with many exceptionally attractive young widows, so it is no surprise that some of the widowers have only one thing on their minds: sex. The meeting, held on Sunday night, breaks up late, so Mrs. Singer had the president ask from the platform if anyone in the group was driving back to Manhattan that night, as someone needed a lift. A man's voice from the floor asked, "Male or female?"

Female, was the answer. Then the voice called out, "Well, I live in Riverdale. She can ride home with me and spend the night. Or, if she is stuffy, I'll drive her to a subway."

A recent widow shared this experience in another group: "I grew up in a very small town where I still live. My husband and I ran a restaurant. I'm now trying to do it alone. One night one of my old boyfriends—now a married man with lots of kids—stopped in and wanted to drive me home. There was a glint in his eye which made it plain that the ride wasn't all he had in mind. I asked him where his wife was. He had the nerve to say, 'Sally is fine. But you get tired of a diet of the same food every night, even if it's steak. I want a change.' I was furious. I still am. I was insulted, too. He wouldn't have dared talk to me that way when my husband was alive."

Another woman, the widow of a publisher, told me that her husband's partner had called to say he would be in her neighborhood on Sunday and would she have lunch? She thanked him, thinking his wife would be with him. But when he arrived he was alone. And he also had an overnight case containing a bottle of champagne and a shaving kit. He took the champagne out and asked her to put it on ice—"I thought you and I might have a little party tonight." When she insisted that he go away, he became angry. "It was as if I was supposed to be grateful to him," she said. Another widow told a married man, "I can't go out with you. You and your wife are my oldest friends." His answer was, "Honey, you wouldn't want to go out with a stranger, would you?"

The theory that all widows are frustrated and longing for any kind of attention is undoubtedly one of those bedtime tales husbands tell each other. One couple, whom I knew long before I met my husband, continue to invite me to their big parties. The next day I invariably get a call from one of their very married guests, wanting to drop over some afternoon. "You work at home, don't you?" I finally pulled myself together enough to ask a divorcée what I was doing to make myself look like such a pushover.

She shrugged. "You've been out of circulation twenty years. You haven't kept up with the sex scene. The men figure you live alone, you have an apartment handy to their offices, so why not? Plenty of married men are looking for dames with setups like yours. So don't react like a virgin. Try it once. You might even have fun."

But even my divorcée friend acknowledges that widows and divorcées feel differently about sex. A divorcée often feels she is "getting even" with an ex-husband. A widow tends more toward shyness even after sexual urges return; she is reluctant to be part of the sexual rat-race. Widowers, on the other hand, may welcome the new freedom. It gives them a chance to play around, have fun, until they meet someone in whom they can become seriously interested. Actually, the sexual needs of most women, and this includes the angry divorcees, are different from men. Most of them want sex that is based on at least mutual affection, if not love. They need the personal one-to-one relationship unless they have brainwashed themselves into the idea that sex is just another pleasant exercise. Sometimes a widow will try to fit into the contemporary pattern of one-night stands, casual sex, friendships formed after bedding down, not before. But when you have been removed from the current sexual scene, except as an observer or as a reader of books, it may be difficult to adjust your attitudes. (And frankly, I don't feel it is necessary. It comes down to the old story: do what your instincts say is right. Don't follow the crowd that may lead you into places you hate.) A woman in one group that included both men and women said seriously, "I was married at sixteen. I've never slept with anyone except my husband. But I have decided—and I have told my children of this decision—that I would insist on an affair before I would consider remarriage."

I expected someone to laugh. But nobody did. So maybe the old-fashioned or slightly old-fashioned standards are still considered okay. Practically speaking, however, the intense need for physical closeness may come sooner than any widow expects. "I need something to hug," one new widow told me. "I'm desperate for closeness." Sometimes widows allow young children to sleep with them in their beds—a mistake and not good for the child, especially when it is a boy. The answer today from the experts is simple: masturbation.

In the days when I was growing up, masturbation had a bad name. I can still recall the feeling of shame that came over me when my mother opened the door of a room where I was studying and found me "playing with myself." She scared me so with tales of something-or-other (maybe idiocy; I banished the horrible fate from my mind) that I stopped right away. Boys who were caught at similar innocent diversions were told, I have heard, that not only did masturbation weaken you sexually, it grew hair on your hands so everybody would know how awful you were.

Today modern parents are brighter, I think, and regard masturbation as no more than a highly effective way for children to investigate their own sexual responses. However, with that taken care of, we have a new shibboleth: masturbation is a failure as a sexual release because it is not the real thing, and sexual relations with a stranger are to be preferred to self-stimulation.

This is nonsense, of course; sometimes I suspect it is being perpetuated by those who would like to see a woman jump into bed just to prove she is okay, a complete female. Masturbation is a far better way of relaxing and inducing sleep than pills, or reading into the night, or listening to TV. But some widows are still afraid of it; one confided to me that she didn't want it to become a habit.

Masturbation is a crutch, yes. Complete, loving sex, shared with a partner, is better. But masturbation is better for health than drinking, reckless driving to let off steam, or the very real dangers of disease from promiscuity. And it will never replace meaningful sexual activity. In fact, the loosening up of blood vessels in the pubic area tends to make a woman more desirous and capable of satisfying intercourse and reaching orgasm.

Sexual promiscuity sometimes is part of the craziness, the restlessness, the frantic searching that comes with grief. Sometimes it is a revenge on the dead man for his philandering or his lack of interest in her. If so, it can be a foolish revenge because he is gone and will never know what she is doing. And satisfying what one widow described to me as her feeling of "inner emptiness" during her depression can be distracting but humiliating. True sexual compatability is a blend of emotional closeness, affection and sharing. It means tenderness, not a series of uncaring bed partners. It reinforces one's ego. Promiscuous sex ultimately leaves a woman more depressed than she was to begin with. One case in point:

A thirty-five-year-old widow in a midwestern town, lost her husband in a car accident. He had been drinking, and there was talk of his affairs with women. Perhaps in anger, perhaps in defiance, she immediately invited a twenty-four-year-old mechanic from her husband's garage to "rent a room" in her house. He paid no rent and shared her bed. Her two teenage children were embarrassed and distressed. She ignored them. The neighbors were shocked. Some mothers refused to speak to her. In six months, the affair was over. He left her and ran away with a twenty-year-old cocktail waitress. Tearfully, she explained, "I don't know what got into me. I was like another woman."

What is the answer? To my way of thinking, the experience of grief, painful as it is, can be a period of growth, an exploration of yourself and your potentials. You will be confused at times, but all the while you will be learning more and more about yourself. You will be lonely and unhappy at times, but were you happy every single moment of every day even in a good marriage? You will be learning new values. You will be finding and making new friends even as some of the old ones are drifting away. Whether you realize it or not, you will be changing, maturing, becoming a different person.

Any change is painful, even changing the part in one's hair. But through pain you will learn humility and sensitivity. You will learn that loneliness has another side: privacy. You will, I think, find the true value of good friends, men and women, just as you discover that'friendship with men is possible, friendship based on mutual tastes and interests instead of sex. You may remarry; and if you are lucky as well as wise in your selection, you may even be happier the second time around than you were the first. At any rate, I suspect you will choose a little more wisely and be more tolerant and less demanding. Or you may decide to enjoy life as a single woman. I have, and believe me, some of my married friends are envious of my freedom and the range of my interests.

Meanwhile, you will take one step at a time, carefully. You will relish progress, but you must not be discouraged when you fail. You will discover risks—but all living is risky. I hope the next chapters will be a practical guide toward your new life, not as a widow, but as a human being complete in herself.

3

STRESS MAKES THE WIDOW A
HEALTH RISK

I WAS under stress. For the first time, I was attending a widows'
and widowers' self-help club. I knew no one. I had come because
I'd seen the notice in a Connecticut newspaper. Signed in, with
my name tag pinned on—they used only first names—I felt like a
fish out of water. First of all, I had misjudged train schedules and
turned up much too early. The handful of women already there
were regulars, too busy setting up tables and chairs to pay
attention to me. Second, I was dressed wrong. I'd put on a cotton
skirt and blouse because of the August heat, and the room turned
out to be air-conditioned. The other women were all wearing
pretty summer dresses or cocktail suits.

From my neutral corner, I watched the new arrivals, including a
woman in a pink knit suit whose name tag said she was Joan. Joan
had brought the cheese for the social hour which was to precede
the period when we would break up into small discussion groups.
She poured herself a glass of wine and went into her self-
appointed role of official greeter. She was a loud laugher. She
made a point of kissing women and kidding men. Joan turned me
off. The fact that she was completely at ease, having a dandy time
while I lurked alone in my corner, made me loathe her.

Finally a quiet, dark-haired woman came to my rescue, brought
me a glass of wine, and tried to introduce me to a few people,
including a man who gave me a quick look and hurried off to
greener pastures. I was relieved when the social hour ended and

my new friend led me to a table where the topic of discussion was to be DECISIONS, DECISIONS. We were all women. The few men had chosen tables where the topics were SEX or VACATIONS. It was my bad luck that the chair next to me was vacant. And that Joan, after wandering around the room a couple of times, dumped herself down in it, with her cigarettes in one hand and an ashtray in the other.

The leader at our table, a widow who was a regular member of the group, introduced herself and suggested we all do the same, telling why we had chosen to discuss this particular topic, decisions. I felt much better when I discovered that the others at my table were far too concerned with solving their own problems to notice me or my clothes. I would have relaxed if it hadn't been for Joan. She hated to let anyone else talk; she kept interrupting, couldn't wait for her turn. When it finally came, she lighted a new cigarette from her old and said, "I'm a nothing. I hate myself. When my husband was alive, I was somebody. Now that he's dead, I am just a big old piece of nothing. I don't know why I am alive. My friends hate me. So do my children."

She would have gone on and on, but the leader gently suggested it was time for the next woman, a blonde named Adele, to have her say. Joan subsided reluctantly, blowing smoke in my face and spilling ashes on my skirt. Adele was a pretty woman, slight and beautifully dressed. She told us, "I'm here because I just can't get myself together. Yesterday I decided I had to clean the house. But the vacuum cleaner wouldn't start. I put it in the back of the car to take to the repair shop, then I remembered that last night when I came home from work the car kept stalling. I took some clothes downstairs to the washing machine and came back upstairs to find out the dishwasher had overflowed. While I was mopping up, the doorbell rang. It was the paper boy, who said I hadn't paid him for three months. I got my purse and was giving him some money when the front door slammed shut. I looked, but my key wasn't in my bag. I stood there wondering what I could do and if I hadn't paid the other bills either, and I started to cry. I think I'd be there yet if the paper boy hadn't told me the garage was open and I could get back in that way."

Before anyone else could say anything, Joan spoke up, "Why clean house? Who cares?"

"I care," Adele said. "I hate living in a mess. I hate it when things don't work. But I can't cope. I just touch a thing and it falls apart."

Joan smashed out her cigarette, missing the ashtray. "You think you have troubles? Listen. Nothing in my house works. I haven't made my bed since my husband died. Why should I? It started when we came back from burying him. The plumbing broke down. There wasn't a drop of water in the house and none of the toilets worked. Since then it's gone from bad to worse." She coughed, wiped her eyes and added, "He loved the house so and took such good care of it and now—it's as though the house was mourning too."

Adele leaned over and touched Joan's arm, "Joan, that's beautiful. It's like a poem. You must be a writer or something."

"I'm nothing," Joan blubbered. And then the tears came. Terrible tears. A Niagara of pain. Suddenly I found myself wanting to put my arms around the woman I had loathed such a short time before.

Like all the rest of the men and women who had come that hot Sunday evening for the meeting, she was alone and afraid. And under stress. Psychiatrists say that when a person is under stress, she becomes a caricature of herself. If she is strong, the strength can turn into stubborness, become hostility. If she is shy and unassertive, she may become a recluse. And if, like Joan, she is active, outgoing naturally, under stress she becomes hyperactive, pushy, smoking too much, perhaps drinking too much, putting what well could be dangerous strains on her already exhausted body.

Only recently have medical men acknowledged that every crisis situation has its effect on the body as well as the mind. Dr. Mardi Horowitz, an internationally known psychiatric expert who is directing a research project on widows at the University of California, San Francisco, says, "Most people underestimate the impact that serious life events have on us." Any change, even a change for the better, like a new job, creates stress. And the stress caused by the death of a husband or wife, plus all the added stresses put on the bereaved by the changes that he or she must make in her life, can be devastating.

Today, *stress* is a popular term. The medical usage of the word was coined by Austrian-born Hans Selye in 1950 when he was a professor at the University of Montreal and published a book of that title, pulling together the threads of thousands of pieces of medical research. He came to the conclusion that stress is the body's response to any unusual demand placed on it. Good stress occurs in situations in which we feel secure, a deadline to meet in a job you enjoy, the challenge of getting a big order to someone who enjoys selling. But stress—good or bad—creates body changes.

Under stress, the heartbeat quickens and the adrenal glands pour hormones into the blood stream, sending them to so-called beta receptors all over the body, initiating the familiar sweats, palpitations, and other symptoms. The heart races, up to 200 beats a minute, almost triple the normal pace and much higher than the pounding of a runner's heart during a race (about 160 beats a minute.)

This sudden burst of hyperactivity serves its purpose in emergencies—for example, when a child is injured and a mother is able to lift a heavy iron bar off his body, a bar she couldn't lift under ordinary circumstances. I remember I was once at a circus rehearsal working in the ring with a photographer. When a tiger got loose, I jumped over a fence that was higher than my head (and I am anything but the athletic type). But constant emotional stress pushes a widow into restlessness, insomnia, activity without purpose. And her body suffers because the emergency system tends to break down from overuse. The protective hormones supplied by the adrenal glands cease to pour into the bloodstream. Bodily resistance is lowered. The widow is actually more susceptible to passing cold germs or some virus that is going around. And any chronic conditions—asthma, arthritis, diabetes, ulcers—is apt to get worse, since these are normally kept under control by the healing anti-inflammatory action of the adrenal cortex hormones.

Undernourished, underprotected by her depleted body defenses, the widow becomes forgetful. The simplest chores seem beyond her. Edward Madara, consultant at the Community Health Center connected with St. Clare's Hospital in New Jersey, compares this depleted feeling to the way men returning from battlefields react. "When I got back from Vietnam," he says, "I felt as though I had been drugged. I didn't know what I was doing or why. For weeks I wandered around in a fog. My body had exhausted itself responding to the stresses of wartime action."

A frequent complaint of recent widows is that, right after a husband dies, the house seems to fall apart. The storm windows fall off. The Venetian blinds collapse. The washing machine breaks down. Actually, what is going on is simply the normal routine of living with its breakdowns and problems. But when she is in a state of depleted energy, she cannot cope with the slightest challenge. Her supply of adrenalin is used up, so every minor mishap is a crisis, and the slightest accident becomes unbearable.

At the beginning of this century, a professor of psychiatry at Johns Hopkins University in Baltimore, Adolf Meyer, began keeping what he called "life charts" on his patients. He found that they tended to get sick around the time when clusters of major events took place in their lives. For example, take an influenza epidemic. Not everybody catches the bug. Some may be mildly ill, some severely and others may have to be hospitalized and even die. What makes the difference? "Resistance" is the classic answer. But resistance is hard to pinpoint. The codeveloper of a well-known test for stress, Dr. Thomas Holmes, explains, "When our resistance goes down, our risk goes up. The routine of our lives is being constantly revised. We have to filter incoming stimuli, assign them priorities and try to fit them into our way of life. If we refuse or are unable to deal with this input, our circuits may become overloaded with a massive life crisis and our systems are at great risk for a breakdown in function." And Holmes quotes Alvin Toffler, who wrote in *Future Shock*: "All change carries a physiological price tag with it. And the more radical the change, the steeper the price."

In the 1940s and 1950s, the late Harold G. Wolff, professor of neurology and psychiatry at Cornell University Medical College, began to expand studies of the emotional states surrounding illness. Dr. Thomas Holmes, who is now professor of psychiatry at the University of Washington School of Medicine, was one of his colleagues. He applied Dr. Meyer's life chart idea to the case histories of more than 5,000 patients. Meanwhile, Richard H.

Rahe, research psychiatrist with the Navy Medical Neuropsychiatric Research Unit in San Diego, California, was studying the relationship between life changes and illness in the health records of navy and marine personnel. These two men have devised what they call the Social Readjustment Rating Scale, known popularly as the "H. and R. Stress Test." It is widely used; indeed, I discovered that the people who apply as volunteers for the Widowed Persons Service are given this test routinely for their own information.

The chart lists forty-three life events and assigns to each a value score which represents the amount, duration, and severity of stress imposed by each item. These scores were arrived at by submitting the lists of hundreds of subjects for grading. Death of a spouse was given the highest rating, 100. And since the changes made in the life of a widow or widower by the death of a spouse are many, widows' scores can run very high indeed. One widow told me, not without pride, "My score went through the roof. Not a man or woman in the group matched it. But somehow, just realizing what a position I was in helped. I had a complete medical checkup right away. And since then I've simplified my life as much as I can."

It isn't just because of bad luck or fate that a widow or widower often comes down with a serious illness after the wife or husband dies. Indeed, studies have found that the mortality rate among the recently widowed is seven times higher than average within six months of the death of the first spouse. Women are more durable biologically than men. They have two chromosomes which protect against life-threatening diseases, while men have only one. Yet even this protection is not enough, especially in widows under forty-five who have, in addition to their burden of grief, to worry about the grieving children, running a one-parent household, and above all, money. Even with a lingering illness, like cancer, when the sick man has time to make a will or establish a trust, the widow often neglects her own health nursing him and overspends her energy trying to cope, so that when he dies she is an easy target for disease.

Mary L. S. Vachon, a registered nurse at the Department of

Psychiatry, Toronto Hospital, Canada, reports that in a study of 375 widows under sixty, done thirteen months after the women had lost their husbands, 32 percent suffered marked deterioration of health. In additional to menstrual difficulties, miscarriages, and problems like insomnia and loss of appetite, these recent widows had three times as many hospitalizations as the control group and spent more time home sick in bed.

What can a widow do to protect herself?

The first rule offered by Dr. Roy Menninger, head of the Menninger Clinic, is to recognize what causes stress. Any widow or widower knows the major cause of her stress. But she or he may not be aware of the other problems that are pushing at her, problems which can be corrected or postponed until she is better able to cope. That is why it is extremely useful for any widowed person, especially a woman, to take the Stress Test created by Holmes and Rahe. Look at the following list and check off those life events which you have experienced within the last year. When you have reviewed the entire list, total the numbers beside the events you have checked.

Life Event °	Value	Score
Death of a spouse	100	_____
Divorce	73	_____
Marital separation	65	_____
Jail term	63	_____
Death of close family member	63	_____
Personal injury or illness	53	_____
Marriage	50	_____
Fired at work	47	_____
Marital reconciliation	45	_____
Retirement	45	_____
Change in health of a family member	44	_____
Pregnancy	40	_____
Sex difficulties	39	_____
Gain of new family member	39	_____
Business readjustment	39	_____
Change in financial state	38	_____
Death of a close friend	37	_____
Change to different line of work	36	_____

Change of number of arguments with spouse	35	_____
Mortgage over $10,000	31	_____
Foreclosure of mortgage or loan	30	_____
Change in responsibilities at work	29	_____
Son or daughter leaving home	29	_____
Trouble with in-laws	29	_____
Outstanding personal achievement	28	_____
Spouse begins or stops work	26	_____
Begin or end school	26	_____
Change in living conditions	25	_____
Revision of personal habits	24	_____
Trouble with boss	23	_____
Change in work hours or conditions	20	_____
Change in residence	20	_____
Change in recreation	19	_____
Change in church activities	19	_____
Change in social activities	18	_____
Mortgage or loan less than $10,000	17	_____
Change in sleeping habits	16	_____
Change in number of family get-togethers	15	_____
Change in eating habits	15	_____
Vacation	13	_____
Christmas	12	_____
Minor violations of the law	11	_____
TOTAL SCORE		_____

°KEY

0–149	Mild Life Stress	— 30% chance of illness
150–299	Moderate Life Stress	— 50% chance of illness
300 +	Major Life Stress	— 80% chance of illness

Don't worry if your rating indicates major life stress. You are not alone. Others have survived with high stress ratings, and it is better to face what is happening than to be in the dark. People may hint that you are cherishing your grief, hanging on to the past. So when they ask how you are, you tend to be evasive, knowing they want a cheerful answer, not the truth. Yet underneath, the pain and symptoms continue.

One cold winter Saturday, I went to the YWCA to attend a meeting of widows, chaired by Lynn Caine (author of the best-selling book *Widow*). Lynn arrived and reached for the paper carton of coffee her colleague had supplied. She said to the group, "I've been grinding my teeth all night. My teeth ache so I can hardly bear it. How many of you are teeth-grinders?"

About twenty hands popped up. Then she asked, "How many of you ground your teeth before your husbands died?" A pause. Three hands. And one young woman said, "I did as a child. Then I started again when I found out my husband had a brain tumor."

We are given timetables for grief, most of them worked out by men. After the first year, the widow is supposed to be much improved, ready to begin a new life. Of course, this isn't necessarily so. Recovery is a strange passage, bumpy at best. You reach plateaus when for weeks nothing happens. You make no progress. Then, without warning, you slip into an abyss. You are down, down, lower (you think) than ever before, not caring whether you live or die. In panic, you reach out for help. This is when your doctor looks at you wearily (he has heard your sad song before) and reaches for his prescription pad. Valium. This is also when your most devoted relatives begin to whisper behind your back.

The other day I met a friend, the brother of a woman in Florida who has been a widow almost two years. He was exasperated. "What in hell is wrong with her? She drags around like a sick cat. She always has something wrong with her, something real, but what the hell? I think she is turning into a chronic malingerer. And she used to be so cute and funny."

"Did you tell her so?" I asked.

He looked embarrassed. "Maybe I did."

I thought, well, we all have to put up with frank criticism from those who love us best, for our "own good." Most of us have learned that tranquilizers, drugs, and alcohol aren't the answers, easy or hard. But when you are trapped in the dark crevices between plateaus, you can see no daylight and begin to wonder if there are any answers at all.

There are. Some of them may sound childish, some even kooky. Believe me, they aren't. They have worked for others and they may for you; in fact, we are learning that sometimes the old ways of handling illness, the power of old remedies and "mind over matter" are better than pills which cloak symptoms and may cause addiction.

First, let us consider some of the most frequently encountered symptoms: menstrual difficulties, insomnia, loss of appetite, psychosomatic pains, and the killer bee of all problems, fatigue.

Mental stress can cause irregular menstrual cycles. In addition, as has been borne out by the experience of ballet dancers who diet constantly, high-fashion models who must keep bone-thin to work, and overzealous dieters of all kinds, menstruation sometimes stops. Studies by doctors have proved that if the body of a woman loses 10 to 15 percent of its fat, her estrogen level drops— hence, no menses. For a long time anthropologists have observed the drop of the birth rate during periods of famine and stress. This may not be due to lack of energy or interest in sexual activity but, rather as Dr. Rose Frisch of Harvard suggests, the fact that diminished fat reserves make the woman's body unfit to carry and nurture a child.

Some widows can't eat; others gorge. A friend whose husband was killed in a commercial airliner accident where the victims were so hard to identify they were buried in a common grave, told me that when she flew out to the services she varied between having no appetite at all and orgies of overeating. I seem to have spent a large part of my adult life on some kind of a reducing diet. Then, like many other widows, I found that not only couldn't I regain the weight I had lost nursing my husband but I kept on losing, because the very thought of food was repulsive. In extreme cases, some widows can't even swallow. And believe me, inability to gain weight or even to keep yourself at a low level can be scary. It was no longer a good feeling to put on a pair of jeans or old slacks and find them falling off. Nor was it pleasing to hear people say, "You've lost weight, haven't you?" I looked and felt like a scarecrow. And I just couldn't eat the kind of nourishing food I felt I should be putting into myself.

At a recent medical meeting, a researcher at Temple University in Philadelphia reported a theory that hormones are responsible. Abnormal craving for food may be linked to the ancient caveman's feast-or-famine way of life. The hormones in the body, released by the pituitary gland, stimulate appetite and were necessary in early days because the cavemen had to survive intermittent periods of starving and eating. Counterbalancing these insulin-producing hormones are other hormones that inhibit appetite. During routine periods of life, these two systems keep each other in check. But during other periods—and he believes these periods are related to stress—the two systems go out of balance. A person may have an unnatural craving for food, which leads to overeating and obesity, or an aversion to food, leading to anorexia (loss of appetite coupled with hyperactivity). People most subject to imbalance of these systems are from thirty-five to sixty.

After fixing meals for a family—even a family of two—a widow loses interest in preparing meals just for herself or for herself and the kids, who would rather have junk food anyway. It gets easier all the time to let them go the pizza and potato chip route while you chew on your own solitary sandwich.

"I used to be the wizard chef," one widow told me. "I worked, sure. But I came home buzzing with ideas for dinner. Dad and I used to spend Saturday morning shopping and I'd make out a list of menus for the week. If I happened to have to stay late, Dad or one of the kids knew what to do. He'd look up the menu and start the potatoes or whatever.

"Now I've lost interest both in cooking and shopping. I go to the supermarket on Saturday morning and sometimes one of the kids will tag along. We usually end up with a lot of junk and fast food. I just can't bring myself to bother to cook a balanced meal."

Another widow told me, "I put food in my mouth and I can't swallow. My doctor says it is all psychosomatic. So what? I still can't swallow. The only food that appeals to me is sweet stuff—fudge sundaes, banana splits, big thick milkshakes. And chocolate. I wallow in chocolate. My kids call me a chocoholic. I know it's lousy nutrition. But just the sight of a vegetable plate sends me to the john to toss my cookies."

Here is a direct quote from a government bulletin on nutrition: "For the most part, man is able to maintain health with a rather large range of nutrient intake. Short-term deficits in nutrients and energy intakes will not jeopardize health since small deficits are easily repleted. Long-term consumption of an inadequate diet, however, will lead to nutrient deficiencies. The most common one in the United States is iron deficiency." And iron deficiency, I might add, also could contribute to cessation of menstruation.

My recommendation, when eating seems to be a chore, is to go back to the favorites of your childhood. Mine happen to be peanut butter, milk toast, and club sandwiches. Don't ask me why, but when I can hardly face the idea of a meal, I can usually wrap myself around a club sandwich.

I'm not going to insult you with a list of foods with high nutritive value. The government will no doubt be doing that any minute for all of us. But I do want to give you the classic elements of good eating that I myself go by.

First of all, eat breakfast—and eat it sitting down. If you are alone, try to pick a place near a window. Don't just drink a cup of coffee and nibble at toast. If you aren't hungry, you can put together a blender mixture that will furnish you with a good supply of blood sugar through the morning and a nutritious start for the day. It consists of a large glass of orange juice, a banana (cut up), any other fresh fruit you have around, maybe an egg. If you are strong of heart, you might add wheat germ and a dab of yogurt. But don't do this unless you are feeling okay. The wheat germ and yogurt, both worthy foods, might put you off. Then you can have your coffee—add milk to it if you can—and your piece of toast.

It is easy to form the habit of living on sandwiches or standing at the refrigerator nibbling on leftovers. But don't let yourself fall into it. Form instead the habit of sitting down to the table at a regular time and eating a balanced meal, even if it comes out of a package that you have defrosted. When you begin to entertain, even in a small way, freeze the leftovers into one-person meals and have enough variety in the refrigerator so that you can choose according to your mood. And, no matter what, eat three meals a day. If you don't eat between meals, and save the candy and other tempting things like cookies until the end of the meal, you will find that your appetite will come back. A friend who was thin to the point of frailty after her husband died, made a point of finishing off her lunch with a chocolate malted milk. Even when she had no appetite, it went down easily, and she sometimes added an egg. Eight months later, standing on the scales at her doctor's, she heard the nurse suggesting that she was a couple of pounds overweight.

Another response to stress is to overeat. I've seen some miserable widows stuff themselves, not because they were hungry, but because it seemed to be a way of filling the empty space inside themselves. And when you combine stress and depression, there just doesn't seem any point to denying yourself food even if it provides only temporary comfort. Here is where the various support organizations like Weight Watchers or Overeaters Anonymous might offer a place to go, and new friends, to give you a reason for getting back to your normal shape.

High on the list of problems any new widow faces is insomnia. If "white nights," as the French call them, are your ongoing problem, pills may not get you back into the routine. Music helps some people. A widow I knew lived in a trailer for six months while her house was rebuilt (it had been destroyed by a fire in which her husband died). Later she told me, "I played music until about 2:00 A.M., when I would fall asleep until about 6:00. Then while I had breakfast I would listen to music again. I was working at a full-time job all this time. I believe music helped me survive on four hour's sleep a night."

All-night movies, reading, exercises are other tricks used to pass the nights, as well as a glass of hot milk before going to bed and no alcohol after dinner. Another trick is never to read in bed or watch television from the bed. It helps if you associate your bed only with sleep. However, it may be difficult for a widow to adjust to being alone in the big bed she had shared with her husband. As my husband grew frail, he was so exhausted when he returned from the office that I would serve him dinner in bed and eat from a tray in the bedroom with him. We watched television from our big bed and eventually, when he was very bad, I bought a convertible sofa and slept in the living room. Changing back to sleeping alone in the bedroom was a tough transition.

Smoking, which has come under so much criticism recently, also seems to affect insomnia. A team of five researchers at the Sleep Research Center of Pennsylvania State University in Hershey discovered in a study that nonsmokers fell asleep after an average of thirty minutes while it took smokers an average of forty-eight minutes. Dr. Martin Sharf, a member of the research team, noted: "Many insomnia patients will light up a cigarette when they can't sleep. And that's the paradox; the nicotine in their cigarette is a well-known stimulant."

What about sleeping pills? Don't be upset if your doctor is reluctant to prescribe them, or if he gives you a prescription for only a few nights. It isn't at all unusual for a widow to consider killing herself. An amazingly perceptive man, an artist who was in his most productive years when he found himself going blind, said, "I was swamped with self-pity. I was like a woman who had lost her husband, with all the self-esteem drained away."

This inner sense of helplessness, the sensation that you no longer are able to control the situation you are in or any situation, is not just in the mind. It is a stress-related disorder with actual physical manifestations. You retreat from life. You do what a psychiatrist has called "cave living," and the deeper you dig into the cave, the more difficult it is to find your way out.

When you have this attitude you may retreat from those who might help most. In addition, the loss of a husband may stir up old feelings of inadequacy, lack of self-esteem. Try to figure this out; try to face the buried hurt. Then choose only to do things you can complete. Don't overtax your endurance. Your obligation right now is to take care of yourself. Recognize that your energy is limited and you only waste it resisting the inevitable.

When you have been taking care of an invalid, the sense of loss at his death is like that when one loses a child. The widow is left with what she feels is no role to play, no feeling of being needed or personal worth. A widow who had nursed her invalid husband for two years before his death, neglecting her career as a medical technician, felt she could not return to the laboratory—she had focused so much of herself on her husband. To fill the gap in her life, she volunteered to take care of a neighbor's spastic child. The task was far too much for her and put her in the hospital with pneumonia. There, at least, she had time to realize that what she needed at this moment was to do things for herself, not for others.

Hans Selye, in his book *Stress Without Distress*, has termed this sensible attitude "altruistic egoism."

Once when a book I'd written on death, *Love Must Not Be Wasted*, had just come out, I was speaking informally to a group at a library. One woman asked me, "Do you think I'm justified in killing myself if I find I am too unhappy to go on?"

I gulped a little because everyone seemed to be waiting for words of wisdom. Finally, I said, "If you don't hurt someone else, you are justified, otherwise, no."

Sometimes just the planning, the procuring of a sufficient quantity of sleeping pills, is the consolation that keeps a disturbed widow going. The old adage that "just the sight of the pill bottle got me through many a sleepless night" is an old adage simply because it is true. Knowing you have the means can be the comfort you need to try to go on for another night, another day.

Two research scientists at the University of California, Berkeley, Carol Huffine and Warren Breed, note that men in their late forties are twice as likely to commit suicide as women, and that by the time they reach their mid-seventies and are sick and/or widowed, they ar seven times more likely than women to take their own lives. The suicide rate for women peaks before fifty and declines steadily after that.

These two obviously intelligent scientists say that they believe the "personality traits" so often viewed as "psychologically crippling" in women may be a key to their survival; in particular they mention passivity, suggestibility, and malleability. I am not at all sure they are right. I have seen too many women today who, once they were able to breathe the clean, cold air of personal freedom, began to find life had more opportunities and excitement than they had previously ever suspected. One widow told me, "At first, I not only thought I couldn't make life alone, I didn't want to. Then gradually, I began to realize how many compromises I had made in order to make myself into a good wife and mother. To my surprise, I not only could resist any impulse toward suicide, I found I was able to counsel a discouraged friend out of the idea."

Anger and a desire to punish also play their roles in suicide, whether it is a way of showing society that it didn't care enough when you were left alone, or of punishing children and siblings for neglecting you. In *Instant Relief: the Encyclopedia of Self-Help*, edited by Tom Greening and Dick Hobson, suggestions are offered to people who have suicidal feelings. They include the following:

- Suicide is never an obligation; you can always change your mind and choose life.
- Suicide is crisis-related; and crises always pass. Give yourself time to decide.
- What are you trying to tell others by committing suicide? Why not tell them yourself beforehand? You may find out you don't need to kill yourself.
- Face the burden you may leave on your children. Children of suicides are statistically at greater risk of also killing themselves.
- If you are sure your suicide isn't a way of punishing someone, don't dump a mess on others. Leave a will. Give as much as you can to others before you take yourself away. Show that you love them.
- If you have no one in whom you want to confide, try calling a suicide prevention center or hot line listed in the telephone book. Sometimes just talking things out will help.

In California, in association with the Coroner's Office, there is a grief counseling service for the survivors of suicide and murder. As any widow knows who has lost her husband by a violent death, there are special guilt feelings and regrets involved here. One widow whose husband was killed in a robbery at the drugstore where they both worked could not stop blaming herself for not being there the night he was killed. "If only" can become an obsession, as in the case of a woman who was working on a night job when her house was robbed and her husband and daughter were murdered.

Suicides sometimes plan deaths to make the survivors feel guilty. One man in Nebraska was so mentally disturbed, he felt his wife was persecuting him. One day she came home and found a note from him on the front door, warning her not to go into the basement alone. She called her sons, who found their father hanging by a noose in the basement. He had left scattered throughout the house suicide notes blaming his wife. Her sons tried to destroy these, but carbon copies had been hidden among her underwear and jewelry.

Many survivors of suicide victims need special therapy. At the end of this book there are the addresses of two groups—one in California and one in Ohio—that specialize in helping the relatives of suicides. Beware of quacks, however. I heard of one therapist who used what he called his powers as a spiritualist to bring back suicides so they could absolve the troubled widows. The widow who reported this to me said she walked out of the séance without paying, whereupon the therapist ran down the street after her, screaming at her until she got in her car and drove away.

Which brings us to another problem that is difficult for survivors of cancer patients to face: the fear that they, too, may develop cancer.

Earlier, I told about a woman in a bereavement group who was afraid to grieve after her husband died of cancer because she was afraid that worry and depression might bring on the disease. From what research has been done in this complicated and mysterious field, we have learned that the opposite is true. A study done at the University of Glasgow, in fact, has suggested that suppression of emotions might make someone more vulnerable to disease—even a disease like cancer—than if he or she had been able to articulate anger and grief.

In an anthology entitled *Jewish Reflections on Death*, Audrey Gordon, who has worked as an assistant to Dr. Elisabeth Kübler-Ross, writes the following:

The working through of ambivalent feelings toward the dead by members of the family is extremely important in order to avoid later psychosomatic damage. I have myself conducted therapeutic interviews with such people, suffering from various forms of cancer and ulcerative colitis, in which the onset of the disease could be traced to a time shortly after a traumatic loss that had somehow not been fully faced up to and resolved. In each case the patient displayed ambivalence and unresolved grief. For example, a woman in her late sixties was admitted to the hospital with severe abdominal pains for which no physiological cause could be found. . . . My conversation with her elicited the fact that she had not attended the funeral of her daughter who had died of cancer four years before. She had never confronted the reality of her daughter's death, and she felt somehow that God was punishing her because she had not gone to the funeral. . . . When we began the grief work and she spilled forth her guilt and her anger at her daughter for leaving her by dying, her physical symptoms began to subside and she was soon able to return home. . . .

In a more tragic case, . . . a twenty-eight-year-old man refused to permit a lifesaving operation to be performed in order to stop the spread of his cancer. His two-year-old only son had died just three months before of leukemia, and the father's grief was so overwhelming that he no longer wished to live. His body heeded his mind's demands, and he died soon after.

A widow whose husband's problems started with cancer of the larynx found she was unable to swallow after his death. Not until therapy plus a complete physical convinced her that the pain was psychosomatic was she able to start eating.

In the early stages of grief, the widow is in a physically and emotionally vulnerable state. The development of symptoms similar to those of her dead husband is not uncommon. Psychiatrists suggest that this may be an attempt to identify with the dead person or perpetuate his memory. I, on the contrary, wonder if it can't be just too much familiarity with a set of symptoms so that, when you feel lousy, you begin to take them to yourself.

It had been over a year since Joan R.'s husband died of a sudden heart attack at forty-four. She made her adjustments. She began to go out with a pleasant widower. Whenever someone asked how she was doing, her answer invariably was "fine." But ever since her husband died, she suffered from chest pains. Her regular doctor examined her carefully and insisted they were psychosomatic.

One of Joan's friends, a woman on the board of trustees of a large teaching hospital, was so concerned that she brought up this problem at a meeting. The consensus: Get another opinion. If that is still negative, go to a clinic and have a complete checkup. There may be another problem causing Joan's discomfort.

The mind does tricky things and can cause pains that turn out to be imaginary. But the best way to get around that problem is to go to a doctor, tell him what you are feeling, and make sure there is no physical cause for your problems. If you aren't satisfied, by all means get a second opinion from a stranger and don't tell him about your dead husband's symptoms. And if you are given a clean bill of health and the pains still persist, you might try therapy.

It may be less easy for a recent widow to cope with what the medical profession calls autonomic behavior. Autonomic behavior is rather like sleepwalking, both of which tend to boggle the mind. I once was doing research for an article on sleepwalking for *Reader's Digest*, and went to Canada to interview a neurologist who was considered an authority on the subject. To demonstrate the simplest form of sleepwalking, he got his two-year-old son out of bed and escorted him to the toilet to relieve himself. "He functioned, but he will have no memory in the morning of having done so," he told me. "Sometimes I ask him a question and he answers, but he will have no memory of that either."

A Chicago widow told me that often, after her husband died, she would get up, dress in jeans and a sweater, and go out to the garage. "I'd wake up in the middle of the night and find myself miles from home, with no memory of how I got there. I thought I was going crazy. I would actually go so far as to hide the car keys when I went to bed. But when I was in that strange state, I could always find them. On top of which, if I slept through the night without getting up, I would often forget where I'd made my hiding place. So do you blame me for getting worried about myself?"

I don't. But autonomic behavior, rather like sleepwalking, is caused by stress. Reassuringly enough, the person seldom does anything she could not do under normal circumstances. For example, a woman who did not how to drive would not try to get in a car. Still, it does lead to some strange behavior.

Two widows, sisters-in-law, whose husbands died within six months of each other, both of massive heart attacks, decided to live together. It was a comfort, because they could compare symptoms. They found themselves doing the same foolish things, writing checks and forgetting to mail them, unable to concentrate. One of the two, a telephone sales expert, stayed home and cared for the children. The other went back to her job as a legal secretary. One day, the telephone saleswoman told me, "I just had to get off the phone and go to the store for milk. It was a compulsion. When I got home and put the carton in the refrigerator, I discovered two new cartons sitting there. I must have followed that compulsion twice before and forgotten all about it. A little bit annoyed, but amused, too, I called my sister-in-law at the office to tell her what I'd done. So do you know what? When Alice came home from work, she had a half-gallon container of milk. It wasn't a joke. She remembered I'd called her but couldn't remember what it was about, then suddenly she remembered it was milk. So she bought some."

This stage does not go on forever. When the body begins to heal, reason returns. But unless you know others behave this way, too, it is easy to worry.

Which brings us to the killer bee, fatigue, that bone weariness that few widows escape. According to Dr. John Bulette, a psychiatrist at the Medical College of Pennsylvania Hospital in Philadelphia, psychological fatigue, which coexists with depression and anxiety, is your body's safety valve for expressing repressed emotional conflicts. He reports that some people who complain of extreme fatigue don't even recognize that they are depressed. They are so concerned about exhaustion they never link it with depression. Vitamins and tranquilizers are almost never the answer, any more than those more familiar crutches, alcohol or drugs.

Although his answer may come as a surprise to the widow who is so weary she can hardly drag herself out of bed, Dr. Bulette recommends exercise to get rid of tensions, mild enjoyable exercise combined with proper nutrition to help your body restore itself. So let's look next at exercise and other ways to combat stress.

4

WAYS TO COMBAT STRESS AND OTHER PROBLEMS A WIDOW MAY FACE

FOR A woman in good physical condition, stenuous exercise like that provided by tennis or handball helps resist fatigue by increasing the body's ability to handle more of a workload. Because capacity increases, you tire less easily. But for the new widow who is suffering from chronic fatigue, who forces herself to get to work in the morning but spends all weekend in bed, who can't get started without a cup of coffee, the start must be slower.

Exercise is the "in" thing today—running, jogging, aerobic dancing, and, of course, tennis. But when you are trying to drag yourself around, it is far better to start with noncompetitive sports like swimming, which allow you to stop if you get tired. The slow, rhythmic Chinese exercise called Tai Chi Chuan—look in your telephone book for institutes that teach it—can be fun, and so can belly dancing, which is taught at most YWCAs. The important thing is consistency. It is far better to exercise half an hour a day at something that doesn't tax energy, than it is to strike out over a weekend and deplete your low stock of energy and discourage you from trying again.

Jogging is fine. But before you start, talk to your doctor. Your blood pressure and weight should be checked, and other factors (such as your smoking habits) considered. And when you start, try short distances at first, gradually increasing until you can run, say, a mile with companions.

Dr. Henry D. McIntosh of Lakeland, Florida, a heart specialist, suggests that at the outset you jog only every other day. He adds, "If you don't feel better five minutes after completing the exercise than before, it's been too strenuous."

After hearing four overly enthusiastic doctors who jog themselves speak about jogging on a television show, I want to also add one bit of advice: Read the jogging books, learn all about eighty-eight-year-old Eula Weaver of Santa Monica, California, who had such bad heart trouble she could only walk 100 feet at a time before jogging, and now today holds Senior Olympic gold medals for the half-mile and mile. But if you don't enjoy it and don't feel better, try something else. And if you are allergic, either keep away from shellfish or forget about jogging. Dr. Alan Schockett at the University of Colorado Medical Center reports that one jogger who had eaten oysters twenty hours prior to running experienced an anaphylactic reaction—hives and the inability to breathe. On another occasion, he had a similar experience, having eaten boiled shrimp five hours before running. He had no previous history of allergy to shellfish.

One of the best forms of relaxation is yoga. Joining a class will not only give you health benefits, but is a way of making new friends. And age and lack of previous exercise is no barrier. However, one yoga enthusiast warns, "Be sure to get a good teacher who will not push you to do anything beyond your capabilities. Yoga is supposed to bring you peace within yourself. It should never be competitive." I asked how one could be sure to get a good teacher.

She smiled. "The way you find a good doctor or a good school for your child or a good kennel for your dog. Ask around. Make a list. Then visit a few classes. Your vibes will tell you when a teacher is right or when he or she pushes too hard."

Another widow who has found yoga the answer for her tensions told me, "I felt like a caged animal until I found that the physical demands of yoga freed me. I recommend it to any widow who can't rid herself of tensions."

You can hardly open a general-interest magazine these days without finding some kind of article on keeping fit with exercise. All of these are good, as are many books and exercise recordings.

But it is hard to exercise alone and be consistent. Fond as I am of swimming, I found that going alone to the YWCA on any kind of regular basis was beyond my power of self-discipline. Joining a health club offers you the chance to meet other women who are regulars so that before long you have new friends who will be supportive and sympathic. But shop around before you sign up; examine the facilities and compare prices. And, above all, do not be high-pressured into a lifetime membership or even a long-term commitment.

Walking is cheap, and good for you. The habit of getting out of the house every day, in rain or snow or gloom of night, can help a widow when she begins to feel the walls closing in and the demons chasing her. And don't discount the benefits of walking. The executive director of the President's Council on Physical Fitness says that three miles of brisk walking will accomplish the same thing as three miles of jogging. But again, it is easy to skip your daily walk if you are late for work or the weather is bad or you feel sluggish. A walking companion puts a certain amount of pressure on you, but human walking companions can be undependable. Here is where a dog can be a valuable health adjunct. In fact, I feel keenly that dogs not only offer a new widow companionship on walks but the best kind of security and mental therapy. (This is my favorite hobby horse, so forgive me while I ride it.)

A recent study of persons hospitalized for serious heart problems (heart attacks or severe chest pains) showed that those who owned pets were more likely to survive during the first year after being in a hospital than those who did not. It didn't matter whether the pet was a canary, an iguana, a gerbil, a dog, or a cat; animal companions seemed to give the patient a reason for surviving.

Dr. Erika Friedman, biologist at Chestnut Hill College, Philadelphia, who did the study of ninety-two patients, concluded: "Some people believe that a pet, unlike a human companion, offers no chance of rejection, which in itself may fill a human need. Studies also show that living a long time is often associated with a complex and varied life style, with hobbies and interests outside of oneself. It could be that the taking care of a pet provides something of this sort. On the other hand, it could be that individuals who own pets are somehow different from those who don't."

Lack of companionship has been recognized as one of the factors often associated with heart disease, particularly in widows and widowers, people who live alone not through choice. Dr. Bruce Max Feldmann, a veterinarian and teacher at the University of California, Berkeley, says, "The family pet plays a therapeutic role, has helped millions of people cope with life in our complex contemporary society." Feldmann gives many reasons for this, including the following: "Pets are unselfish; they give much and ask little in return. They love and forgive unconditionally. They are ego-boosting and offset feelings of inadequacy. By their very nature, pets encourage active participation in life rather than passive observation."

As a longtime dog woman, I think that dogs especially can help a widow, whether she lives alone or has children living with her. One reason my nondoggy friends give for not owning a dog is that they are so much trouble. True. A dog owner has to keep regular hours, take the dog out—exercise him on schedule—feed him. If she goes away, she has to make arrangements for someone to take care of him. That can be a nuisance; but, as most dog owners will tell you, it is worth it, if only for the protection and security they offer you and the children. Human beings can let us down. Dogs involve no risk; whatever you do they love you. The only problem is that giving your heart "to a dog to chew," as the saying goes, means that the death of a pet can be as traumatic (or nearly so) as that of a member of the family. You can't replace a loved pet, but you can get another puppy or kitten to ease the pain and bring young life into your household. And in a family where there is only one parent, a pet—particularly an all-suffering and loving dog— will help unhappy children, give them a means of releasing tension, by joining in silly games, and a way of getting rid of emotion-provoked restlessness. And when there are problems of communications, the family dog can act as someone every member of the family can talk to without fear of contradiction or interruption. Often a child will tell the dog things he wouldn't say to his mother; she can learn a great deal if she simply listens in on those conversations. And for adults and children, dogs offer unflagging companionship.

A recent widow wrote me, "Cindy (a cocker spaniel) wouldn't eat and kept sitting by the door, waiting for Don to come home. It nearly killed me. But now she is willing to go to the bedroom with me at night and she is beginning to eat. Just worrying about her helped me with my own grief." And she added, "A dog is certainly one of the family."

Another widow who lives alone with her two dogs in a high-rise apartment in Ohio, writes, "When I come home from work, I never walk into an empty apartment, as so many single women do, because the dogs are there, waiting to be taken out, to be fed, to be loved and played with. I find that women alone without animals tend to take life more seriously than you or I. When you take dogs seriously there's less seriousness and room to worry about other things."

Maybe that's what Dr. Friedmann, the Pennsylvania biologist, meant when she theorized, "It may be that individuals who own pets are somehow different from those who don't."

Whether you decide to take up tennis or simply walk the dog five times a day, in planning your activities as a woman alone it is important to realize that under stress you simply do not function as usual. Pushing yourself will only create additional problems. This goes for all of your everyday activities, in fact. In a lecture to women about conquering stress, Dr. Kenneth Greenspan, of the College of Physicians and Surgeons at Columbia Medical Center in New York, made a statement that I hope will be as much help to you as it was to me: "Don't sweat the small stuff; and you'd be surprised how much is small stuff." There are certain obligations which every widow must discharge, responsibilities which must be met. But if you can find someone to help you with these, by all means take advantage of the offer. Disposing of your husband's clothes, giving them to someone in need or sending them to a charity for a tax deduction, may be less painful if a friend or relative helps you. A family lawyer can take care of many details, such as notifying insurance companies and probating the will. Don't attempt major decisions if they can be postponed. As for other obligations, here are four steps that may help:

1) Do one thing at a time. If you are paying bills, pay them. Sit at your desk until you have finished. Don't waste your energy by running to the kitchen to see if you need to shop, calling someone about a problem in your car, and the like. Concentrate on each job as it comes.
2) Pace yourself. Don't rush at things; that is when you can make mistakes. If you find yourself getting tense and shaky, that is also when you can make mistakes. Take a break and relax. Lie down. Go for a walk. Don't answer the telephone or the doorbell; this may only confuse you and bring on new problems.
3) Evaluate. Decide what is important. Put the rest aside.
4) Stop worrying about what might happen. Take each day as it comes. A boss of mine used to say, wisely, "Most of the things you worry about never happen. It's the things that you don't worry about that can throw you." Even so, at this crisis in your life, it helps to realize that most things are small. People aren't; they are the ones who need cherishing.

Sometimes the pressures to do something come from parents, relatives, children. Helena Znaniecki Lopata, in *Women as Widows*, reports that many of the over 1,000 women she studied complained they felt outside influences were brought to bear on them about changes they neither wanted nor were able to make. And some of these changes, she further reported, were actually more for the benefit of the person advocating the change than for the widow. We have all been through this. A married son feels guilty because his widowed mother is left alone. He wants to make room for her in his own house. But his wife, unable to face the idea of having the older woman around all the time, convinces him his mother would be better off in a retirement home. So together they push for that and, unless the older woman is able to fight back, she is sometimes railroaded into a decision absolutely wrong for her.

One of the classic warnings that should be delivered to every widow along with the death certificate is: Do not make any major decisions, whether they entail moving out of your house or inviting someone to live with you, for as long as possible, at least a year. Hardly ever are financial circumstances so dire that the sale of a house cannot be postponed until you are in a better frame of mind to know what you want, and what will be right or wrong for you.

On the other hand, if someone supportive and attractive comes along and wants to marry you, don't let the opinions of others sway you too much. I am thinking of the situation of Benita Colman who, shortly after the death of her actor husband, Ronald Colman, decided to marry another actor, George Sanders, who was known even to his best friends as a difficult man. They suspected he thought she was richer than she was and was after her money. But against all opposition she followed her instincts, and the marriage turned out happily. They were better suited to each other than anyone else could have guessed.

Loneliness can push a new widow into mistakes of judgment, however. At a time when the widow's ego is badly battered, and friends seem to be deserting her, she may stumble blindly into what might be called a marriage of convenience. Oddly enough, this can also be due to secret arrogance, a desire to show old friends that she is still of value to someone. Instead of falling into this trap, instead of succumbing to the idea—however common this is—that old friends have failed you, it is better far to go out of your way to keep up some of the old closeness. Not that you should lean too hard or become overly dependent; simply do a little more than your part in reaching out to people.

Dr. Roy Menninger, who deals continually with patients' loneliness at the Menninger Clinic at Topeka, Kansas, says, "We must recognize the value of others not simply in terms of giving us solutions but in terms of helping us understand what is happening to us, of giving us comfort and confidence. Most of us deal with our relationships to others in terribly casual ways. We do not spend time with each other. We do not systematically work at trying to understand the concerns and the troubles that people close to us are struggling with. And therefore, when we have a need and look for help, it's nowhere to be found."

He also adds, "One of the things that is very clear to us, in working with patients, is the extent to which their capacity to handle stress is very often a function of their social connections. We know that the individual who has a number of connections or relationships, of ties to others, is far better able to handle pressure than those without it."

Which brings us to the subject of grudges. You can't sit in on a group of new widows and widowers without hearing about the sister-in-law who didn't visit your dying husband at the hospital, the old friend who never wrote a line to you after your husband died. Then suddenly, out of the blue, comes an invitation to a christening, a holiday party, some kind of sentimental occasion. Your tendency, like a hurt child, is to say no, to hell with it. But think again. If you accept, and forgive, you are not only helping them, you are increasing your own strength and self-reliance.

One more bit of sound medical advice which, in a roundabout way, has also to do with your vulnerable ego. Doctors recommend that any elective surgery, even dental surgery, should be postponed until you are in better shape emotionally. This applies most particularly to plastic surgery.

When your ego is at low ebb, it is a temptation to try to make yourself look better. Protruding ears, a large unattractive nose, freckles and hanging jowls and wrinkles suddenly become terribly obtrusive. A widow may get the twisted idea that her problems will be solved overnight if her freckles will disappear or the bags under her eyes can be removed.

Plastic surgery is so usual now, and so much discussed on television by actresses and singers, that it seems to be something everyone should consider. Few people, however, know what is in store for them in terms of discomfort, rehabilitation, and expense. The American Medical Association (AMA), in conjunction with the American Society of Plastic and Reconstructive Surgeons, has published a booklet about cosmetic surgery in which they give the following information:

Plastic surgery does not produce instant results. No matter how minor the operation, living tissue is cut, moved, and reshaped. Such disruptions obviously may cause pain, discomfort, swelling, discoloration, and often bleeding. Reactions are temporary but all cuts heal by scars. Surgical techniques are designed to minimize the scars but sometimes an obvious scar is left, either due to the way the patient heals or the location of the scar. Older people may heal more slowly, but younger people are more susceptible to scarring. Other complications—which a reputable surgeon will not fail to mention—are infection and the remote possibility of paralysis.

There is a saying among surgeons that there is no such thing as minor surgery; every operation has to be approached as major because of complications that may arise. A patient who comes for plastic surgery is screened to be sure she is in good enough physical condition and routinely asked about hidden conditions or diseases which might cause complications. Yet even this does not guarantee an uneventful procedure.

A widowed friend of mine, a dance teacher in apparently excellent health, was persuaded by her teenage daughter to have her face "done." The argument was, "Mother, you've looked so tired since Dad died. This will perk you up."

The dancer agreed. One complication, which might have served as a warning signal: the surgeon selected, one many of her friends had used with good results, could not schedule the operation for six months. The dancer was impatient and told him she couldn't wait and would go to someone else. Miraculously—or so it seemed to her—the nurse called within a week to say the doctor had had a cancellation and could take her in three days.

She passed her physical examination, but during the operation she had a heart attack. Whether this would have happened if she hadn't rushed into surgery, and had been under less stress, is a question nobody can answer. But she was in intensive care for days and her activities were curtailed for months afterwards. Today she thinks that her need to push the doctor into doing the operation when she was emotionally and physically exhausted was a mistake.

For those who do not expect miracles, plastic surgery can make a great difference. A Detroit plastic surgeon is quoted in the AMA booklet as saying, "If the patient feels that his appearance has improved, his personality improves and others respond with a better attitude toward him." So, if a widow can afford the services of a good plastic surgeon—and they come high, especially on the two coasts of our country—the temptations are also high.

A Chicago widow who had been thinking of plastic surgery because she does a great deal of television work, decided to wait for a year after her husband's death. She did everything by the book. She shopped around, asked her friends to recommend doctors, and had a thorough checkup by her own internist beforehand. She even dieted at the surgeon's suggestion, and lost a few pounds so that her rather full face was slimmer. The results have been good, and she is pleased.

"However," she wrote me, "don't fool yourself that it is a minor operation. I was tired for weeks afterward. I couldn't sustain my usual pace. When I was out in California I talked this over with a client of mine who has been 'done' twice and who encouraged me. When I told her my surprise at the discomforts and weakness following the operation, she kept nodding. Finally I asked her why she hadn't warned me. She said, 'You wouldn't have listened because I knew you'd never be satisfied until you had it done.' "

My comment is: if you really feel driven (as my Chicago friend obviously did) to have plastic surgery, at least wait a year. Time won't take care of bumpy noses or Dumbo ears, but rest and exercise and good nutrition may erase some of the lines of fatigue and strain, and surgery may not be necessary.

While you are resisting the surgeon's knife, I also want to urge you to resist another impulse: the desire to run away, to take a cruise or go someplace in the sun to "relax." Relatives and friends often urge the new widow to get away, which I fear can be an unconsciously selfish gesture, a way to get her off their backs. Even a trip south with old friends may emphasize your change in status. Right after my husband died, I went back to a resort where he and I had often taken a cottage, at the urging of a couple who had sometimes gone with us. The difference in my position was painful. Not only did I have a room alone in the hotel, to which I retired at a certain hour each afternoon to watch television alone and cry; I was also expected to act as a baby-sitter for my friends' four-year-old daughter when they wanted to go out to a nightclub. Today, that wouldn't bother me. But at the time I felt it only emphasized my new position and my lack of worth.

A solitary vacation can be even more devastating. When you add the strains of travel and the stresses of being alone among strangers, a so-called vacation can do a new widow more harm than good.

A friend of mine, whom I shall call Jennifer G., had made reservations for herself and her husband on an African cruise when he died suddenly of a heart attack. Friends urged her to go anyway ("It will do you good"). She was able to cancel the double cabin, reserve a smaller one, and get some money back. The single cabin was below the water line, which gave her claustrophobia. Unable to sleep, she walked the deck at night, thinking of throwing herself overboard. A few couples tried to be friendly, but Jennifer was in such a state she could not respond. She caught a cold, which developed into pneumonia. Jennifer went right from the ship to a hospital, where she spent weeks recovering from her vacation.

Laura H.'s husband had been an invalid for more than a year after a heart attack. She kept her job on a magazine, hired a visiting nurse, and tried to create a stress-free atmosphere for her husband at home, meanwhile worrying frantically herself about diets and decisions at home, deadlines at the office. She also withheld the truth from their fifteen-year-old daughter about how sick her husband was.

Her husband died suddenly one day, when he was alone. Laura went to pieces. Her editor suggested she needed a rest. So she and her daughter went to Florida. The girl was so miserable she spend all day hiding in the room, unable to make contact with the other teenagers. Laura had just sense enough to cut the vacation short and fly home. "The only happy moment was when I shoved my summer stuff in a chest and brought out a warm sweater and slacks and went back to the office, where I had familiar work and friends."

What about the various "new" methods offered to us for combatting stress (some of which have ancient roots)? I have talked to a number of widows who found themselves much helped by meditation and various other practices offered by organizations and lecturers. Dr. Menninger, who has had experience with most of these techniques and systems, says that some serve a legitimate purpose, but that he is concerned that the leaders of such groups too often fail to recognize the limits to what they can do, so that conditions needing medical attention may be left untreated. My opinion is this: if the course or treatment offered is free, or costs very little, you can afford to experiment. But it is wise to have a thorough checkup by your own doctor before you give yourself too wholeheartedly to any venture, no matter how alluring, especially if it is expensive.

High blood pressure can be a problem with new widowed persons, and there has been considerable talk in popular magazines about a technique called biofeedback. Biofeedback is a way by which the mind learns to control bodily functions such as blood pressure, migraine headaches, colon movements, gastric-acid secretions.

Method in biofeedback training vary. At the Long Island Jewish Hospital, patients have learned to control tension headaches through electrodes applied to their foreheads that record muscle tension. When tension is high, the machine attached to the electrodes emits beeps. As the patient consciously relaxes, the number of beeps slows down and the headache eases. The principle of this is to make the patient aware of his tenseness so that he or she does not need the electrodes to reduce it. In other hospitals, in experiments with migraine patients, temperature sensors are taped to the patient's finger and forehead and a meter shows the difference between head and hand temperature. The patient is asked to relax and to will the blood vessels in her hand to relax so that the hand temperature will rise. When this happens, the meter needle moves to show more blood going into the hand. And with a redistribution of blood flow, the pressure is lessened in the head and the headache is eased. The meter gives the patient an easy way of learning that he or she can control body functions. Afterward, when the technique is learned, it can be practiced any place, any time, without equipment.

It must be emphasized, however, that much research in this field has been highly experimental. Before you enroll in one of the advertised institutes or join a therapist's group, it would be well for you to ask your doctor to check credentials.

Another approach to the control of stress is a method called holistic medicine. Holistic means "heal" in the old sense of "making whole again." In the vanguard of this nonmedical movement is a professor at the University of Hawaii, Dr. Mitson Aoki, who teaches a popular course on death and dying. Dr. Aoki was born on the big island of Hawaii, the son of a plantation carpenter, and raised a Buddhist. He moved to Honolulu as a child, attended the Honolulu Bible Training School, and converted to Christianity.

For depression, for mental distress, for pain, tension, and anxiety, and as a preventive measure to ward off illness, he urges that this holistic exercise be done three times a day. With relaxation and imagery, the patient concentrates on his own immunization process. Aoki says, 'The Chinese call it *chi*, the Japanese call it *K*, Hawaiians call it *mana*. In our Western culture, it is the spirit of God. What it does is eliminate tension-related obstructions to the flow of universal life force in the person.

The first step is to relax the total person. He urges that this not be forced or made difficult. "Go with it, flow with it. Sit comfortably in your chair and close your eyes, the better to direct yourself inwardly." Then visualize one part of the body at a time, the right foot, the leg, then the left foot and leg, the upper torso, jaw, mouth, and forehead. With your eyes closed, imagine yourself in some beautiful spot. Count to five, open eyes. Dr. Aoki says that the reason you will feel refreshment is that you are actually letting the life force flow in, activating belief systems in the body and mind, seeing yourself whole. This removes anxiety, which makes pain worse, and allows the force to heal the body. (Part of Dr. Aoki's work has been with cancer patients, helping them to visualize the life force healing their bodies.)

Increasingly, doctors are giving lung evaluation tests as a routine part of physical examinations. They, too, are realizing the importance of learning how to breathe deeply. Here are two exercises given to me by medical men to increase lung capacity. I recommend them when you feel too exhausted to get out of bed, when you are so jittery you can't sleep, and when you feel you can't face anything.

First, lie on your back on the floor, in a relaxed position, with a heavy book—the unabridged Webster's or (my favorite) the combined works of Shakespeare—on your diaphragm. Breathe in, watching the book move up with your breath, hold it, then breathe out in a rush. Start gradually, until you can do this twenty times without feeling oppressed.

For the second exercise, sit comfortably on the edge of your chair, eyes closed, legs uncrossed, back straight, your hands resting easily on your lap. Imagine that the area from your groin to your ribs is a bright red balloon which expands when you fill it with air. Exhale deeply. Hold it. Then inhale slowly to the count of seven, keeping the image of the balloon filling from the bottom to the top. Hold it. Then, slowly, exhale, picturing the balloon deflating. Do this until you feel revived or deeply bored. A friend who uses this "balloon trick," as she calls it, says that while she is doing it, she tells herself she is letting out the bad air and letting in the good.

Jane Boutelle, author of *Lifetime Fitness for Women*, gives a simple exercise for stress and tension that you can do any place, even at a board meeting. Without turning a hair, you simply pull in your stomach as far as possible toward your spine and push up, straightening yourself from the seat to the top of your head. "Just think in and up," and in a few seconds you will feel better.

Boutelle and other fitness therapists believe that the stomach muscles are very important in any exercise or posture, because "if the abdomen is weak, it provides no support for the spine or lower back." Lydia Back, author of *Awake! Aware! Alive! Exercises for a Vital Body*, gives another quick exercise which can be done in bed before you get up. You place your feet firmly on the mattress, knees bent slightly. Then put both hands under the thighs, meanwhile pulling yourself up to a semi-sitting position. The test of how you are doing is not the number of times you can repeat this exercise but the length of time you can hold the semi-sitting position. For widows who find that the hardest part of the day is getting out of bed and starting to face whatever is to come, this not-so-easy exercise is a way to get the blood stirring. And a chance to feel the small triumph of managing to hold the position a little longer each morning.

The two traditional ways to react to stress, as mentioned earlier, are increased drinking and dependance on drugs. Alcohol is a depressant, and is likely to send an already depressed widow or widower down into the pits. The chemical fix of drugs—Valium, Librium, and Miltown—can be temporarily useful. But there is the very real danger of addiction, as there is with overuse of alcohol.

Two organizations—Alcoholics Anonymous and the less well known Valium Anonymous—can do wonders for the widow who admits to herself that she has a problem. Sometimes the fear of losing something valuable—a needed job or the affection of children—may push her into realizing how much she is hurting herself. But the problem may be emotional, as happens sometimes with people who are grossly overweight and ask themselves, "What if I were thin and still unloved and lonely? Then it would mean that what is really at fault is that I am a lousy person." I am told that the drug and alcohol self-help groups take into consideration these personality problems, and that part of the therapy consists of rebuilding the ego, one's image of oneself.

Having seen an old friend of mine, a talented poet in Wisconsin, take her widowhood through the alcoholic route, I want to mention a group that helped her. She was visiting her parents in San Francisco when they noted how often Mervis was blacking out, sometimes after as little as one glass of wine. Mervis had never been a drinker, but they discovered she was using alcohol as a way of forgetting what had happened, that she was welcoming the blackouts. And, of course, she was becoming a closet alcoholic. They found she had hung a bottle of vodka inside the fireplace of the basement guest room she was occupying.

Mervis refused to go to AA. But she was willing to attend meetings of a group called Responsible Drinkers, a self-help organization in that area. Now back to her occasional glass of wine for dinner, Mervis tells me that Responsible Drinkers has other chapters. (See Appendix B for the address of the main branch.)

Eventually, if do-it-yourself or groups do not help, a widow may consider therapy. Therapists come in all shapes and sizes; some interesting new ones combine exercise or relaxation techniques with emotional therapy. A good therapist can be helpful, and you can almost recognize a good one by the fact that he or she does not insist on your coming forever. If you go, ask in advance what the charge is. If it is under $5, you can take a chance. But often the fee is much higher. I heard of one poor woman who went to a therapist because she simply couldn't function. While she sat there weeping, the therapist wrote down a number of suggestions about where she could apply for a job. Then, while the woman still wept, she said, "That will be $25."

I do have another passing thought, as one who feels that the understanding and sympathy you will get in small groups of widows is usually of more help than the one-to-one sessions with a trained therapist. I read that two-thirds of the patients who seek help from therapists are women, but that 90 percent of all psychiatrists are men. I sometimes wonder if we aren't inheriting a lot of male prejudice against liberated women when we go for help. As a reporter, I have heard too many male doctors talk about women as castraters and ball-breakers. Of course, not all women are great, either. I've met some bitches, including one who was a psychiatrist. But I think you, as a woman, can get a line faster on a female than a male can.

Just making up your mind to do something to eliminate stress from your life will make a difference. Visiting a yoga class with a friend, joining a health club, going to a lecture will be a step forward. Starting a regular regime of exercise or walking will improve your mental attitude. As one recent widow said to me, "It takes a little more effort to be a self-starter than it used to. But you feel better about yourself once you are committed."

5

WHAT THE NEW WIDOW
SHOULD KNOW ABOUT MONEY

THE following item is from the *New York Times*:

A $40,000 check was found in a women's restroom in Grand Central
Station and returned to its widowed owner, a Conrail spokesman said.
The spokesman said the check, for United States Treasury Bonds, had
been found by a matron, Nora Henderson. A few minutes later a
woman, who asked to remain anonymous, called about the check and
was told it had been found. The woman, who had been recently
widowed, said she had traveled to the city to reinvest her money.

I know why the poor woman wanted to remain anonymous. If
she had come all the way to New York to go to the Federal
Reserve Bank and then lost the check in a washroom—I can feel
for her the shame, the embarrassment, and the horrid feeling that
she shouldn't be out alone.

In a period of uncertainty such as this woman must have been
going through, it is easy to do foolish things. And when money
worries are added to a widow's many problems, she can hardly be
blamed for being in a state of near-panic. Widows today, at least
the ones I've encountered, are by no means idiots about money. A
lot of them have jobs handling money. In addition, they have
wheeled carts through supermarkets working their hand cal-

culators, figuring out whether bargains are really bargains or just come-ons. They know only too well about the devastating effects of inflation. Many of them had to go to work even though their children were toddlers, to keep the family afloat. They have worried about the big tax bites taken out of earnings and the increasing costs of everything, especially college education. But until their husbands died, they didn't have to worry alone. They had a partner to sustain them, to comfort them, to put an arm around the waist and say, "Honey, at least we have each other. Let's forget the bad news and go to a movie."

Everything changes when your husband dies.

The *Christian Science Monitor* reports that the average drop in income for a widow is around 44 percent, according to a survey made by Duncan and Copeland, Inc., and the Life Insurance Marketing Association in Hartford, Connecticut. She may get a lump sum of insurance. But it will not look as large as it did back in the days when her husband took it out, and they may have borrowed on it. She may have half of the pension he would have received, if he had reached early retirement age. And they may have some investments, or real estate. But there are taxes: income taxes, duties on his estate. And if she goes on living in the same place, the basic expenses will diminish very little. She will have rent or the mortgage, the car payments, electricity, gas, food, and clothes for herself and the children. Plus medical expenses. Plus schooling. Plus a lot of other things she forgets about until the bills come in.

So, in a state of shock already caused by her husband's death, she worries about money. And goes a little berserk.

I recall with shame what I did.

My husband had been very sick for two, three years, terminally ill for a year, in and out of hospitals. I paid such an assortment of bills that last year for doctors and consultations and private nurses and ambulances and special equipment that I was dizzy. I couldn't do my own work. I stopped thinking, sitting by his hospital bed because I couldn't face the future. And while he lay dying for many weeks, in a coma, I sat in the visitor's room at the hospital and worried about money.

I was not convinced I could ever work again. I had lost weight until I was no longer thin—I was skin and bones and looked like hell. For the first time I began to worry about growing old and the competition from younger writers and editors. My morale went to pieces. I rode the subway home late at night because I didn't dare spend money on a taxi. I even hoped I would be mugged because that would finish me off and solve a lot of problems.

One night an old friend of my husband's, a bachelor, came by the hospital. He had known Dan was sick, but not how sick. Embarrassed, he asked me to have dinner with him. After one drink, I poured out all my financial worries. Under the circumstances he could hardly be blamed for suspecting I was either trying to borrow money or marry him. He summoned a waiter and quickly ordered dinner. Then he leaned back and said icily, "Well, other widows have gone to work to support themselves. You aren't helpless."

I never saw him again, a relief to us both.

I must admit my husband and I spent a lot of money. We traveled. We went out a good bit, for which we needed lots of good clothes, or thought we did. He loved to make big gestures, expensive gifts of trips or money to old friends who had been good to him when he was a struggling sports writer. We were broke when we were married and everything had worked out. So we really never thought much about money until he got sick. I remember telling him early on, "Thank God we can afford private rooms and nurses." When I finally had to think about the future, he was beyond concern for anything. Sleepless nights did not make me any more courageous or clearheaded. The insurance agent told me I should invest all I had in an annuity—"to take care of you in your old age." So did my husband's boss. An uncle wrote that I shouldn't touch the insurance, but should leave it with the company until I decided what to do. Friends blithely told me, "Of course you'll get Social Security, all widows do." Well, all widows don't, not unless they have reached sixty or have dependent children living with them, or are disabled. In my case, my total payment from Social Security was a check for $225 for death benefits.

A lawyer who handles estates tells me that the main concern of new widows is that they simply have no idea of how much money they will have after the will is probated. Actually, having gone through similar uncertainties, I can only say that the months during which the estate is settled is in reality the breather the widow needs, the period when she can finish her preliminary grieving and climb slowly back to reality. The best advice a widow can have is that time-worn cliché: don't do anything drastic for a year. If you need money to live, you can usually get enough out of the estate before it is settled. The lump sums should be parked someplace, to earn interest, in short-term certificates of deposit or treasury bills. Selling (or trying to sell) a house is the worst mistake you can make until you know where you want to live or whether it is even necessary to get rid of your home. Meanwhile, the vultures gather. It is easy to spot the obvious con games, the people who send sets of books saying they were ordered by the deceased, or who try to collect debts they say are owed them. But watch out for the fake Internal Revenue agents who telephone or ring your bell offering deals by which you can avoid audit or save money by paying them your husband's back taxes. Always ask for identification; all legitimate audits or visits from the IRS are arranged by appointment. If anything looks phony when the so-called agent arrives, have him or her wait outside your locked front door while you call his office. And if the agent doesn't check out, call the police. The IRS says the problem of bogus government employees is a constant one, and widows are often targets.

And beware, even more, the relatives and good friends who eye you as a rich widow and come hat in hand, asking for loans to tide them over a short period. Your best answer, which should be truthful, is that the money is tied up in term accounts and can't be touched. You may lose a friend, but I fear you may lose him anyway as soon as you discover that he can't pay back the money as promised.

Your main problem may be with the legitimate beggars, the good old IRS, which still thinks we are back in the days when men were always breadwinners and the little women sat home and darned socks and washed diapers.

Harold Clurman, professor of taxation and business law at New York University, says, "If a wife dies first, I know from practical experience that the husband doesn't have much difficulty proving he was the breadwinner so that the property doesn't go into her estate. But if the husband dies first, even if the wife worked, the burden of proof is on her to prove that she paid her share of the property."

The ruling is that jointly held property will be included in the estate of the first spouse to die unless the survivor can prove that he or she used personal funds to pay for it. As Harold Clurman noted, this is never difficult for a husband. But a wife must produce personal checks, cancelled, or some other proof. Since the 1976 tax law revisions, a husband could have fixed this, if he had filed a gift tax return so that when he died only half of the appreciated value of the house would be included in the estate, whether his wife worked or not. The law allows a one-time marital gift tax deduction; however, returns would also have to have been filed each year when half the mortgage amortization or home improvements exceeded $3,000, since each time a payment was made it would be considered a gift, and a spouse can only receive $3,000 a year tax free under current rules.

But who thinks of things like estate taxes when the two of you are sailing along in the prime of life, having a good time? Not me. Not my husband.

When he died, I ran into an if-I-had-only-known situation of my own. I had worked all our married life. Sometimes I made a lot of money, other years the pickings were slimmer. My husband, whose salary was steady, gave me a household allowance that was supposed to include personal expenses like clothes. So when my checks came in, I handed them to him for investing. I endorsed them to him and they went into his checking account. His office had a pension plan for executives, into which it paid a certain amount each month, which he matched. The money he put into his office pension plan invariably came from my checks. Neither of us thought anything about it. The pension fund was our investment for the future, when we retired.

Once in a while he would remind me, as I endorsed a check to him, that if he should die I would get the money in the pension fund. There were regulations attached, of course, including the fact that any widow of an executive could not earn money while receiving the fund if she worked for any company that competed. My husband had that clause waived, because my free-lance work for other magazines might be considered competition for his company.

The day after he died, I was called up to the offices of his company. I was told that, as his widow, I would receive half of the money in his pension fund, paid to me over a period of five years; if I remarried during those five years, the money would stop. When I got home, I realized that I would also have to pay income tax on the pension fund money. What burned me up, and still makes me feel stupid, is that I had already paid income tax on the money that went into the fund. Now I was going to have to endure double taxation because I had no proof that the checks I had endorsed to my husband had gone into the fund. Unfair? No, bad planning and stupidity on my part. I could have taken that money and put it in a savings account and, over the years, collected interest on it instead of being in a position of owing the government.

Another way of destroying a woman's ego is the IRS appraisal of household furnishings. When my uncle died, during World War II, two men turned up at my aunt's home and began appraising the value of her tables and chairs and china so it all could be added to his estate. She was horrified to learn that her furniture and dishes belonged to the estate now, not to her. In my case, the two appraisers were women, nice women, who nodded when I told them that my bits and pieces of marble-top tables and the like were family pieces—from *my* family. But that, I think, was because we really had nothing of great value. If we'd had valuable Oriental rugs or paintings or a coin collection or expensive jewelry, I doubt if even my nice females would have been generous enough to take my word that they were mine. I would have had to produce evidence of purchase in cancelled checks or evidence in written form from my family saying they were inheritances.

Of course there are ways to reduce death taxes and put money and investments into trusts to avoid probate. But unless you know what you are doing, these maneuvers can backfire. Another uncle put the house in his wife's name, figuring he would die first. He didn't, so the house was in her estate, and death taxes were collected on it.

When a man is in the prime of life and earning a top salary, he may think of putting something aside for retirement, but he seldom worries about dropping dead. He has insurance. And although it is for his wife and children, he pays the premiums, which means that the lump sum goes into his estate when he dies, unless he has had her take out the insurance and the premiums were paid by her, with her own checks. Which (my lawyer tells me) isn't usual, because men don't like to relinquish control. For one thing, the time might come when he would want to borrow on his insurance and she might not agree. For another, there is such a thing as divorce.

So when he dies in a accident, or has a sudden massive heart attack, she may have good reason to worry about money.

A Chicago lawyer who does a great deal of estate work told me, "My clients in their forties or early fifties aren't thinking about death. He is in the prime of life, earning a peak salary, and his wife is usually working, too, contributing to the heavy expenses, children in private schools, trips, real estate, probably a second home for vacations, dependent parents. With the help of two paychecks—sometimes three if the wife was married before and her previous husband is paying child support—they still aren't putting much aside. Nor do they worry about it. Their attitude toward money is both smug and daring. Then when the unexpected happens and he dies or is killed, the wife doesn't know where to turn. Her smugness about money vanishes. Often she just falls apart."

He added, looking at his own attractive wife, "Women need more money than men. Men don't have to have their hair styled, they don't throw out clothes and good shoes and handbags because they have gone out of style. And it is very hard to get women to economize where their children are concerned. They want their kids to have what other kids have."

This lawyer has three children, all in private schools. He and his wife have a big house in the suburbs of Chicago and a "little place at the lake." They travel extensively and take the children with them—to Europe, to the Orient, to Africa. He says, "I'm loaded with insurance, and I have a revocable trust fund, a living will. But in these crazy times, I sometimes wonder what it all will be worth in another ten or twenty years. My wife and I agree that the best thing we can do for our children is give them the best possible education and the experience of travel. These tools may be worth a lot more than the money I will leave them."

Maybe he is right. Who knows? In any case, it is hard to save money nowadays, and few couples try. They have gone into debt with a feeling of false security. After all, they are investing in homes, real estate, stocks and bonds. But if the husband dies, his widow can be left in a quandary. Big houses are becoming increasingly hard to sell, the market is unpredictable, and she doesn't know which way to turn.

The second piece of advice I can offer may sound foolish, but I'm going to offer it anyway: Don't panic. Estate taxes aren't all that horrendous. The government today is giving more breaks to small and medium-sized estates, and widows have the benefit of an expanded marital deduction. You will still have to pay the income tax your husband owed at the time of his death and have to file for the portion of the year in which he died, and pay death duties to the federal government and perhaps to the state. You may not need a lawyer, if the estate is small and everything is left to you. But even if you have a lawyer and he or someone else has been named the executor, you should not let anybody else take over completely. The money your husband left is for you and the children, and it is up to you to get as much of it as you can.

You are under no obligation to accept the lawyer who drew up the will to take the estate through probate. He may assume he will get the job, but he has no rights at all unless he was named as executor. You may like him and want to retain him. But you have every right in the world to ask about his fee and to comparison-shop, just as you would if you were buying a car, and let him know that you are shopping. Sometimes he will cut his original fee. Or recommend a younger lawyer.

You must also be careful not to let emotions sway you into spending money for a lavish funeral. Many undertakers are honest and helpful, especially in smaller communities where they are known and plan to continue to serve the area. But funeral costs, like everything else, have gone up. And some funeral directors will try to push a grieving widow into spending more than she should. The cheaper caskets may not even be on display, so you will have to ask for something less expensive. In the old tradition, the widow was shielded from the grim task of selecting the coffin, partly for this reason. Today a widow often wants to do this herself and sometimes, when her husband is terminally ill, will even make arrangements in advance. It is one way of facing reality during the anguish of a prolonged illness and her husband may, if he is able to, help her make decisions.

If there are specific instructions in the will regarding the service or burial, she probably will try to follow instructions as closely as circumstances allow. But she is not bound to do anything that seems impractical or distasteful. Or follow instructions that will bring distress to others.

My husband used to say, only half-jokingly, "When I die, I want my ashes put in a bottle of Grant's eight-year-old and floated out to sea." After his death some of his friends expected me to do just that. I couldn't. And I didn't accept his ashes, because we were not religious and I didn't know what to do with them. Although he had told me he wanted no service, I didn't feel I could do without some gathering. So a group of our closest friends and his colleagues at the office gathered briefly at the home of another friend, and a young priest, a friend of one of his editors, said a few words.

I remember that the funeral director did try to upgrade me when I was ordering a coffin,. When I told him I only wanted a simple casket because no one would be present at the cremation, he didn't accept my verdict with much grace. However, unless you literally have money to burn, selecting an expensive casket for cremation is ridiculous.

Cremation is being selected more and more, simply because of lack of space in cemeteries. Some widows I met have regretted doing this. They feel that death would have seemed more real and final to them and their children if they had gone through the traditional rite of burial. In the Jewish religion, the grave, the raw gaping hole in the earth, is supposed to be a symbol of the raw emptiness of the mourner, just as the service is supposed to encourage outpourings of grief, to make the mourner aware of what she has lost. A widow whose second husband was cremated because he asked in his will that it be done—"I want a clean disposal"—was never forgiven by his children of another marriage. She told me she now wishes she had not followed his instructions.

As near as I could find out, the cost of a conventional funeral runs from $1,200 to $22,500. Cremation may be from $150 to $350. A great deal depends upon the locale. Embalming is not required for cremation as I write this, except in one state, Massachusetts. But it is necessary if you plan to ship the body by train or plane. If you are planning on cremation, find out if state laws permit you to send the body directly to the crematorium, bypassing the funeral parlor. It is also wise to inquire in advance if they insist upon embalming. If they say this is a house rule, find another crematorium. There is no reason to let them sell you an expensive container for the ashes. You can supply your own. If the ashes are to be dropped at sea, a floral arrangement on the cardboard box is sufficient. Or, if you prefer, nothing at all.

Guard against the so-called "package deals" that some undertakers like to offer. They can include frills that a widow neither needs nor wants. The best time to settle any discussions about money is *before* you give permission for the body to be released from the hospital or nursing home.

There is nothing mysterious about probate. All that you need do is file the will, as soon as possible, in the proper probate or surrogate court. Any adult can qualify for administrator or executor of the estate. If you have been named as executrix in the will and the estate is small and uncomplicated (everything left to you, the car and other property held jointly), you may be able to dispense with a lawyer. Find out where the courthouse is located, ask to see the probate court authority, and get instructions on how to proceed. You may be told that the court does not have time to spend coaching amateurs. But you are within your rights if you insist. And in recent years several states have adopted the forward-looking practice of encouraging executors of small estates to go through probate without lawyers.

If your husband did not leave a will, he is said to have died "intestate." Each state has different laws about handling this situation, but in any case, you will not be saved time or money if there is no will. Usually a widow gets from one-half to one-third of the estate, but there can be many restrictions imposed by law to protect the survivors against all imagined forms of human greed. In some states, to protect the rights of children, the law will divide the estate between mother and children and insist that the amount due to the children be kept intact until they are of age. Or sometimes the court will decide to give your husband's parents half of the estate.

An executor was chosen because your husband felt that he or she would handle affairs honestly and efficiently. The job of the executor is to pay taxes and "guard" the assets as best he can, then distribute them to the heirs or to a trustee named in the will. An executor is paid a fee, although a close friend or relative will sometimes waive it. However, considerable work is involved, so banks and lawyers named as executors usually charge the maximum fee allowed by the state. If the widow was named as executrix, she will of course save the fee. But she also has her responsibilities. She must not let the lawyer do as he pleases. If he makes a mistake or files late, for which there is a penalty, she is the one responsible by law.

Sometimes your husband's choice of executor was a poor one, which is again why a widow should not look aside while others take charge of her money. He may not be as efficient or as careful as your husband thought he would be. So you must watch what is going on. If you think the executor and the lawyer are dragging their feet, press them to move more quickly.

After the will is filed for probate, your husband's property will be inventoried and the full value of the estate determined. There is no probate for property left outside a will, trusts set up before death, property (such as a car jointly owned), or U.S. savings bonds. All these assets can be paid immediately to the beneficiary or the joint owner. Income taxes must be paid. If you did not participate in keeping tax records, this can be a painfully illuminating experience. A friend of mine had to go to her husband's office to search through all his papers, which, as it turned out, his successor had already removed from the desk and stored away in boxes.

Death certificates must be obtained by your lawyer or, if you are functioning without a lawyer, from your funeral director. There is a small charge for each, and you will need a separate certificate for every person or institution to be notified: banks, Social Security, insurance companies, recipients of transferred property, and the like. You should order about ten; you may not simply get one copy and xerox it yourself, as the death certificate must have a proper seal.

Insurance, fire, and casualty policies must be checked immediately to find out when they should be paid and when they expire, and put in your name. Sometimes, if you are a widow with a dependent child, the law will permit you to go on filing jointly with your husband for two years after your husband's death if you were entitled to file a joint return when he was alive, whether you did or not. You should determine whether this applies to you and whether it will be to your advantage. The federal estate tax is due nine months after the death date.

Under current inheritance laws, a widow can claim a marital deduction of $250,000 or half of the estate, whichever is greater. And with the new 1981 credit allowed, if your husband's gross estate—that is, his estate minus debts and expenses—does not exceed $425,000, you as his widow will not have to pay a federal death tax at all.

For example, if your husband died with a gross estate of $400,000 and left everything to you, the breakdown will go this way:

Gross estate	$400,000
Less debts, expenses	40,000
Total	$360,000

Marital deduction	$250,000
Taxable estate	$110,000

The tentative tax would be $26,800. But under the 1981 exemption ruling, you will be allowed a credit of $47,000 so you will owe no tax. If current plans to increase the estate tax exemption go through, 99.6% of all estate taxes filed could have no tax.

You also must make a point of asking your husband's employers if there are any insurance benefits due you, if there is a final salary check (you may find it figured down to the last penny) and what your pension benefits, if any, are. Before the Employee Retirement Income Security Act of 1974 (ERISA), private pension plans did not have to offer benefits for widows. Those that did required the husband to sign a paper agreeing to take a reduction in his pension if he claimed widow's benefits. Now by law, pension plans must provide something for widows, at least if the husband dies after having reached what is considered early retirement age (fifty-five in most plans) and has signed a form agreeing to take reductions if he retires early. Few plans give widows benefits if the husband dies before he is fifty-five. Profit-sharing plans and other types of pensions not covered by ERISA may not provide widow benefits at all. The usual benefit for widows is half of what the husband would have received.

You may also qualify for worker's compensation if your husband was killed on the job, in performance of his work. This is paid for by the employer. Worker's compensation is not taxable, and you can get it along with Social Security. If your husband was a veteran, contact the local office. Benefits change as regulations change, but currently the widow of a veteran gets a $250 burial allowance if he is not buried in a national cemetery.

Social Security laws and benefits are subject to change and you will have to apply to the local Social Security office nearest you to find out how much you will be receiving. At this writing, various widows' groups are hoping to have changes made so that widows will receive more generous benefits. But if your husband died before he reached the age of sixty-five, currently you will not get as many tax credits as you would have if he had lived to 65 or over and paid taxes up to time. A widow with dependent children living at home will receive family benefits up to a certain maximum that changes according to regulations and her status. For example, if she works and earns over a certain amount—also variable—part of her benefits may be subtracted, but on occasion this amount can be added to the amount her children receive. Benefits for children stop when they reach age eighteen unless the child is a full-time student and unmarried; then benefits go on to age twenty-two. Elderly parents, if they were supported by the dead man, are eligible for payments until the family maximum is reached.

If all this sounds complicated, it is. And a word of warning: sometimes the person in the Social Security office who adds up your claim is not as informed as he or she should be. If you feel your benefits have not been tabulated correctly, you have every right to ask to see the manager in charge of the office. If you still aren't satisfied, you can appeal your case to the government. A widow without dependents must wait for her Social Security benefits until she is sixty, at which time, if she is not earning over the maximum, she can elect to take 71.6 percent of the benefits due her. If she waits until sixty-two, she will get 82 percent. At age sixty-five, she can take 100 percent of her husband's benefits, or her own, whichever is greater. Remarriage before she reaches age sixty means that the Social Security she gets from her husband will stop, but if the marriage ends in divorce, she can have it restored. After the age of sixty, she has the choice of taking the benefits of her dead husband or those of her new husband.

When you apply for Social Security, you will need a copy of your husband's death certificate, his Social Security number, the name of your husband's employer and the approximate earnings of your husband for the year of death, as well as your latest income tax return, your own Social Security number, your birth certificate and those of your children.

Edward F. Balmer, a lawyer who heads a financial marketing consultant firm in California, publishes an interesting magazine that is distributed through banks, called *Dollar $ense*. I asked him what advice he would give a recent widow. This was his answer:

First, do nothing drastic. Hang on to real estate until you know if you want to move and where. Before you make any decision, look into the tax situation in the area where you think you might like to live. If that is satisfactory, it is sometimes possible to exchange your house for another. This is a tricky field, but if you know what you are doing, it can be a practical and economical move.

Second, stay flexible. Keep your assets liquid, in short-term deposits or certificates. You may have to move on a dime, or a quarter.

Third, keep records, not only for tax purposes, but also for your own information. Know where your money is going, and why.

Fourth, put any lump sum you receive as from insurance, in short-term certificates with no more than a maturity of two years. If you leave it right now with an insurance company, your interest rates will be very low. You can do better with banks or federal securities.

Fifth, always keep enough money in a no-touch savings account that is immediately available for emergencies. Have enough between that fund and your short-term investments, so that if necessary you could live for half a year. You can, if needed, borrow up to 90 percent on savings held by banks.

The American Council of Life Insurance urges widows to make a complete search of all papers left by their husbands, as certain policies—paid-up annuities, for example—are often forgotten. Also, policies that you think have lapsed may have built-in protection, so that they have value even though payments were stopped.

All these are details, and some information may come too late to be of use. In that case, it will warn you to be more careful in the future. Edith Sands, who teaches finance at Long Island University Graduate School, says not to worry about past mistakes. "A widow will probably do some wrong things, listen to people who don't know, and get bad advice. Or she may forget. But that mustn't discourage you. Just chalk it up to your initiation fee because you must learn to go it alone, handle your own money, for the simple reason that nobody can know what you want as much as you do, and nobody cares as much."

Eventually, you must learn as much as you can about investing, and there are many courses especially aimed at teaching women how to handle money. But a new widow seldom has the patience or concentration to get her money's worth. She must tackle one thing at a time, listen, and not be afraid to ask questions. She may discover that she has a greater flair for investing than she ever suspected.

An old friend in Wall Street tells me he has long believed that women have better money sense than men. "They have instincts," he says. "I hate to play poker with women, because I can never tell what they are going to do, and I invariably lose my shirt."

Meanwhile, he tells women, "Make yourself as much of an expert as possible. Read the financial pages. Study money magazines. And don't believe everything you hear or read. Do what you feel comfortable with, make up your own mind. After all these years on the street, I am really sure of only two things: You can't go broke taking a profit. And the experts are often very, very wrong."

IMMEDIATE DECISIONS

When someone dies, creditors and tax collectors have first claim to the deceased's "gross estate." Whatever is left for the family is called the "net estate." Life insurance benefits, however, are not subject to attachment by creditors; they become available immediately after death without waiting for the probate of the will. Such benefits are also not subject to federal income tax and, if ownership of the policy has been transferred before death to the wife, they are not subject to estate taxes.

In addition to the insurance, a widow may receive through her husband's employer a lump sum of money from her husband's pension fund. She will be required to pay taxes on this amount. But for the moment she will be in possession of a sum of money that should be earning interest for her. Until she knows more about her financial situation, it should be "parked" in places where it will be safe, earn interest, and be available quickly if she discovers that she needs money.

Banks are the obvious answer, but the interest paid by passbook savings accounts is less currently than you can get from money market funds, treasury securities, and certificates of deposit. All of these have advantages and disadvantages, and sometimes a widow who is not ready to make decisions would rather accept the lower interest offered by savings and NOW checking accounts that pay interest.

Money Market Funds: When you want to invest as little as $1,000, you can pool it with hundreds of other people and invest in one of the many money market funds. Some specialize in blue chip stocks, others in government and corporation bonds, others in tax-free municipals. The advantage of money market funds is that there is no sales commission or redemption fee, and you can, unless rules change, withdraw your money at any time by wire or a check of a certain size (usually $500 or more). You are credited with your share of the interest daily; administration fees do vary, but average about one-half of 1 percent of interest earned.

The drawbacks are that, unlike treasury securities or bank deposits (which are insured up to $100,000), these funds are not federally guaranteed, so that you would be ill advised to invest your total principal. And, although some funds include treasury securities, which are not taxed by state or city, you will have to pay federal, state, and city taxes on the income from the funds, in every state except (currently) Nebraska. Sometimes withdrawal funds may also be slow in coming, as your funds may not be located in your area. But there is no penalty for withdrawal.

Treasury Bills: Although bank deposits are insured up to $100,000, some pessimists warn that in case of a national panic and a run on banks, it might not be possible to get money out for a time. Even the pessimists agree, however, that aside from digging a hole under your house and filling it with gold coins and installing guard dogs on twenty-four-hour duty, treasury securities are the safest investment any widow can make, if safety is your first concern. The interest, as noted, is exempt from state and local taxes, although not from federal. And for the recent widow who wants to park her money until she finds out where she stands, treasury bills, with a maturity of three or six months, are sound ways of guarding money. There are also treasury bills that mature a year from date of issue, but the three-month and six-month bills are easier to buy and usually considered better for the new widow.

Bills are sold at a discount. This means that you pay less than the full value, but receive full value at maturity. At present the minimum denomination is $10,000. The difference between what you paid and what you get back is the discount, and you get a check for this.

You deposit the check in a savings bank and it earns interest; that is what is considered your yield. The discount you receive is not taxable when you get it but when the bill finally matures. For instance, hoping for a tax cut in the next year, a canny friend bought six-month treasury bills in July, knowing that they would mature in January when there might be a tax cut, so that she would owe less tax on them. She lost nothing by doing so, so it was a safe gamble—the best kind.

The one-year bills—actually they mature in 359 days—are sold every fourth week, so they are not as easily available as the three-month and six-month bills, which are sold at auction every week, usually Monday, at 1:30 P.M. But if you are faced with heavy taxes immediately after your husband's death, the one-year bills might be a way of throwing the discount you received into next year's income tax. This, however, is a matter for your accountant or CPA.

When you buy three-month and six-month bills, you have your bank make out a check for $10,000 (or more, in multiples of $5,000) to the Federal Reserve, or else have them give you a certified personal check. In this way, you are submitting your order blindly, accepting whatever rate the professional competitive bidders set at auction. You can get a general idea of what your bills will yield by examining the rates published in the financial pages of your newspapers. After auction, you will get a check for the difference between the actual purchase price and the amount you gave the Federal Reserve. And when the bill matures you get the full amount.

During periods of rising short-term interest rates, the yield of treasury bills rises. In the spring of 1980, when the Treasury sold six-month bills at an average discount of 17.29 percent, lines at the Federal Reserve Bank in Liberty Street, New York, are said to have resembled the lines of baseball fans trying to buy World was 14 percent, and the rates have been as low as 1 or 1.5 percent over those offered by savings banks' regular passbook accounts. The lucky investor who bought one six-month $10,000 treasury bill on March 24, 1980, for example, received a discount check of $739.70—the difference between the purchase price and the value of the bill when it came due. When rates on bills run little above those offered by regular passbook accounts, it is hardly worth the trouble entailed in buying them. But at slightly higher than average term bank certificates, they still remain a safe and liquid way for a widow to park her money, free of city and state taxes.

You can buy treasury bills through banks, for a small fee, or through brokers (to whom you usually pay a little more). Or you can get them direct from the Federal Reserve at no additional purchase fee. The way to do this is to ask your bank for the address of the nearest Federal Reserve Bank or branch. You can either go in person or buy by mail. If you go in person, and have a check made out to the Federal Reserve, be sure to write your name and your Social Security number on the face of the check before you leave the bank. Checks made out to you and endorsed to the Federal Reserve, are not accepted. If you want to buy by mail, ask the Federal Reserve nearest you to send you forms and instructions. There will be a number you can call about pending offerings and another number for a recorded message giving the auction results. The *Wall Street Journal* also publishes the results each Tuesday.

Certificates of Deposit: Under law, there are no limits on the interest rates that can be paid on certificates of deposit of $100,000 or more, although there are on certificates of smaller amounts. The rates are linked to six-month treasury bills and limited to investments of $10,000 or more. Rates are changed weekly, on Tuesday, and are usually posted prominently in banks. The drawback is the relatively rough penalty of three months' interest if the saver withdraws the money before maturity. Be aware that interest on CDs cannot be compounded, but you can get around this by opening a savings or NOW account in the bank and having the interest transferred to it, where it can earn compounded interest.

Do not let your insurance agent or a misguided friend hurry you into putting your husband's insurance money into an annuity for yourself. The sum you receive monthly from an annuity (depending upon the size of the investment and your age) will never increase with inflation. However, for older widows, a mother, or a mother-in-law, the gamble may be worth it. You just might fool the odds and outlast your money.

In the meantime, you should always have a few thousand dollars in the bank that are quickly accessible; some financial advisors call this the "appendicitis fund." This should not be included with other savings, and should never be touched except in an emergency. It is your guarantee that you won't be caught short if you or one of your children should be in an accident or fall sick.

Closing Your Husband's Business: A small business is often controlled by a stockbroker's agreement that requires stock of the deceased to be sold to the business or surviving partners. This is why it is not always a happy arrangement when a business partner of your husband's is named executor of the will; his interests may conflict with yours. Your husband should have carried life or term insurance to cover the cost of buying out, if you should wish to buy the business, or the company itself should have carried partnership insurance. Be sure you investigate thoroughly before you blindly agree to anything, and have a lawyer to protect your interests.

Joint Tenancy: A widow will find that stocks, registered bonds, coupon bonds, and bank accounts held in joint tenancy will be cleared and turned over to her once she has obtained the necessary waivers from the state and sent them, together with the death certificate, to the agents involved. United States savings bonds issued in the name of two persons with the word "or" between them can be cashed by the widow. Proof of identity is all that is necessary. Clearing title for an automobile that was listed in the name of husband and wife is usually a simple matter of presenting the death certificate and saying she believes herself to be entitled to the ownership. The procedure varies from state to state, however, so you will need to inquire.

Real estate may be more complicated, as noted in the beginning of this chapter. It may be necessary to prove that the survivor contributed to the purchase of the property, or received half of it as a gift. Out-of-state property that is held jointly with the right of survivorship passes to the survivor without delay and before the will is probated.

Insurance: Examine all your fire, casualty, and other insurance policies to find out when they were last paid and when they will expire. If the car insurance is in your husband's name, notify the agency immediately. Usually they will allow the coverage to run to term, then renew it in your name. In some cases, they may be willing to lower the rate if you alone will be driving the car, don't smoke, and will be driving only locally to markets and the station. But don't count on a reduction. Some agencies even regard widows and divorcées as high risks on the ground that they may be emotionally upset, and this will increase the premium.

Credit Cards: When your husband dies, notify the various organizations whose credit cards he carried. If you wish, you can ask that one or two be converted to your legal name. (A widow who applies for too many credit cards may not be considered a good risk.) The best way to destroy credit cards is to cut them up, put the shreds into an envelope, and toss it into the jowls of a sanitation truck.

Credit: Right now, look at your department store charge cards. I've just done exactly that and discovered that they are all in what I always thought was my legal name: Mrs. Daniel D. Mich. Since I have been finding out about credit and credit ratings, I have discovered I am wrong. That is merely a social title, and as such belongs to my husband's ex-wife just as much as it belongs to me. Now I understand why, when I first applied for an American Express card in the name of Isabella Taves Mich (which is my legal name), it took so many months to get it. Although I had earned money since the time I graduated from college, as a credit risk I didn't exist. When Dan died, the stores let me keep using my charge cards—I suppose because I had always paid the bills promptly with my personal checks. With some of the utilities, I didn't bother to change the listing, which was in his name. I just went on paying bills, as always. In fact, I sometimes wonder if he is dead, so far as credit ratings are concerned; every once in a while I get offers from credit organizations offering him loans and fancy credit-card privileges. Once or twice I have accepted in my name but heard nothing.

Don't be as foolish as I was. From the beginning, establish yourself as a financial identify. Change your charge cards so that they bear your own name—Mary Jane Doe or Mary Thompson Doe, not Mrs. John J. Doe. Apply for a Master Charge or Visa Card in your own name. American Express keeps their files confidential, and so do phone companies and utility companies, so their records don't count toward your credit rating. Nor do your checking and savings accounts, the premise being that you opened them as a means of getting to the most important step in the process: actual borrowing or use of credit. Also, if you took your husband's name when you were married, any previous credits you accumulated probably will not count.

Then, just to find out where you stand, get a copy of your credit file. (The Federal Fair Credit Reporting Act of 1970 gives you the right to look at it.) In order to do this, ask your bank the name of the bureau it uses. Write them and tell them you want a summary of your credit rating. Include your full legal name, your name before you were married, your married name, your social security number, birth date, all previous addresses for the last five years, your signature, and four dollars.

If you find your rating is low, what can you do about it besides applying for a credit card and your charge cards in your legal name? Well, you can try to open a checking account attached to a "line of credit." (This is sometimes known as "overdraft checking" or "no-bounce" checking.) With this, you can cash checks for more than your actual balance up to your credit ceiling, paying interest on the extra amount just as you would on a personal loan. If you want to speed up the credit rating process, you can also try to take out a loan. The Citibank booklet "Borrowing Basics for Women" suggests that if you are doing this specifically for your credit rating that you put the money you borrowed into a savings account and use it to repay the loan. After you establish a good repayment record for six months, you could repay the outstanding balance before it is due. Depending on the difference between the interest you get from your savings account, and the interest you pay for the loan, this may be an expensive way to establish your credit rating.

However, although it may read like madness to the uninitiated, this is the way the money world works. Dr. Jo Ann McGeorge, project director of HUD's credit program, gives this advice to widows: "Most women have been taught to be frugal, to save. When you are alone, the first thing you do is forget about being frugal. The name of the game is debt. You've got to have a credit line, and the easiest way of getting it is to take a loan and pay it back on time. And you've got to keep this up if you are considering a major purchase, like property or a car. You've got to show that you are in this regularly." In other words, as a broker from Paine Webber scolded an audience of women, "Don't have a love affair with a bank account."

Speaking at a seminar for business women, Patricia Flaherty, a vice-president of the First National City Bank, said, "Debt is leverage. Use someone else's money to increase your assets." Then she added cheerily, "Debt is a kind of enforced savings. But no more than 20 percent of your income should go into serving a debt, excluding your mortgage."

If you have been employed at the same place for a number of years, this will help your credit rating. (Bad luck for those who dropped out to raise children!) Living in the same place for five years or more also helps. But your husband's borrowing records don't count in your rating, not even if you cosigned the note.

Of course this is for the future, but bear these facts in mind because your credit rating as a woman alone is important. And don't let yourself now, or at any other time, be talked into cosigning a loan for a friend or relative. If he or she defaults, or doesn't pay promptly, this goes on your record. And it is better to have no credit rating at all than a black mark against you.

If a department store asks you to reapply for credit after your husband dies, do so and be sure you pay all bills promptly. If a widow skips two monthly bills in a row, that may be considered proof that she is not stable. So, no matter how upset you are, do not lose bills. One way to avoid this is to pay them immediately when they come in. A charge account, once lost, may be hard to get back. If for any reason, you plan to be away for more than a month, notify the store in advance.

Since the passage of the Federal Equal Opportunity Act and federal laws prohibiting credit discrimination, discrimination against widows has supposedly stopped. But landlords may take advantage of a widow, refuse to rent to her on other pretexts, or try to get her out of the building. Use your lawyer here. And speaking of lawyers, be sure you get one who has expertise in the area of estate-settling, as one without it could make costly mistakes. As a rule of thumb, a lawyer will receive as fee around 4 percent of the first $25,000 and less as the size of the estate goes up. But I have a suspicious friend who warns that some unscrupulous lawyers "milk" the estate by running up unnecessary expenses. It is a good idea to use a lawyer you know and trust, or one who is known and trusted by good friends or business acquaintances.

It also may be a good idea to remove your stocks and bonds from the brokerage account where you and your husband kept them until you are ready to decide what you want to do about future investments. A temporary (or perhaps long-term) answer might be to open a custodian account with a bank. For a fee (tax deductible), depending on the size of your portfolio, the bank will keep your securities, clip coupons, and open a checking account for you into which the dividends are deposited. They will also give you regular reports on income, notify you when bonds and notes mature, and execute commissions. But they do not offer investment advice, except for an additional fee.

Life Insurance: If you have young children or older parents to worry about, you should have protection for them. If you are working, your firm may offer a good insurance deal. Otherwise look into term insurance. Term insurance is pure insurance. You buy it to provide your family with a death benefit if you die prematurely and for no other purpose. Unlike straight life insurance, it does not include a savings element, so you can't cash in a term policy and get some money back. It is also the cheapest form of life insurance. Commissions collected by the salesman are less than half of those he gets for whole life coverage, so don't listen too hard when he tries to knock down term insurance, saying that it does not have a cash-in value and that it goes up every year or every five years depending on the policy. And for those over forty-five, it does go up fast. Remember by that time, your children will be grown and you may not have the responsibility of caring for aged parents. But as with any type of insurance, shop around. Do investigate savings bank life insurance, which is available in some states and is usually a good buy.

Health Insurance: If you and your children were covered under an insurance plan at your husband's office, this will probably run out within thirty days after his death. Unless you replace your health insurance, you may be without coverage at a time when you are most vulnerable. An individual policy may automatically cover you and the children after the death of a spouse, but check to make sure. Check, also, to make sure that your premium rate is lowered since one less person is insured. Widows who initially neglect to take care of this should notify the company and ask for a refund.

Major medical insurance is not cheap, but knowing that you are covered will probably help you sleep nights. If you can join a group policy at your office or with any club or organization of which you are a member, costs will be lower.

Benefits can range from $10,000 up to a million, or can be unlimited. Most policies make use of what is known as "deductibles" and "coinsurance." The deductible is the amount you must pay before benefits begin. Generally speaking, it can range from $50 to $5,000, but the higher the deductible, the lower the premium you pay. After the deductible, the insurance company commonly pays 80 percent of the remaining costs up to the maximum benefit. You pay the other 20 percent. Some policies now assure you that your out-of-pocket expenses cannot exceed a maximum amount, usually $1,500. After that cutoff point, the insurer will pay all expenses up to a maximum limit of your policy.

Before you buy a policy, it is a good idea to shop around. Choose one with the highest deductible. Also check the following points before you buy:

- Is coverage excluded for preexisting conditions? If it is excluded for more than a year, that is too long.
- Does the policy specify any medical conditions for which it will not pay? You should be aware of this.
- Are both illnesses and accidents covered?
- Is there a waiting period during which time the policy will not cover new illnesses? The waiting time should be as short as possible, thirty days or less.
- Does the policy cover all illnesses and accidents requiring hospitalization?
- Are service benefits (full coverage) specified in the policy, or is there a stated amount that will be paid (indemnity type)?
- If indemnity benefits are provided, will they cover a major portion of the fees typically charged by surgeons in the area where you are living or are most likely to receive treatment?
- Can the policy be cancelled by the insurer? If so, when and for what reasons?
- What provisions exist for renewing the policy when you reach 65?

The Social Security program was expanded in 1978 with the enactment of Medicare, which offers hospital and medical insurance protection to people aged sixty-five and over. Practically everyone is elegible, but those who are not can purchase the hospital service (Part A) for a fee that is currently $69.00 a month. For most people, it is free. The medical service (Part B) requires a modest quarterly payment, linked to current medical costs.

Medicare is also available to people younger than sixty-five who have been receiving Social Security disability payments for twenty-four consecutive months and to those with permanent kidney damage. If you are a widow aged fifty or older and have been severely disabled for at least two years, but haven't filed a claim based on your disability beause you were getting Social Security checks as a mother caring for young or disabled children, you probably can get Medicare, but check with your local Social Security office.

The address of your Social Security office is listed in the telephone book. You can write or call for information, but a personal visit is recommended when you apply for benefits. When you apply, as a widow, for survivor's benefits, do so immediately so that you will begin receiving your benefits promptly. Applications for Medicare should be made several months before you reach your sixty-fifth birthday. Booklets available in the various offices will explain schedule benefits, and the personnel will explain your rights and help you fill out forms. If you are not satisfied, ask to see the supervisor.

Taxes: You may not use a lawyer to guide you through probate, but with taxes, you need an accountant, a CPA, or a tax lawyer. The tax laws are complex, the forms are confusing, and some of the rules which the IRS goes by are reminiscent of—if not the Dark Ages, then the baby boom days when woman's place was still supposed to be in the home. The single-income family, where only one parent receives a paycheck, at this writing gets all the tax breaks. Although even the men who passed the law that blessed the joint return with only one income, now realize it is utterly out of date—over half the married women in this country work—they are slow to make any changes that will reduce income from taxes.

However, as a widow you can get a modest tax break because of this ruling. For two years after your husband's death you can file a joint return, provided that you were entitled to file a joint return in the past, whether you did or not; that your child or stepchild lives with you and qualifies as a dependent; and that your home is the child's principal residence for the entire year, except for temporary absences (school, camp, etc.).

States vary in their inheritance taxes, and some levy taxes that are not deductible from federal estate taxes. In cases where there are two homes in different states, fixing the legal domicile is a consideration in state taxes, and you may find yourself paying in both. The federal estate tax return is due nine months after the date of death, although it may be filed earlier, if possible. Usually the executor will receive some word from the IRS within six months as to whether the return has been accepted as filed or whether an audit or any additional information is requested. In cases where the estate is complicated or the lawyer is pressed for time, an extension can be applied for. However, partial distribution can be made in the interim, provided the executor is sufficiently protected by a substantial reserve of assets to meet any additional levies. Social Security checks can take as long as three to four months to arrive, and if possible a widow should not have to use insurance or pension money for daily living.

The rule that only a husband is liable for his wife's debts, but not vice versa, may cause a widow problems if it is retired, as many think it should be. Not long ago, in a path-breaking case in New Jersey, the hospital where a man died sued his estate and widow for a bill amounting to over $25,000. Under prior common law, the widow would have been excused, even though she was left with a house that was valued at more than the sum owed the hospital. But the court had a more modern attitude and saw both partners of a marriage as sharing equally in its assets and liabilities. Although the hospital won the case—and the court made its ruling prospective for future cases—it did not penalize the widow in actuality, but freed her of obligation. Other courts might not be so generous.

State and federal tax returns must be filed to cover income earned by the deceased for the previous year; if returns have been filed but taxes have not been paid in full, this must be taken care of before the due dates. In addition, income taxes must be filed for that part of the tax year preceding the time of the husband's death. Here is where an accountant (preferably one you have used before) can help in deciding whether returns should be filed jointly or separately. He can also help you estimate your financial position in the future. Single parents, if they are taxed at the "head of household" rate, pay more taxes than if they can file at the "marital" rate. This is particularly hard on middle-income families, as the child-care tax credit covers only a small percent of expenses, up to a maximum of $2,000 for one child, $4,000 for two. And married couples filing jointly can deduct $400 of interest from taxes, but the single parent only $200.

Steps are being taken to correct this inequity, but don't hold your breath. As noted, the government may acknowledge inequity, but it is much harder to cut taxes for a special interest group than it is for business. And, just to give you the bad news in one lump, Paul Strassels, who used to be an IRS man and now heads his own financial advisory concern, warns in his book *All You Need to Know About the IRS* that all you have to do to increase your chances of being audited is to die. In fact, it is standard procedure to audit the last two or three income tax returns preceding a decedent's death—all the more reason to have an accountant, a CPA, or a tax lawyer standing by.

FAMILY MONEY MATTERS

Budgeting: It used to be old-fashioned to budget. Now it is coming back into style, for obvious reasons. And it is the only logical way for a widow to get her financial house in order. After some soul-searching and a realistic review of your life-style, you can outline a personal pattern. It may not be the most fun thing you ever did, but a sensible budget—if you adhere to it—will go a long way toward giving you peace of mind. For when you are blinded by money fears, you tend to forget what things are really of value.

In reviewing your financial situation, you should know what you owe and what you own. Philip Popkin, financial advisor and partner in Prudent Services of Braintree, Massachusetts, says, "Next, take a look at your spending habits. Are you an impulsive philanthropist? Do you read and enjoy all the magazines to which you subscribe? Are your hobbies income-producing? And as for credit cards: Never charge a purchase you cannot pay for in full when the bill arrives."

We hear a lot about the "cash-flow" forecasting used by corporations. You can use the same method in your budget. The purpose is simply to predict when and in what quantity cash will come in and when and in what quantity expenditures will have to be made.

In setting up a cash-flow budget, you should make a planning sheet to cover the period of a year. On it you should write the total inflow and outgo of funds during the past year, using cancelled checks as a guide. Then in two other columns, put down what you expect will be coming in this year, and leave space to note what actually did come in. This will show you the periods when you have special cash—such as dividends—coming in, as well as those periods in which you have heavy expenses, for taxes, insurance premiums, etc. On another sheet, again ruled off in three columns, list your committed expenses for each month under different headings: food, housing, insurance, medical expenses, clothing, gasoline, utilities, etc. In the second column, list what you think you will have to spend this year, and leave the third column blank for what you actually do spend. Then, on a third sheet, again in three columns, list discretionary expenses, money you would like to spend for trips, vacations, entertainment, eating out. If you wish, you can buy ruled paper set up for cash-flow budgeting and punched for loose-leaf binders.

Budgeting isn't complicated once you set your mind to it. You will also find out exactly where your money went last year. Most people have no idea how much they spend on clothing, for instance, or on impulse buying. Once you see where the major share of your money went, you can begin to make adjustments. You may be spending a lot of money buying "bargains" at stores that turned out to be clothes you never wore or needed. Fast foods and junk foods for the kids may be an excessive drain. If you have your projections down in black and white, you are far less likely to spend money you don't have, or get into trouble using credit cards recklessly.

The point of budgeting is not to put yourself in financial prison. Sara Welles, editor of *Consumer Views*, published by New York's Consumer Affairs Department, says that even in a tight budget some room must be left for savings, not only as a cushion against losing your job, but also as a means toward long-term goals. "Savings are something you pay yourself," says Welles, "and you should take that money off the top." She also suggests that to offset the grimmer aspects of budgeting, one item should be included for treats, special occasions, splurges.

A major point: Once you have done your own personal accounting and soul-searching, get the children in on the act. A survey of 750 students at Purdue University during the 1978–79 academic year found that more than half never used a budget and two in five didn't—or didn't know how to—reconcile their checkbooks. This, I fear, is not only part and parcel of the credit-card society of the seventies. Parents have tended to bail their children out financially, just as they themselves have gone to the bank for easy credit when they've gotten into trouble. Not surprisingly, the result is widespread financial ignorance among our young people.

Children and Money: Any child old enough to have an allowance should be in on budget discussions. Be frank but don't frighten children. Try to maintain your sense of humor. You aren't punishing them by letting them understand that they, as well as you, will have to learn how to manage money and pay for their own pleasures by baby-sitting, delivering newspapers. It is not a bad way to prepare them for the real world. More and more, in schools, emphasis is being placed on career training and money management. So you don't need to feel guilty about acquainting even a young child with the realities of money. A Baltimore-based group, working with the Maryland Council of Economic Education, has put together a syndicated TV program on economics for preschoolers called "Romper Room." Sandwiched between the usual children's fare, this brief program deals with economic basics such as "What is a good? What is a resource? How do they compare?" Dr. Saul Barr, the council's executive director, says, "They (the preschoolers) are making economic choices in their daily lives, starting with what they eat for breakfast. Are they going to choose a cereal that is better for their health or one that tastes better? Are they choosing an expensive brand or one moderately priced? The children who watch these shows will not only see how they are influencing the economy but will learn their roles in it and what the roles of other people are."

The publication *Dollar $ense*, in considering children and money, makes the following recommendations:

- An allowance should never be tied to a child's behavior. Nor should it be linked with the responsibilities that a child is given in the home—like taking out trash, helping with the dishes, mowing the lawn—for which he is not paid. For certain special chores, which you would have paid for if you had hired an outsider, he should receive the going rate.
- The allowance should be reasonable for a child's needs, taking into consideration his age, where he lives, and your circumstances. It also should be reviewed on a regular basis (possibly during the family budget sessions). It should be paid on the same day each week. and you must resist the temptation to bail him out toward the end of the week; otherwise you are introducing him to the credit-card way of life.
- Older children can, through allowances, learn about "hidden costs." For example, a child who spends his last cent on an electric toy should learn that he won't be able to play with it until he comes up with the money for batteries. Grandparents should be discouraged from helping out.

Savings for Children: Grandparents, aunts, and uncles have long perpetuated the pleasant practice of giving a child money toward his education. But $25 savings bonds, because of their low yield, have been out of favor for some years. However, recently rates have been raised and the terms of maturity shortened on Series EE bonds. Series EH and Freedom Shares Savings Notes will also benefit from the increase. And for a child, the gift of small savings bonds is a way of deferring and even escaping taxes.

First, the bond must be registered to the child as owner. (If you have a cautious financial mind, you can make yourself the beneficiary of the bond in case of the child's death, but not co-owner, or you will be taxed on half the bond interest.) For the first year in which the bond earns interest, you have to file a Form 1040 income tax return for the child which puts him on record with the IRS. But in subsequent years, unless the child has other forms of income, it will not be necessary to file. Only when the child becomes subject to income taxes, and is paying on other incomes, will he have to report. Series EE bonds are available for $25 each and mature in 11 years, when the investor will receive slightly more than $50.

Another way of helping a child save money toward his education is to establish a short-term irrevocable trust for him, to last ten years and a day. The income is paid to the child, who pays no taxes in his bracket, and in ten years the principal reverts to you. You must never add to the trust. In case you want to increase the amount, you must establish a new trust. To revoke it, all parties have to agree to pay back taxes.

Parents: In the days before Social Security, a great many elderly parents had to depend on their children for support and housing. Then Social Security gave these older people independence. Now, with inflation, a widow may find herself in the position of having to help out. But don't, if you can avoid it, give your parents cash. There are better ways to handle it.

You can loan them money at a certain interest fee and have the note state that any unpaid interest be taken out of the estate. Then, because debts have priority you will get the sum back right away, plus interest, from the estate. You can also set up a short-term trust for them, ten years and a day. The income of the trust, while it is in effect, is paid to them. They are in a lower tax bracket or perhaps pay no tax at all, so in this way you save tax money and get your money back at the end of ten years. (However, if the interest amounts to more than the permitted gift exemption, there may be a gift tax.)

In the days of large families and big farmhouses, inviting aged parents to live with you was no problem. Today it would be, for both parents and you. A widowed mother poses a particular problem to a widow (see chapter 8, "Life without Father").

Although it may be a temptation to invite the widowed mother into your home to care for young children, this can be harder on her than it is on you. As we grow older, we put down roots, and they grow stronger and deeper. Moving an elderly woman from a house where she has lived for many years is a tremendous emotional wrench. A friend who tried it with her own mother now blames herself for killing her. Although she did everything possible to make her mother feel at home, using her own furniture in her room, and letting her have her own equipment in the kitchen, her mother was so unhappy she died within a year. Of course, if your parent or parents become so old or fragile that living alone is impossible, you can place them in a nursing home and take them as income-tax deductions under the "head of household" category.

But there are ways to help them keep their own homes. You can, for example, buy the home for a minimum amount, take out a mortgage on it, and then rent the house back to them—again, for a small amount. In this way, you can get tax breaks for the mortgage and for depreciation and maintenance. Be sure your lawyer is on hand for this, however, for the IRS looks warily at the practice of renting to relatives.

You should also know about reverse mortgages. In California, elderly people can arrange these plans. Under one plan, a man sells his house but can stay there for life. He gets monthly payments from the buyer until the purchase price is paid off. Under another plan, the retired owner keeps ownership of the house but takes out a mortgage, getting the money in monthly installments instead of a lump sum. In Carmel, California, the Fouratt Corporation (a real estate and insurance firm) helps elderly home owners by finding a buyer who wants a long-term gain or a home when he retires. He buys the senior citizen's property at a discount, in exchange for agreeing to pay all maintenance and insurance bills. Then he also buys an annuity for the senior citizen that will continue payments if he is still living after the equity payments for the property have been exhausted.

Pensions: Employers are not required to furnish pension plans, nor to continue them after they have been established. Most governments (federal, local, and state) offer pensions, as do some private employers. Under ERISA (the Employee Retirement Security Act of September 1944), plans must meet certain standards. Defined benefit pension plans give equal monthly or lump sum payments to men and women. Defined pension plans discriminate against women because although the lump sum payments are presumed to be equal, the monthly payments are lower for women because they live longer than men do.

In planning for her future, the widow should have some kind of pension plan. If you aren't eligible for one at work, you can open an IRA account and save taxes on the amount you pay in until you retire, when presumably you will be in a lower tax bracket. You can deposit 15 percent of your income up to $1,500, and take a total tax deduction of $1,500. While rates are subject to change, the interest yields are based on the bank's eight- to ten-year saving certificates; current rates are 8 percent a year, compounded daily and credited monthly when principal and interest remain in the account. If you make withdrawals for any reason other than becoming disabled before the age of fifty-nine and six months, you will pay a 10 percent penalty tax on the amount withdrawn. In the future, the ceiling on tax exempt contributions may be raised.

If you are self-employed, you can set up a Keogh retirement plan and put in 15 percent of your income up to a maximum of $7,500 a year. This figure may also be increased.

For grown children who are working but having a rough time making ends meet, a widow might start an IRA account as a Christmas present. You can give a child up to the allowable tax-free gift each year. If, say, you deposit $1,500 in an IRA account for him or her, he can take the amount as a tax deduction from his or her salary. If you wish, you can continue to pay into the account until your child is in financial shape to take it over. In the case of a married couple where the wife isn't working, you can start a spouse account with up to $1,750.

Wills: You do not have to have your affairs in perfect order to make a simple will. And as a widow you must have one just to make sure your money goes where you want it to go. But do have it drawn up by a lawyer, and be aware that you can have the witnesses testify before a notary public that their signatures are valid. (Sometimes when a long time elapses between the signing of a will and the death of the person making it, witnesses vanish and must be searched down, which is expensive.) Handwritten wills, even when properly witnessed, can be contested by heirs: a postman in Virginia who never married left a handwritten will giving his three-million-dollar estate to aid the blind. Out of the cold came thirty-five relatives to contest it.

Before making your will, you must do two things. The person you name as executor must be asked if he or she will take that job. Your children should also be consulted about a choice of guardian. You may hesitate to do this for fear of upsetting them. But even four- and five-year-olds may be secretly worrying about what might happen if you should die, too. Explain, simply, that you will not die for a long time but this is simply a statement of preference about whom they might wish to live with, in case of an emergency. It is of course also important to choose a guardian you can trust completely. You should choose someone young enough to raise your children and who would be willing to take them. It is not a responsibility to be taken on lightly, so give the person or persons you select time to consider.

Adieu, childhood: When is your child no longer a child? The answer, according to the Health Insurance Institute, is when he or she is no longer listed on a family health insurance policy. This usually takes place when the children reach the age of nineteen or when they marry, whichever comes first. That is when they must obtain their own coverage if they want health insurance protection. But do check your policy. Some will consider children dependents up to age twenty-three or even twenty-five if they are full-time unmarried students relying on you for support.

Testamentary trusts are effective at death. They are left to hold money for a child, or children, until they reach a certain age. Under certain circumstances, a husband will leave his widow such a trust, under the (usually false) impression that she does not want to "bother" handling money. Trusts are also sometimes set up if a widow remarries and wants to make sure her children will get her money when she dies. "Living wills" are revocable trusts. They may be set up if you are ill and fear that someday you may not be able to handle your money yourself; putting it in trust, with perhaps a bank as trustee, is assurance that your bills will be paid and investments managed no matter what happens. They are also sometimes used when you have considered leaving money in trust for your children and want to see how an institution operates before committing yourself.

6

INVESTMENTS FOR
THE WOMAN ALONE

THE other evening, I sat as a not-so-silent guest at a friend's house and heard her and another widow talk about investments. My hostess has a good job in television. The other widow works on a newspaper. They didn't know the difference between certificates of deposit and treasury bills—which is where I felt called upon to explain—but they were talking happily about tips they'd had on hot stocks in the market.

We all have our own emotional attitudes toward money. One of the classic stories about money is credited to Baron Rothschild. When someone asked him for investment advice, he asked in turn, "Would you rather eat well or sleep well?"

The thesis of investing is that the greater the risk, the greater the reward can be. And when you take risks, you must be able not only to bear the suspense but to get a kick out of it. A very smart widow who makes a lot of money in the market told me, "Of course I like the fun of gambling. But remember that to me money that isn't cash dollars doesn't seem like money. If it did, I couldn't buy stocks. The minute it becomes cash, that must be spent on food, shelter, warmth. I become paralyzed with the idea of taking risks with that money. Beyond my budget, my year's cash flow, the rest of my money is just figures in a book, and I run my house and my budget just as if I were managing a corporation, being an effective comptroller, manager, and treasurer preparing to submit an annual report. With the money I put into the market, I don't worry. I love the excitement of winning, but in my heart of hearts I know I am not really making money for myself but for the government."

Jane Bryant Quinn, author of *Everyone's Money Book*, likes to quote Mark Twain's admonition about staying out of the market in certain months—January through December. And a Wall Street investment counselor, when friends ask him for free advice about what is going to happen in the market, will quote J.P. Morgan: "It will fluctuate." The publisher of a financial digest that is directed at the trade told me, "Over the long haul, you'll never beat the odds at Las Vegas; over the short or long haul, you have a reasonable chance of coming out ahead in the stock market. But you can't be greedy. It is said that only floor brokers take the last eighth [of a point]. Before buying a stock, read the last annual and quarterly reports. And remember that a tip on a stock is no better than a tip on a horse, and a system to clean up in the stock market may be no better than a system to break the bank at Monte Carlo."

Then this same publisher smiled and confessed, "The most money I ever made on a stock was when, by mistake, I bought something I didn't intend to—it had a name similar to one on which I'd received a very hot inside tip. Which proves that tips are nonsense, unless you really are on the ground floor. By the time you can follow a tip, the smart ones are already out, having planned to take their money and run, as soon as the tip boosted the market another ten points."

In the old days, a widow could divide her money between blue chip stocks, widow and orphan investments, and a savings account, and feel secure. Today, with double-digit inflation, a woman alone can't just put her money in the bank and a few "safe" stocks and go away, unless she is so rich that her money will outlast her. You have to make your money work for you, make it earn interest, dividends. You may never catch up with the inflation rate, but you aren't giving up, either.

However, Edward J. Rudman, president of Boston Financial Strategies, says, "If you are a widow with a small amount of money and young children to educate, swallow hard, accept the loss of purchasing power and do not expose your principal to substantial risk." In fact, no large investment trust will be interested in a portfolio of $250,000 or less because it isn't large enough to achieve diversification, nor will the investor be able to live with his money tied up and the possibility of one or more investments going sour. Theoretically, investment advisors are experts in the market and know their way around. But even if you go with a big, prestigious firm that has a fine reputation, you run the risk of having your investment counselor lose interest in your modest account if he hits a hot streak and attracts a lot of business. Besides, when you take on an advisor, you also inherit his prejudices. Here are two examples of what can happen:

Twelve years ago, a widowed friend in California turned over $300,000 to an investment firm that was very prestigious. The head man seemed delighted to have her account and mentioned various ways in which he would help her money grow. She remarried and moved to England. Last year her husband's tax man questioned some of the decisions made by her trust. On his advice, she made a surprise visit back and discovered that the original advisor had moved on to million-dollar accounts and hers was being managed by a very nervous young man. She wanted to take her money away from the trust on the spot but found out there would be a considerable penalty if she did. Confused, she went back to England to think it over and ask advice there. Sometimes a hungry counselor with his own small firm will pay more attention to a small account because your money is important to him. But beware—if he becomes a star, and moves on to bigger things, he may forget about you and turn your money over to underlings.

Several years ago, on the advice of a lawyer, my husband and I hired two "brilliant" economists to advise us on how to invest the money we were making. In several gloomy sessions, they told us that they were certain a depression was coming and that our investments should be made with a downturn in mind. Meanwhile, Wall Street was booming and all the other investors were making money but, said our economists, "you'll be glad and they'll be sorry." Well, after a couple of years of losses and no recession, we fired them. By the time the recession came, my husband was dead and—I hope—the economists went broke following their own prejudices. But maybe not. Maybe they are down in Washington telling the president what to do.

It seems to me that it is better for a woman alone to make her own decisions about how she wants to invest her money, so that at least she is comfortable with what she is doing and understands where her money is. Money isn't the most important thing in the world, but knowing that you have a certain amount between you and the wolf (and knowing where you can put your hands on it) can give you a feeling of security. Of course, being at heart a Cassandra Milquetoast, I am speaking of my type of widow. I loathe gambling, and feel very comfortable with treasury securities.

However, I realize I am not typical. Sometimes today a widow comes into her own for the first time when she begins to handle money. My friend Karen L. is such a woman. She and her husband both taught at a midwestern university, he in economics, she in the psychology department. He was considerably older than Karen, and had two children from a previous marriage, so they decided not to have another family. They had a beautiful home, which was his hobby. He didn't care for traveling, so the only trips they took were in connection with his other hobby, bridge. They attended masters' tournaments and Karen finally, in desperation, learned to play tournament bridge, too.

He died suddenly of a massive heart attack. His affairs were in order, of course. He left trusts for the children and the house—worth a considerable sum—and some blue chip investments for Karen. She was offered a considerable amount of money for the house and land, and was able to sell the buyer most of the furnishings. With that money, and his insurance, she decided to go into the market. It had always interested her, but Hugh had taken care of investments for them both and never even consulted her. She told me, "I took a small carriage house on a big farm, which I rented very cheap. I gave most of the good pieces of furniture I didn't sell to charity, for a deduction on income tax. Then I read a few books on investing and took a seminar. I decided I liked a certain stock; the expert running the seminar laughed at me. But I put all my money into it and it did remarkably well. I got out at a big profit and went into another. That wasn't such a big success, although I got out before I lost money. Now I've decided to diversify. I have a couple of ideas about certain companies. And I ask you, why not? I have my tenure and my pension. His kids are taken care of; anyway, they think I'm crazy. I'm having more fun than I ever did, traveling, guessing about the market. I feel more alive than I have for years. And if anybody asks me if I play bridge, I say no. I am a different woman."

There are no simple rules to follow in investing. If there were, the stockbrokers and the experts who write the books and columns and market letters wouldn't be working; they'd be out lolling on the yachts. But there are options, and by options I don't mean the dangerous kind of stock market gambling options, I mean choices. It is your money and you alone must decide what to do with it. Meanwhile, for what it is worth, here are a few choices for you to consider:

Treasury Notes and Bonds: Treasury notes have maturity dates of one to ten years. Anything over ten years is called a treasury bond. Notes and bonds are sold in minimum denominations of $1,000 or $5,000 and pay interest twice a year. You can buy notes and bonds when they are issued at the Federal Reserve or you can look up the listings—prices fluctuate—in the *Wall Street Journal* and order through your bank or broker. When you buy in this way, you will be required to pay a premium of one-thirty-second or one-sixteenth percent over the asking fee, for anything under $100,000 is considered an odd lot. The interest on treasuries is exempt from state and local taxes, a consideration if you live in a state or city where taxes are high. They are also for women alone who want income, maximum safety, and protection.

A widow who was considering buying an annuity instead decided to buy ten-year treasury notes. She did so figuring that if interest rates went up again, she could sell the notes at a loss, have a capital loss on income taxes, and still make money.

Term Bank Accounts: If you are able to put aside small amounts of money once in a while and do not want to tempt yourself by having them too readily available in a regular savings account, you might consider the term certificates offered by banks. They usually run from ninety days up to eight or ten years. Currently popular is the two-and-a-half-year term deposit (based on government two-and-a-half-year treasuries): you can invest as little as $500, rates of interest are in line with those offered on short-term treasuries, and the length of time you must lock up your money is not too long.

Money Managers Who Accept Small Sums: If you have a secure job, a pension, no dependents, and $200,000 or so that you would like to invest, there are money managers who will give you personal attention. But watch out. Be sure the firm you are considering is registered with the Securities and Exchange Commission and ask to see the file on it, which is available to prospective clients. You are also entitled to ask for the names of other clients as references. Fees will vary, but that is not too important; if the manager does well, even a large fee is insignificant, and if he does poorly, even a small fee is too high. Also, if you decide to use one of these smaller investment advisors, do give him or her a chance, for at least two years, before pulling out. In other words, don't pressure for short-term results, although in my opinion after two years you should know enough to manage your own money.

Now, if you do decide to manage your own money, whom should you trust for advice?

Banks or Brokers?: My financial magazine publisher friend says, "If I were a widow, I would listen to them both but reach my own conclusions. Brokers can be more dangerous—their job is to earn commissions for the firm and for themselves, so they tend to churn accounts. But their knowledge is better, as they have access to better analysts than do banks. My personal belief is that bankers know less about securities than brokers and also tend to be more cautious. I could go on and on about this, but I return to my earlier premise that with a little training, availability of information and experience, a woman may do better than any bankers or brokers in deciding how she should invest her money."

In *Everyone's Money Book*, Jane Bryant Quinn writes: "If you don't know about investments and have only a small amount of money, it's best to do business with one of the large national or regional houses. The big firms have competent research departments that provide investment reports on many companies." But if you don't mind doing your own research, the investment research firms often use *Moody's* and *Standard & Poors*, financial periodicals that publish current and historical data and opinions on companies and securities, which you can buy or find in any business library. Sometimes, I am told, brokers simply photocopy these reports and send them to customers. And in some cases, the research opinions they quote blithely are colored by the bias of another expert.

When you deal with a broker, you pay a commission on each transaction. The commission varies from firm to firm. If you want, or think you need, a certain amount of hand-holding, big brokerage houses often offer special deals or discounts to encourage small investors who look like they might be good customers in time. But there are also no-frills discount brokers who charge a lot less, have no research services and no carpeting on the floor, and simply execute orders.

Before you even think about brokers, however, it is wise to take some kind of an investment course, just for the basics. See Appendix A (p. 253) for a list of books that may be useful. On request, The Stock Exchange and the Brooklyn Business Library will send you a list of books you can take out from your own library.

Free Advice: Don't ask a broker or an investment advisor who is a friend, or whom you have met socially, for advice. For one thing, it is bad manners. You don't approach a doctor at a party and ask him to look at your tonsils. For another, if he does break down and his advice is bad, you will naturally blame him, when the fault is yours. This bracket even includes relatives and lovers. There is an oft-told tale of the big business creature who would invest his mistress's money—for services rendered. As long as her nest egg kept increasing, she was happy. But after he made one big mistake, she promptly threw him over and went all over town telling his friends and clients how stupid he was.

Debt Securities: For the small investor, the Federal National Mortgage Association regularly sells debt securities ("Fannie Maes," from *FNMA*) in denominations ranging from $1,000 to $10,000. These are not direct obligations of the U.S. Treasury, but financial experts consider them nearly as safe, and the yields may be higher than on comparable Treasury obligations. Investors must purchase through a commercial bank and usually a handling fee, between twenty and forty dollars, is involved. You do not get a paper certificate, but the purchase is recorded through a computer entry, and you receive interest payments by check or direct bank-account deposit. Because these are medium term, usually ranging from five to twelve years before they mature, widows who don't want to have frequent financial decisions to make may find these investments satisfactory.

Mutual Funds: Andrew Tobias, author of *The Only Investment Guide You'll Ever Need,* recommends mutual funds for women going it alone in the stock market. So does Jane Bryant Quinn, who says, "If you try to do a rough comparison between your performance and mutual funds . . . you will probably find that the good mutual funds are far more successful than you are. You may wish to stop fighting them and join them." Rosemarie Sena, senior vice-president of Shearson Hayden Stone, Inc., adds that it is difficult for individuals with less than $25,000 to invest in the stock market because "there cannot be sufficient diversification."

In a mutual fund, you pool your money with thousands, sometimes millions, of other people, and a professional manager invests it. There are mutual funds for all types of investments—bonds, stocks, gold, and so on.

Closed-end funds, which sell only a certain number of shares, are listed on the exchange just like General Motors, and are bought and sold like stocks. Open-end funds, which take new investors at any time, are flexible, so you can withdraw whenever you wish. If you sell for more than you paid, you get a capital gain; for less, you have a loss. Dividends and interest are usually distributed on a quarterly basis.

A "load" is a sales charge. Funds that are sold by stock brokers usually charge 8 percent load, which means your fund has to go up 8 percent before you have a profit. When you buy a no-load fund, you pay net asset value, which is the value of all the investments owned by the fund, minus any debt, divided by the number of shares outstanding. No-load funds are bought directly from the management and have no sales charge, although some, to discourage in-and-out investors, have an exit fee. There is no difference in the way these funds are conducted so, Tobias suggests, if you feel two funds are otherwise equal, why pay a load? All funds charge an annual management fee, usually one-half of 1 percent, but sometimes more.

Just two words of caution. First, don't expect mutual funds to be high risers; at any moment, one can fall on its face. And just because a fund did well last year is no reason to buy. A survey made over a period of ten years showed that if you bought the fund that did the best the year before, you would have made less money if you had bought last year's worst fund.

Tax-Free Municipal Bonds are isued by cities, towns, villages, states, territories, housing authorities, port authorities, and other political divisions for maintaining facilities at schools, power plants, sewage systems, and the like. In a community where money is scarce or tight, when commercial banks are charging relatively high rates for loans, those who issue bonds have to pay the buyer more interest than otherwise in order to make the bonds marketable. A municipality with a high credit rating can command a lower interest for its bonds than one with a heavier debt load or some other credit-reducing factor.

If you are a resident of the state that issues the tax-free municipals, they are exempt from city and state taxes as well as federal taxes. For this reason, even when they aren't paying high interest rates, they are in great favor with people in higher income brackets.

However—and there is always a "however" in investing of any kind—in recent years so many large cities have found themselves in budget trouble (New York is a prime example) that there is a very real danger of bankruptcy when you buy tax-free municipals. Project notes (short-term investments used to finance urban renewal and housing) are not subject to federal income tax but, warns one wary widow, buy only those "guaranteed by the full faith and credit of the U.S. Government."

Mortgages: With mortgage rates so uncertain, if you have a mortgage on your house, especially one secured some time ago, don't pay it off with your insurance money. Use that for investment that will bring in interest, and establish your credit by making mortgage payments regularly.

Real Estate: Big gains in the value of real estate in the past few years may mean that, at least on paper, the most important asset a widow may have is her house. And economists say cautiously that "barring economic or real-estate collapse" they expect this trend to continue. Their reasoning is that more and more single people, divorced or unmarried, want to own houses, and that the children born during the baby boom of the fifties are now grown and producing their own families, albeit smaller ones.

This may mean that big houses will not sell as rapidly as smaller ones. Still, if you are in no rush to sell and can wait it out, you may do well. Children often feel displaced if a widow sells the family home immediately; even college-age children, who soon will be on their own, cling to the security of the family house after they have lost a father. I had one widowed friend whose daughter—who had been accepted by a prestigious Eastern college—offered to stay home and go to college in Nebraska if her mother did not sell the house in which she had been born. In order to keep up a big house, however, you must count on a certain sum for maintenance. And, as children do grow up and leave home, living alone in a big house can be depressing. But before you sell, make sure you have someplace else to live.

When you find a buyer, if you reinvest the sales proceeds within eighteen months in a new house, or build and occupy a new home within a period of two years, you can postpone payment of the capital gains tax or perhaps pay none at all. Smaller houses tend to appreciate in value as fast as, and perhaps faster than, big ones, and if you can get a long-term mortgage, you can use the available cash for college for your children, or for investment. But if you are close to fifty-five, you might want to wait until you reach that age in order to take advantage of the one-in-a-lifetime tax break offered to people age fifty-five or older who have used a house as a principal residence for at least three of the previous five years. According to a law passed by Congress in 1978, you can exclude from federal income tax the first $100,000 of gain from the sale of a house. The exemption can be used only once in a lifetime, so if you use it now and buy another house, you will have to hang on to it or sell without benefit of the exemption. The gain (or profit) in a sale is the difference between the sales price (minus selling expenses and improvements made with a view to selling) and the seller's so-called "basis"—the original price plus the capital improvements that have been made. If the difference is any amount up to $100,000 and the other tests are met, you could avoid all capital gains tax.

The lure of a condominium or a cooperative, where somebody else cuts the grass, may be strong for a widow. But be careful. Newer buildings are often flashily attractive but shoddily built. Older ones tend to have serious internal problems with plumbing, leaks, and the like. Before you buy, it is wise to hire a home inspection company to cast a professional eye over the apartment. Costs at this writing run from $125 to $225, a small amount when you consider the possible headaches you may save yourself. In addition, if you are buying an apartment in a condominium with grounds and a pool area, be aware of the rising costs of maintenance of these areas. If there are teenage children in the building, vandalism might be a problem, despite the fact that yours is supposed to be a luxury building. In one condominium in Hawaii where the smaller houses cost $150,000 to $250,000, the teenagers wrecked the furniture in the pool area twice. The only answer the tenants found was to remove everything from the pool to discourage sun-bathing. There were also problems between parents of young children, who wanted the streets open to skate boards and roller skates, and the older owners, who longed for peace and quiet.

Investing in "raw land"—wilderness land—may be a temptation, especially if it is in an area where there is a potential for growth. But if you intend to hold the land for future appreciation rather than to build, the risks may be great. Though land values may in general rise, there is no assurance that one's own piece will have appreciated when you want to sell. The land can become a financial burden, tie up cash, and necessitate dealing from afar with problems that can be handled properly only from close by. When future buyers are considering your raw land, roads and cesspools, perhaps sewers, wells, and the cost of bringing in electricity all enter into the problem. And you cannot ignore the carrying cost of land that is providing no income. Property taxes may be low when you buy, but no one can ignore what happens to neighboring land and its possible effect on yours.

Gold: In recent years gold in all forms has produced investment yields far outpacing stocks and bonds. Gold trades all over the world and generally advances in price when people are nervous about inflation, business, and the stability of governments. Paul Sarnoff, New York director of research at Conticommodity Services, Inc., says, "Gold shares, which our company does not trade in, are fine. But any pension fund or institutional money manager who invests in physical metal is courting disaster." He does not feel that individuals should be similarly constrained, but many other experts do. Gold can drop in price very far and very fast. Unlike stocks, which can decline in price but in most cases continue to pay dividends, gold pays no income and could cost you money in storage fees and insurance. And safe deposit boxes, where most people store gold bars and coins, are not insured. If you store your gold there, and thieves break in—they have been known to, when so many people use the boxes to store cash and jewels—you have no recourse unless you also have insurance.

You can buy gold in bars or coins. The most popular coin by far is the one-ounce South African Krugerrand, followed by the one-ounce Canadian Maple Leaf, both of which sell for up to 4½ percent more than their gold content. The United States started to sell gold medallions in 1980 and plans to continue with two new medallions for each following year for four years. The price is pegged to the prevailing market price of gold, plus a $12-an-ounce charge for production and distribution and a premium of slightly less than 2 percent at the moment. But this can change.

Gold bars and coins can be bought from banks, metal and coin dealers, and some stockbrokers. The daily price is listed in the financial pages of most newspapers and you will pay a small markup over this when you buy.

If you are buying gold jewelry for investment, be wary. Something called "solid gold" may be solid but it isn't necessarily pure gold. Only gold labeled 24-karat is pure. A 14-karat gold ring may be gold, but its metal content is only fourteen parts gold and ten parts something else. An 18-karat chain is only 75 percent gold. The word *solid* only means the object is not hollow.

Investing in Orientals, Jewelry, Antiques, etc.: Some people are borrowing money to buy diamonds, expensive works of art and the like, gambling that they will pay off in cheap inflation dollars when the time comes to liquidate the debt. This is risky even for rich people, but it is a snare and a delusion for the woman alone. In the first place, unless you are on the inside with the experts, you don't know whether you are getting something that will rise in price. And in the second, even if it does, that doesn't mean you will necessarily make a profit. The average person—you—buys at retail and pays the retail price. It is the only safe way for someone who is not an expert. But if you want to sell, you will probably have to do it through a dealer, so you will receive the wholesale rate. Finally, there is the law of supply and demand. Just because your collection of Royal Copenhagen Christmas plates is listed as being worth a certain amount in the catalogs, this doesn't mean you will automatically get that amount when you try to sell. You have to find someone who wants them.

Another point, for the woman alone or the one who is head of a household with young children or older parents: the danger of theft. Insurance is expensive, particularly on these so-called collectibles. Thieves today know what is valuable and what isn't, especially when it comes to jewelry. The woman alone can be a vulnerable target, if she keeps cash or expensive jewelry in the house. A forty-four-year-old widowed friend of mine was in an automobile accident and rushed to the hospital. Two days later, when she arrived back at her home in a quiet suburb, she found that burglars had ripped off everything of value. My sister-in-law in California, widowed not quite a year, has a dog and is careful to have special locks on all her doors. But the dog is old, and recently has become deaf. When she was out one Saturday night, thieves crawled in the "doggie door" she had cut, opened the back door, and walked out with her jewelry and sterling silver, everything in her liquor cabinet, her pots and pans, and even a roast in the refrigerator.

It also must be noted that wearing gold jewelry—even costume jewelry—on the street or when you are using public transportation, makes you a target for the gangs who reach up and snatch anything that looks as if it might bring a few illicit dollars. A friend coming out of a movie the other evening had her gold chain snatched by a young man on a motorcycle. He rode up on the sidewalk, grabbed, and was gone before she knew what had happened.

Penny Saving: It is not true, says Andrew Tobias, that a penny saved is a penny earned. On the contrary, when you earn a penny you pay income tax on it, but when you save a penny, you have a 100 percent profit. Tobias is a great believer in waiting for sales in drug stores and supermarkets and then stocking up. He even stores cans under tables when he finds a particularly good buy. He tries to rotate their use but says he doesn't worry about botulism, that there have only been three fatal cases between 1920 and 1975 out of 775 billion cans sold, and he only worries about cans that are leaking or those that are bulged out at the end.

To me, this attitude seems a little too relaxed for comfort. But you can put dates on your cans and stack them according to age, the oldest in front. You also may do better with store brands of items which, like generic drugs, tend to be cheaper. And no-name brands of items like detergent, tissues, and nuts have proven satisfactory in my experience.

But you don't even need to go so far as to store toothpaste to save pennies. Frozen dinners, shaped hamburger patties, all the little gimmicks that purport to save time for the busy shopper, also cost more, and the convenience isn't worth it. If you sent your kids shopping, warn them of these easy pitfalls. Caution them about soft drinks that contain additives. Cakes and cookies that they find on grocery shelves are loaded with fat, to preserve them. It's no great chore to bake a cake at home and it will be better and cheaper. Health food shops usually charge a premium. You can do just as well if you shop around at the supermarket.

You may not get rich this way. But don't knock it, either. Buying in bulk saves time and gasoline. Buying carefully, making sure that the big economy size is really a bargain—learn to use a pocket calculator—is good for your pocketbook and your kids' arithmetic. When you teach yourself and your family to get full value for cash paid out, you are learning how to use money, which is the secret of sound, profitable investing.

And just one further—and last—word from my publisher friend about charity deductions. During the year, he keeps a file of requests for money. In December, he evaluates the begging letters—to which he has already sent postcards saying they are under consideration—decides how much he wants to donate to charity (his CPA is in on this) and what causes he considers most deserving, and sends out checks. In this way, he has the use of the money during the year and still has the advantage of the tax deduction.

7

CHILDREN AND GRIEF

A WOMAN, even though she has lost a husband, the father of her children, is still a mother. Her needs, however, are different from those of her children. She must build a new life for herself. While death always means a personal threat to the survivor, an adult no longer requires only one or two major love objects. But her children's needs have not changed, particularly if they are young. They must have security, reassurance that life will go on and that she will not desert them. A child needs someone to care for him, to fulfill his wants, and to help him grow up and build his own personality.

There never was a child who did not need an adult, nor was there ever a child, no matter how seemingly secure, who did not fear abandonment by the person or persons taking care of him. No matter what the age, from infancy through puberty, the fear and threat are there. In her involvement with her own anguish, a widow may not recognize how terrified her child may be, how worried about the future.

Depending on age and personality, children use various devices to call attention to themselves and their needs. Young children may cling desperately to their mother, revert to babyish habits like thumb-sucking and bed-wetting, and behave boisterously. Older children may become injury-prone, develop physical ailments, become unmanageable at school or even behave in a delinquent manner.

Acceptance of death is difficult enough for adults. The younger the child, the less he can separate himself from his mother. A baby cannot tell the difference between temporary and permanent separation from her. While the death of a father, a secondary love object, does not have the direct impact of mother loss, it can have the effect of removing the baby's mother from his care and substituting another, a baby-sitter, relative, or friend. Toddlers, who try to rouse a dead kitten or pet canary by shaking it, cannot comprehend death. Even children of nursery-school age, although they can grasp the basic meaning of death, may not be able to comprehend that their dead father will not return. If they do, they sometimes identify with him by playing dead, or they may develop an excessive fear of death.

Christy was five years old when her father died of a heart attack. When she came home from nursery school, her mother told her the sad news. She nodded and hurried to her room to get her favorite doll, and played with it all afternoon, seemingly unaffected. She was told about funeral plans but did not want to participate. Weeks went by and Christy never mentioned her father. She became increasingly hard to handle, impatient, giving to fighting with other children, destructive at home. One day when she had deliberately smashed a favorite teapot, Christy's mother, tried beyond endurance, spanked her harder than she intended. Christy screamed, "Just wait until my daddy gets back— I'm going to marry him and make you get dead!"

Randy was eighteen months and his sister Liza three years old when their father was killed in an accident. Jane, their mother, wrote me, "Liza has started bed-wetting again and has terrible nightmares. She doesn't want to do anything I suggest. Randy won't let me out of his sight. Even when I go to the bathroom, he pounds on the door and screams. And Bitters, our old dog, sits by the door waiting for Tom and won't eat. The awful part is that I am so exhausted and emotionally drained, I simply haven't the patience to cope. I find myself screaming at them all, resenting the added burden they put on me."

Finally, to give Jane a break, her parents came and took the children. As soon as they left, the dog ran away. Neighbors helped Jane hunt for him in vain; after several days they decided he was gone for good. Then one day she had a call from the drugstore where Tom had worked. "There is a little dog outside trying to get in. We think he might belong to you. He seems to be looking for Tom. Every time he sees a tall man he runs up to him."

Jane went down and got Bitters. She reported: "I think the dog decided Tom had divorced us and was down living in the drugstore, where we often picked him up at night. When Bitters realized he wasn't there he seemed really glad to see me. He no longer sits by the door and has begun to eat. Last night he even followed me into the bedroom. That experience helped me understand what the children are going through. They are trying to hang on to me and make me notice them because they think Tom has deserted them and they are afraid I will disappear, too. I should have realized this before, but I was so overwhelmed by what had happened to me I wasn't thinking straight."

Harvard's Phyllis Silverman, who has done so much pioneer work with new widows, says, "You can't replace a lost parent, but you can help the family continue as a unit."

That is to say, you must, in words and actions, let children know that although their father is dead, their needs will be met, that you will continue to supply support and love, that your life as a family will go on. To a baby or toddler, your familiar face and body will offer comfort. With a slightly older child, who can comprehend death but probably is not capable of accepting it, talk to him. Silverman says, "Whether the child understands or not, your reassuring voice will help. Don't be concerned with spoiling. Concentrate on how you, as a surviving parent, can meet his needs."

All children are selfish little animals. They have to be, to survive. The younger the child, the fewer tools he has to master anxiety. And the young child's very real fear is that he or she will be deprived of essential physical and emotional gratification. One four-year-old boy, when he was told his father had died, shocked his grandparents by asking, "Who will take me to have my hair cut?" What he was really asking was, "Who is going to take care of me now?"

There is a temptation, in the chaos and agony of terminal illness and death, or the shock of sudden death, to send young children away to be cared for by friends and relatives to "spare" them. Under the theory that "they are too young to understand," a dilstressed mother really is saving herself because she doesn't have the strength to cope with her own grief. But sending children away, even to beloved relatives, may create fears that you will desert them, too. Relatives, particularly grandparents, can and should play a key role in your children's lives, providing not only the security of an extended family but giving them alternate male figures with whom to relate. But you must not turn over the primary nurturing role to anyone else at a time when the children are so bewildered.

"Sometimes I get so mad at the kids I want to give them away," one exhausted young widow said. "But then I realize they are acting up because they need me, and it is a wonderful feeling to know you are needed." Ann Kliman writes in *Crisis*, "When we nurture children in times of extreme stress, we are reassured of our ability to manage our lives and our feelings of helplessness and inadequacy are lessened."

Anna Freud, in a study of children in England during the bombings of World War II, discovered that those who stayed behind with their mothers in bomb shelters were both better adjusted and healthier than children who were evacuated to safety. Just being part of a continuing family, even in a dangerous situation, and facing hazards with their mothers, was better than being taken away at a time when they were already missing their soldier fathers.

Children do not grieve as adults do, because they have no memory bank of experience to relate to grief. They are bewildered by the tears of adults. Tears are "babyish" and the sight of their mother, the only authority figure left to them, in tears may be distressing and frightening. But it is of no help to a child to suppress your grief because he seems disturbed or frightened when you cry. Rabbi Joshua Liebman, author of a wonderful book called *Peace of Mind*, which he wrote just after World War II, when there were so many grieving war widows with young children, noted the following:

> A child should never be needlessly frightened . . . but what is a supreme illusion among men is that children cannot stand grief and sadness, that under all circumstances they must be coddled and sheltered against the winds of reality. No, the truth lies in exactly the opposite direction. The child can stand tears but not treachery, sorrow but not deceit. The little girl or boy should be dealt with in a straightforward, honest fashion; he should be allowed to share in a family's woes as well as its triumphs. The little organism is much tougher than we think . . . It will not break under honestly presented grief. It may break under the burden of exclusion and exile from the family circle, under the heavy load of adult evasions, half truths, frozen emotions, hypocritical pretenses.

Explain to your children, if you wish, that you won't always be crying but now you must because you are sad. Not to see you shed tears over the loss of someone you both loved is to deny a child his birthright as a human being, the ability to express sadness at loss. In order to grow up into a mature person emotionally, a child must also work through his own grief and loss, and you are setting an example for him. Liebman says, "We are all baffled children . . . [But by] accepting rather than avoiding intense feelings of sadness, by expressing emotions rather than suppressing them, by readjusting to the environment bereft of the loved one and by beginning to form new relationships . . . a true grief strategy has been discovered and the danger of future neurosis averted."

The most important thing you can offer a baby whose father has just died is consistency. Child psychologists say that very early in life, the baby learns the difference between having and not having, between here and not here—"all gone." And anxiety about separation from love objects is also present early. Justin Call, professor and chief of infant, child, and adolescent psychology at the University of California's Irving School of Medicine, believes that by the age of six months, in response to a loss such as separation from his mother, an infant is capable of feeling depression, expressed in sleep disorders, bowel difficulties, and refusal to eat.

In the hectic pace of events surrounding terminal illness and death, it is often necessary to turn over the care of young children to someone else. So long as the baby is in familiar surroundings with his own crib and toys, he will not suffer. But be aware that he needs you. Even though you are unhappy, it is still important that he know that you aren't "all gone."

Of course, if in the past you have turned over the daily care of the baby to a grandparent or housekeeper, it is best to continue this same routine for a while until the baby feels secure again. This substitute parent does not and should not play the role of an additional parent, but at this time it is best not to disturb the routine. Transfer to a day-care center, or to the home of someone new, might add to the child's bewilderment.

Past the age of three, children seem to be able to realize that when a dead pet is buried in the earth, he does not mind because he does not need air to breathe anymore, and that it does not hurt him to have earth piled on him, since he cannot feel. By the time a child is four, however, his fantasy life is so vivid that it is hard for him to distinguish between pretend and real, between what is happening and what might happen. That is another reason why it is important not to confuse a child with myths or half-truths about what happened when Daddy died. Ann Kliman, who has worked with many bereaved children, warns, "The grimmest reality is rarely as terrifying as their own fantasy."

Young children believe that they are omnipotent, and that the world exists solely for them. Kliman tells the story of a small child who was so angry at his mother that he took a baseball bat and went out and hit the lamp post in front of their house as hard as he could. All the lights in town dimmed, then went out. It was the 1965 blackout in New York. But the little boy was sure he had caused it by hitting the lamp post.

Small children often get so angry when they are punished or denied something that they tell their parents, "I wish you were dead." Then when disaster strikes, they feel guilty. One little boy of four had resented sharing his mother's affection with his daddy and fantasized a world where his father didn't exist and he had his mother all to himself. When his father died suddenly, the little boy felt he was to blame. His way of handling the situation was denial. He insisted his father was not dead, but hiding, and that he would come back. What he did not say—aloud—was that he also was sure his father would come back to punish him for his evil thoughts. When his mother told him, over and over, that his father could not come back because he was dead, the child then decided that his father would appear in the form of an animal and hurt him. He developed an inordinate fear of all animals—birds, cats, squirrels, especially big dogs.

A therapist at one center explained the death of a two-year-old's father to him in this way: "Daddy was in an airplane and it fell and he was hurt so badly that he died." That evening, when the child's mother was putting Jimmy to bed, he threw his arms around her and whispered, "Mommy, I didn't push him."

Ted, five years old, was taken to the intensive-care burn unit of a large city hospital after the family house burned down, killing his father and injuring his mother so badly she was hospitalized elsewhere. The boy refused to eat and stared listlessly at the wall all day. Social workers explained why his mother could not visit him, and even arranged to have him talk to her by phone. But Ted grew more and more remote. Finally a psychiatrist was able to find out that Ted was sure his mother was angry at him because he had not been able to rescue his father when the fire broke out.

Children of different ages cope differently with grief. An older child, for example, has developed relationships with other children, uncles and aunts, teachers. But from six to ten, most children, although they recognize death as final, in their reactions unconsciously protest against the acknowledged reality. Much depends on a child's maturity, what kind of a home atmosphere exists, the strength of his mother and his relationship with his dead father. "Some two-year-olds have a concept of death, while some five-year-olds do not," says Dr. Robert Furman, Director of the Child's Research Center in Cleveland, Ohio, who is making an ongoing study of death and young children.

Physical symptoms—sleepwalking, asthma, facial tics, nervous stomach, sleeplessness, headaches, eating disorders—often occur in preadolescent children. But these troubles, worrying as they are, improve and disappear as the child again becomes adjusted and secure. Delinquent behavior—fighting with other children, impudence to teachers, running away from school, setting fires— is another way of expressing anger and protesting.

Nine-year-old Rickie had always been an outgoing, bright boy, a good athlete who also made excellent grades and was liked by students and teachers. But during his father's terminal illness he set fire to the principal's office and ran away. (It turned out that he was trying to burn his report card because his grades had fallen.) When the police found him and brought him home, his mother was both relieved and angry. She shouted at him, "Don't you care that your poor daddy is dying? Why do you have to do such things and cause him and me extra worry?"

Rickie reacted with unexpected fury, ran in his room, and slammed the door. One of the policemen said, "The boy said his father was sick, but I don't think he knew he was dying until you said so." His mother, when she felt calmer herself, was able to go Rickie and explain that they hadn't told him his father was going to die because they didn't want to worry him. She held the boy in her arms and comforted him—and herself—while they both wept.

In a study conducted by Phyllis Silverman, two-thirds of widows with dependent children reported that the children were having some kind of difficulty. But Silverman and other experts who work with widows feel that professional counseling is not the answer unless a child is unable to function. Sending an already upset child to a stranger for help can be devastating. In a household where one parent may be too ill to think of anyone but himself, and the other is overburdened with worry, the child may be crying out for attention in the only way he knows.

Children's outbursts of anger can be very trying to a recently widowed mother. "My twelve-year-old son is so angry at me for letting his father die, I can hardly bear to have him around," I heard one distressed widow complain at a group meeting. Anger says, "Why did this awful thing have to happen to me?" "Why did he go and die when I needed him so?" Or, "Why did he desert me if he loved me?" It may be directed at the dead man, or the doctor, or God—or you. And if it is directed at you, it means that you receive double the amount of anger, because there is no one else on whom the child can unload now that his father is dead.

It is essential to recognize that anger is actually a healthy sign, a sign that the child has accepted death and is ready to survive, albeit not without telling the world how unfair life is. Also, bear in mind the complications of the child's position: the fact that he is dependent on you, and knows it, puts him in a frustrating situation. In the case of Christy, who wanted her dead father to return and "make her mother get dead," she was both angry at her mother for letting her father die and afraid to express her anger directly because she needed her mother.

A Cancer Care report, *Listen to the Children*, says that young children have a sense of personal danger even before death when a parent is ill. In the families they studied, one parent had terminal cancer; two-thirds of the children had sleeping problems, difficulty concentrating at school, and trouble getting along with other children. Some retreated into sullen silence, others caused trouble by getting into fights. The more prolonged the illness, the more severe the symptoms. But—and this is significant—the most excessive regressive behavior, ranging from reversion to babyhood, inability to walk or dress themselves, to actual delinquency (in the six-to-ten group) was seen when the child was not told the prognosis.

When a mother can't sort out her own ideas about death and what lies beyond, it also becomes difficult for her to decide what to tell her children. Author Earl Grollman quotes a sophisticated religious school teacher who, when asked to explain death to her students, said, "Before I can teach children about death, someone has to straighten me out!" But you can be honest with them and say, "I don't know." When you draw back from discussing death with your children, you are hurting them and sometimes yourself. In order to be able to mourn, a child must accept death as final. Erna Furman, in her book *A Child's Parent Dies*, says, "When a child's parent dies, he faces an incomparable stress which threatens the future development of his personality.

This danger can be averted if the child can be helped to mourn as fully as possible."

She goes on to say that the older the child, the better will he be able to accept death and to mourn. Also, the more mature and healthy the child and the family relationship, the better will he be able to adjust eventually. Yet a child can mourn only when he feels so secure with his remaining parent that he no longer needs to worry about himself and can focus his attention on grief for his father.

Just because children don't react as adults do to the death of a father, do not think they do not care or are "too young to understand." Dr. Robert Furman, of the Cleveland Child's Research Center, dismisses the notion that any child is incapable of grief. He warns, "It is important to make a sharp distinction between a child's not mourning and his incapability to mourn."

My friend Lorraine had twins, a boy and a girl, who were a little more than nine when their father died of a brain tumor. The girl was sad and wanted to be comforted. Her brother merely nodded when he was told and went back to the book he had been reading. Lorraine was terribly distressed because he was not more affected. What he was doing, although she did not realize it at the time, was protecting himself by accepting the overwhelming news bit by bit. Many children, even children well on the way to puberty, do not have sufficient maturity to pay constant attention for very long. (And, it is to be noted, boys often mature later than girls.) In the case of this twin, he had expressed as much emotion as he dared and had hidden away in a book to recuperate. Slowly, he got over his feeling of shock and was able to talk about his father's death with his mother.

Patience is needed in a situation like this. You must hold yourself open for the moment when such a child is ready to talk. It may take a long time, but you cannot push. If a child starts to talk, then draws back, let him be. A silent hug will tell him you will wait until he is ready. And do not worry if he needs to talk at an inconvenient moment, such as a family dinner, when he whispers "I miss Daddy" or something equally indicative of his desire to talk about it. Excuse yourself so you can have a few minutes of private conversation. Then wait, although it may not be easy, until the moment comes again. "It will," therapist June Wimpy assures us. "It always does. You must simply be alert and not miss it."

Unresolved mourning may mean a child will eventually need the help of a psychiatrist. Erna Furman tells of a four-year-old girl who was not told of her father's death by her mother, but rather by a playmate whose mother had attended the funeral. She showed no grief symptoms until two years later when she acquired what was diagnosed as an "hysterical" stiffness of her neck and became hyperactive. The psychiatrist concluded that the neck stiffness was related to the stiffness of the dead body of her father and that the hyperactivity was a way of warding off her own death. Children who are never given the opportunity to grieve can grow up into men and women who are crippled emotionally. Francine de Plessix Gray, the writer, in discussing the mark left on her as an adult by her unresolved grief after her father's death when she was a child, quotes François Mauriac: "Upon the death of a parent, a child is like a reed bent by a heavy storm. He may straighten up or he may not, he may live permanently in a stooped condition, a condition of enfeeblement."

We used to pay too little attention to the grief of children. If a child didn't cry, that was all to the good; if he reacted with temper tantrums (as my husband did after his mother's death when he was four) he was punished. But large extended families, and the presence of brothers and sisters, meant that most children knew what was going on through the grapevine. Today with one- and two-children families, children are more protected, and adults often try to soften the blow of death with myths, euphemisms, and half-truths.

But it never works. For, as Earl Grollman says in his book *Explaining Death to Children*, the gap between "what the adults say or do and the underlying feeling that children sense, is likely to cause more confusion and distress than if the parents tell the child the truth."

The desire to "protect" children, especially young children, is human. A nursery school teacher, Marguerita Rudolph, tells an interesting story about the reactions of parents toward death in her book, *Should the Children Know?* One of her pupils, four-year-old Rachel, died during the school term. She asked the parents of her nineteen other pupils to come to a meeting to discuss what the children should be told about Rachel's death, and how.

The first suggestion, made by a mother, was, "Tell them Rachel moved. After all, this happens quite often." Silence followed, indicating general agreement.

Then another mother, apparently not quite convinced, had another idea. "I think they would accept it if you said Rachel went to visit some relative out of town. Taking a trip is a great thing for a child—it sure is for Peter."

A voice from the back of the room asked, "But wouldn't they ask when she's coming back?"

A pause. Then still another parent spoke up. "Say 'after school is out,' and by that time they'd forget."

A father asked Mrs. Rudolph, "Can children of four and five years of age understand death?"

She answered, "No, not in the sense they can understand something they themselves have seen or experienced."

There was an air of general relief. One parent spoke for most when he said, "Then why worry them with something that's beyond them? Tell them Rachel has gone somewhere. This way you'd keep the knowledge of death from them."

At this point, Mrs. Rudolph objected that if she did this, she would be aware that in speaking with the children she would be concealing something from them. And several parents agreed that children do recognize when you are holding something back and might even imagine something far more terrible had happened to Rachel, something too awful to talk about.

In the end, with the consent of the parents, Mrs. Rudolph told the children that Rachel had died. She had known that the children had feared something had happened to Rachel because they never mentioned her absence or talked about her. She finally was able to encourage them to admit they had noticed Rachel's absence.

Mrs. Rudolph said, "Rachel isn't here—because something very sad and very unusual happened to her. She died last Monday."

In the discussion that followed, she made clear that Rachel wouldn't—couldn't—come back. She answered questions about where Rachel would be buried and about Rachel's mother's grief. In the end, the children decided Rachel's name should be kept on the attendance list, "for remembrance," and in deference to their decision, the school administration did not fill Rachel's place in the class for the remaining months of the term as they would have done if she had just withdrawn from school.

During the parents' meeting, the problem of religion came up. One father, a clergyman, suggested that he thought Rachel's death should be the occasion of offering the children religious belief. "This is an opportunity to tell children that God is in command of what has happened. Rachel is now in His hands and she is in heaven."

Mrs. Rudolph's answer was that the families in the school were of different religious beliefs, and some had no official religion, so that as a teacher her explanation would have to be in nonreligious terms.

When a widow finds religion a comfort, she may want to share this with her child. But psychologists warn that a child's capacity for abstract thinking is not yet developed. Instead of receiving solace from your religious concepts, he may misunderstand and be frightened. (Dr. Robert Furman puts it more bluntly: "The surest way to make an atheist of a young child is to tell him of a God who takes away someone he loves.")

Mentioning "eternal sleep" may only make a child fearful of going to sleep. A young widow with a little girl of three explained Daddy's absence by telling Nicole that "Daddy went to sleep." Some weeks later, she was lying on the couch watching Nicole play, and closed her eyes. Suddenly the child was on top of her, trying to pry her eyes open. Nicole's imagination had turned sleep into an enemy that took Daddy away, and the sight of a sleeping mother sent her into panic.

Telling a young child that "Daddy is in heaven" or that "God took him" may also terrify him. One five-year-old who had been told that God took her daddy was afraid to sleep with the window open even though it was the middle of summer, because she was afraid God would come and get her, too. A boy of six and a half was told that his father had gone to heaven when he was killed in the crash of his private plane. He told reporters when they came to interview the grieving family, "Why is everybody so sad when Daddy's gone to heaven and is so happy?" But a few months later, the disturbed little boy tried to kill himself so he could join Daddy in heaven and go fishing and have good times.

It is far better, even with a toddler, to be honest. Instead of telling him only what you think he can take, or understand, tell him the truth. The child will accept what he can understand and ignore the rest. If he really is too young to grasp what you are talking about, he at least will react instinctively to the fact that you are not holding back. And if he understands even a small part, much is gained.

A widow who had behavior problems with both of her children after her husband died told me, "He said in the will that there should be no service, and he requested cremation. I sent the body directly to the crematorium and did not accept the ashes, as I could not decide what to do with them. So his death never had any reality for Jeb and Nancy. Intellectually, they have accepted the fact that he is dead, but emotionally they are still mixed up. If I had it to do over again, I would have a viewing, some kind of a service, if not a religious one, and I would have a grave where I could take the children."

Sometimes when a man is dying of cancer, for the sake of the patient, the facts are not spelled out to young children for fear of disturbing him. But it is unfair to older children not to be aware of what is happening. They should be allowed to visit a dying father, even if the experience is painful. In many hospitals today, the hospice concept allows even small children to visit dying patients. Experts believe that children who are allowed to participate in these family hospital visits and even assist in funeral arrangements have fewer traumatic adjustments to make than children who are more protected.

In cases of sudden death, as through fires or accidents, the child may be witness to scenes that leave horrible scars on adult memories, but it has been found that if the child is encouraged to talk about what happened, he is able to endure almost anything. A good friend had a call from her husband saying he was ill, could she please come into town to get him. He had a one-room studio in a building near his office that he used when he did not have time to go out to the family home in the suburbs. She drove in, taking their son, nine-year-old Mike, with her. When she arrived, her husband was dead and the police were there. Not only did Mike see his father wrapped in the makeshift shroud that the city hospital attendants had brought with them, but he helped them take the body down in the tiny elevator. It was so small that the body had to be held upright, and Mike insisted on doing that. Afterward, when Mike's mother told him she was sorry he had to have such a painful experience, he told her, "I felt as though I was helping Daddy."

Many people today think of funerals as barbaric. Cremation is more usual than burial in a cemetery plot. But whatever kind of a service is held—even one of those near-parties where food and drink are served—children should not be excluded. Earl Grollman says, "A youngster should have the same right as any other member of the family to attend the funeral and offer his last respects and to express his own love and devotion. . . . To deprive him of his sense of belonging at this very emotional moment is to shake his security."

Some people think that children should attend the religious service and not the burial, some reverse the order. I have known widows to ask that the church service be shortened so that the children would not have to go through a long ordeal. What you do, or don't do, is a matter of your own opinion and your knowledge of how much your children can take. But, as wiser people than I have said, children are closer to the primitive. Even though they may feel sad, they enjoy the mock burial services they hold for pet turtles and birds. The absence of a certain amount of ceremony may seem wrong to them.

So long as a child is told in advance what to expect and is given the option to be present or not, he will not be unduly upset. And instead of sending him away from the after-funeral gathering— the event that may turn into a cocktail-party farewell to the dead man—it is better to tell him what it will be and why it is being held. He may not want to stay until the end, but he should be allowed to greet friends and relatives, and to be as much a part of the gathering as he wishes. Of course, if a child does not want to attend the service or the burial, he should never be forced. Instead, he might stay home with a relative or neighbor who is a good friend, and help answer the doorbell and telephone. But if older brothers and sisters are going, even a toddler may feel hurt if he is left out.

A child will ask questions afterward, even if everything was explained beforehand. Do not be afraid to say "I do not know," if he asks about what happens after a person dies. It is better to be honest than aim at poetic conceptions which are hard for children to grasp. Your husband may live on in your heart and in your children. But a child needs concrete answers. And if he wishes, he should be encouraged to talk about his own concepts.

Most children—and adults, too—indulge in fantasies, wishful thinking, about the return of the dead man. But adults, except in rare instances, know they are daydreaming. To children, especially young children, the idea that a daddy will return can be very real, again because they have no memory bank of experience. I am told that when little John Kennedy returned to the White House for the first visit after his father's death, he asked, "When is my daddy coming back?"

Children should not be discouraged from telling you their fantasies. An honest discussion with you will go a long way toward helping them separate fantasy from reality. If your child dreams recurrently that his father has come back to him at night, and tells you his daddy really isn't dead, you can explain it was a dream and that you, too, often dream of Daddy. If he tells you Daddy called up and said he would be home for dinner, you must explain that Daddy is dead and will not return but you, too, often wish you could see him again. A book for children, *The Black Dog Who Went into the Woods*, answers the fantasy question in a warm and nonrejecting manner that might be of help to a young child who has lost his father. It is the story of a beloved family dog who goes into the woods to die. At breakfast, the family members tell about their dreams of the dog coming to them in the night. But Benjamin's dream is the most vivid because, as his older brother explains, "I think he came to Benjamin because he could still talk to him." This blend of fantasy and reality might give a child comfort when he is floundering for explanations.

The need for comfort and closeness is so urgent in young children at this stage that it is a temptation to allow them to share your bed, especially if they have nightmares or difficulty sleeping. This, a mother of a three-year-old boy admitted to me, was for her a substitute for sex, and she wisely seldom indulged herself. Since Daddy always slept with Mommy, if the mother takes a child into bed with her she tacitly confirms the myth that the child can replace the father. Especially for a little boy, sleeping with mother is far too stimulating. And it can lead to future problems. He may develop such a strong sense of guilt that he can never enjoy a healthy relationship in later life with another woman. With a little girl, it creates a dependency that is not wholesome. It is far better to sit with the young child until he falls asleep and then leave a light on or let the child know that you will be nearby and check on him before you go to bed.

It is a comfort for children of all ages to know you need them and you should be affectionate. Don't be afraid of touching. Sometimes children in their teens need hugs as much as younger kids. But adolescence is difficult. Don't be too dismayed if they seem to pull away from you.

In a Cancer Care workshop, I heard a mother complain that her thirteen-year-old daughter had completely rejected her since the death of her father. "Terry sits and stares into space. When I ask her a question, she either ignores me or walks out of the room. If she does speak to me, it is only to complain. One night she was very angry at me because I had given her daddy's camera to his mother. She had enrolled in a camera course at school and needed one. I didn't like to ask Jerry's mother to return what to her is a keepsake, so I suggested to Terry that we get her a camera for her birthday. She said okay, but she wouldn't go with me to pick it out. So of course the one I chose was all wrong. I told her to take it back and exchange it, but weeks later I found it on her closet shelf.

She told me she didn't need it, as she had quit the course."

The therapist suggested, "Give her time. Share whatever you can with her, like a TV show or a movie. Wait—and the moment will arrive when she will open up and tell you what is really bothering her."

It did. What worried Terry was the thought that her mother, now that she was the single breadwinner in the family, would expect the girl to be in charge at home, become a permanent baby-sitter for her little brother, and take over the shopping and heavy cleaning chores her father had done. When her mother assured Terry that this was not the case, Terry of her own accord volunteered to do the grocery shopping after school and even start dinner on the nights "when I don't have a date."

When Edythe's husband died, their son Jules was fourteen and their daughter Leslie was twelve. Both children had been very close to a warm and loving father. But Jules refused to act as one of the pallbearers. He was silent and withdrawn during the service and refused to attend the gathering of friends at their home later. As time went on, he was sullen toward his mother, and picked fights with his sister, telling Leslie she was ugly and that nobody would ever marry her.

Edythe's brother, who had often gone fishing with the boy and his father, invited Jules up to his fishing cabin in the woods the weekend before he was to go back to school. They were alone, but the boy was no more communicative than he had been with his mother. Then, on the last day, Jules caught a fishhook in his hand, and his uncle had to do impromptu surgery. In his pain and distress, Jules blurted out that he was in a trap. Now that his father was dead, he was going to have to be the "man of the family" and fill his father's shoes, and he wasn't ready. His mother's request that he be one of the pallbearers had frightened him.

A boy in adolescence is at the stage where he is wanting to pull away from his parents, particularly his father, yet he needs his father as a role model more than ever. If at this point his father dies, it can be very threatening to think that he must be his father's substitute. Just as his lust for life is developing and he is coping with vast body changes, he is thrust into a role that he is not ready for and shouldn't be asked to assume.

Edythe, who had no such thoughts in mind, was startled when she found out what was bothering her son. She told Jules frankly that she regarded him as her son, that he would always be her son, and she certainly didn't want him to turn into an adult right now or take his father's role. Jules was so openly relieved that when he said goodbye at the airport he hugged his mother and his sister and even threw his arms around Uncle George and kissed him.

With a girl who is approaching adolescence, the situation after her father dies can be complicated by the fact that, although she still needs her mother, she needs to pull away from her and be on her own. In the case of fifteen-year-old Renée, this created confusion because she felt responsible for her mother. Her mother, as it happened, was an actress of considerable reputation, and far from helpless. But in order not to be the star at home, she had made a great point of her husband being the head of the household, the one who kept things running. And Daddy's next-to-last words to Renée had been, "Take care of your Mom."

Renée decided her mother should remarry. There was no shortage of opportunities, for her mother was a beautiful woman. But in order to ease the path, Renée also decided she should get out of her mother's life. She ran off with a boy who came from a very different background, and insisted on marrying him, saying she was pregnant. It turned out she wasn't, but she stuck to the marriage until, after a dozen years and three children, she finally filed for divorce. Now, with little education and three children and in bad health, she is dependent on her mother and her mother's new husband.

Joan was nine when her father died in an accident. She reacted with such violent anger that her mother asked the school psychologist to talk to the child. With him, Joan was calm, talked about her father freely and happily and claimed she was okay. But she always spoke of her father in the present tense. When asked about her fights with her mother, she shrugged, "She just cries and carries on to get attention. It makes me mad, she is so silly."

The psychologist said, "You mean you think she is taking your father's death too hard." Joan nodded, smiling. Then she confided that the doctors were just doing an experiment to see how she and her mother would act if they were told her father was dead. When the psychologist asked how she knew this, Joan said confidently, "Dad wouldn't leave me. He loved me too much."

It seems strange that at her age Joan could believe so sincerely in her delusions. But denial of death of a father seems common in girls and especially common in those who are approaching adolescence, when a developing young person is forced to withdraw a large part of her emotional attachment to her first love, her father. Under ordinary circumstances, once this stage is passed through, the girl is happily ready and eager for new loves and attachments. But if a father dies at this point, the abrupt loss is sometimes too much to face.

Sally, a year older than Joan, had always been a tomboy and a poor student. But after her father died, she began getting good grades, behaving well in classes, doing everything to make her teachers approve of her. Her mother was gratified but mystified. One night, however, when Sally was talking to her mother, it slipped out that her father had promised her a reward several months ago if her grades improved. Now she was sure that if she got a good report card, her father would come back.

Mary's father died when she was fourteen. She and her Dad had been very close. He had often told her lovingly that when she started to date he would check out the boys to be sure no harm came to her. Almost immediately after her father's death, Mary started going out with a series of older boys who had the reputation of being wild. When she was sent to the family doctor for a talk, Mary confided that if she were bad enough, someone (her father?) would come to help her.

It is harder to be patient with adolescents and preadolescents, because in so many ways they attempt to be grown-up. But in this important crisis time they require the same understanding as younger children. One night I attended a widow-and-widower group where a doctor was the main speaker. When he asked the audience to mention their main problems, the most frequent complaint was about the behavior of teenage sons and daughters. He came up with several suggestions. One was to try family therapy, when you and the children and perhaps a grandparent go for counseling and act out your problems. Another was to have the child talk to someone whom he likes and trusts, a favorite teacher, an aunt or uncle, a family physician. He also suggested that teenage rap groups, which include children of divorce as well as those who have lost parents through death, might be of help (such groups can sometimes be located through hospitals or mental health organizations). In summation, he looked around the room and said, "You just have to do your best. When weren't the teens difficult?"

8

LIFE WITHOUT FATHER

———

ACCEPTANCE that a father or husband is dead will not come in a few minutes, either for you or for your children. The younger your children, the more they need your guidance and strength. Older children, from ten or eleven on, have more resources and can actively seek the help of others—teachers, friends their own age, relatives. But every child must mourn and it is your role to encourage the painful, but eventually healing, process.

Mourning is the way a child frees himself for new love investments without forgetting the old. You can help by putting framed pictures of his father, especially pictures taken with the child, in his room. As time goes on, make it a point to give the children things their father used and treasured—books, a watch, a favorite tennis racket or fishing pole. This will help the child integrate his memory of his father into his own growing personality.

"Be patient" and "Time heals" may sound like banal clichés of advice. But time *does* heal, and in the meantime one of your prouder tasks is to preserve for your children the picture of their father as a real and loving person. Tell them funny stories about him to which they can relate. Don't be morbid about it, but show home movies of special occasions when you were all together as a family. Talk about Dad's foibles, lovingly, so that he does not turn into a man on a pedestal.

There will be times when your child is doing something special, graduating with honors, winning an award, when you will be proud and wish his father could be there to share the moment.

This is something a child should feel, too. It is the heritage you are able to give him. A widow whose youngest child was just seven when her father died told me that one day Judy was listening to her two older brothers talk about their father and said, "I only wish I could have had a longer time with him."

If you are able to preserve such a memory, you will not only have given children a priceless gift, but you will have your own reward. Psychologist Betty Stone, who specializes in working with children who have lost parents through death, says, "There is magic in living through the first year of grief together, making each season and each anniversary a new concept and then going on. Easy? No. But a growing and enriching experience."

Nor is being an only parent easy. At the end of the day you are alone. There is no one to share your worries, laugh with you when the children have done something funny, help you pick up the pieces. Worst of all, there is no one to talk to but the kids, and sometimes they don't want to talk to you. Don't let it become a crushing burden, however.

Furthermore, just because you are a single parent, you don't have to become a paragon or a super-mom. Real discipline does not mean punishment. It means rules, structures, and order. Children are more secure when they have rules. But at this difficult period, for them and for you, you must be especially aware of your own tensions and anxieties so that you are not too demanding or restrictive. Avoid conflict over trivia. Let the bed-making lapse and the tidying-up go, at least some of the time. Avoid nagging—but if something serious comes up, don't be afraid to face the issue head-on. You don't need to overcompensate by allowing late bedtimes, limitless TV, indulgences they don't need or deserve.

Of course discipline was easier when there were two parents presenting a solid front. The mother of twin girls, for example, found herself challenged when she discovered that their boy-friends were bringing beer to the house. "Daddy wouldn't have minded," the girls chorused. The new widow's answer was straight and direct: "Well, Daddy isn't here and I am and I don't like the idea. So it has to stop."

Picturing a dead parent as all-permissive is a good ploy, if it works. Saying "Daddy would have let me go to the out-of-town game" or "Daddy would have let me stay as late as the other kids" is a way of trying to get around you. But sometimes it is just testing. Sometimes your son or daughter really doesn't want the ploy to work. The important thing is not to be afraid to say no. Try to be as honest and fair as you can. Listen to their opinions, consider their demands. Keep channels of communication open. But remember that, being children, they will take advantage of you if they can.

Being human, you will also make mistakes. You will react in anger, overreact on occasion, because you are exhausted and tired of coping. You will say the wrong thing, like "Your father would have whacked you for that." And sometimes you will be unfair.

Don't worry about your less than perfect behavior. An explosion of anger often clears the air. If you have been out of line, an apology afterward is all that is necessary with older children. With young ones, a reassuring hug and kiss will tell them that you love them and everything is okay.

Children can get along with one parent, so long as that parent supplies their needs. But they will feel better about the situation and themselves if you show them that you need them, too, by giving them responsibility and letting them share in decisions. Psychiatrist Helen DeRosis, author of *Women and Anxiety*, says that parents over the last twenty years have done so much for their children that the children lack the feeling of being needed by the family.

In the old days, children of poor or pioneer families had the advantage of knowing they were needed to contribute their share. They grew up an integral part of family life. Too often in families today, children are praised only for their social and athletic skills or their ability to get good grades. When a father dies, you have the opportunity to bring your children closer into the family unit by giving them meaningful duties, tasks that were performed by the father like cleaning the basement or bagging up the garbage. Responsibilities should not exceed the child's ability. The whole point is to give him or her the experience of success so that self-confidence can grow and pave the way for him to become a responsible adult.

As a single mother, your role is to offer dependability, to be there when the child needs you. But it is easy, after you have lost a husband, to become frightened and overprotective. Your worst fears were realized when your husband died; now, irrationally, you wonder what other blows fate has in store for you.

Growing up can be precarious. At any moment, something terrible can happen, a playground accident, a mugging, sexual assault. But a mother hovering over her children can't protect them from the unexpected. In order to face the world as it is, children need to develop confidence, positive feelings about themselves. Trust them as you have in the past.

Sometimes a child will want to identify with his dead father. One widow in a group workshop told of her daughter who had never tried to draw while her artist father was alive. After his death, she took over his studio. She never was able to learn how to manage perspective, but she did develop a rather charming primitive technique. A new widow told me that before her husband's death, her son, fourteen, had always watched from the sidelines while his handy father fixed things around the house. Soon after the funeral, Helen went out to go to work and her car wouldn't start, so she took the bus. At noon she had a call from her son. Charles had looked at her car and thought he knew how to fix it, but he had to buy some spare part. All day Helen waited apprehensively wondering what kind of a mess she would find when she got home. To her amazement, the boy had the car running again.

There is a delicate line between support and suffocation. Children should be encouraged, as soon as possible, to go on with their normal lives. Even the younger child, whose first instinct is to cling, should be gently persuaded to spend time with grandparents, a favorite aunt, his old playmates. Sometimes going with him to the playground or birthday party, then waiting until he has joined a game or seems occupied before you leave, may supply the bridge he needs. But be aware that children can be unwittingly cruel. The mother of a child whose father was killed in a plane accident told me that she didn't find out for years why her son hated going back to school. Then she learned that the kids in his class used to tease him by pretending to be airplanes coming in to crash, just as they taunted a boy whose father was a drunk by acting tipsy. Your child may not want to report on what his playmates are doing. But it is your job to find out what is going on by making it easy for him to talk to you. Teachers should be alerted, too.

You cannot live your life in your children. They must grow up and leave you. When I was a child in Chicago, we had a neighbor, a widow, whom we called Aunt Rose. She devoted her life to Frankie, her son. Now Frankie is married and living in Brazil with his wife and children. He comes home once a year on a business trip and sees his mother, but she doesn't go to South America to visit because she and Frankie's wife don't get along. Not long ago, Aunt Rose told me, "I made a mistake. Many times, men asked me out. I always said no because I thought my job was to raise my fatherless child. Nor did I take a job, for the same reason. I think if I had had a career or had remarried, I wouldn't have ended my life as a lonely old woman who is a burden to her only son."

Today we are more aware of the hazards of possessiveness and sacrifice. Yet sometimes when we are confused and bewildered we make the mistake of letting other people take over our lives. In times of crisis, family ties are very important. Relatives can be lifelines for widows and their children. But do not pass your responsibilities on to them. The reentry of Mom into your life can be a way of avoiding reality. Whenever a widow blames her mother for taking over her life and children, she may be admitting that she really wanted—at least in the beginning—to retreat to the passive role of being a child again. And when you invite a divorced or widowed mother to share your home and take care of your children, you may be simply abdicating your role as a mother. And you may also be doing your children no favor because the changes she makes in the household, with the best of motives, may be hard on children already upset by the loss of a father.

At the age of forty-seven, Don G., a popular newspaper columnist and TV personality in a midwestern city, dropped dead on the tennis court. His funeral was a semipublic event. The mayor and governor attended, and loudspeakers were installed outside the church so that those who couldn't get in could hear the service.

A friend reported: "Cindy and the children will be all right, but it was a shocking blow. It broke my heart to see them at the service—Cindy and fifteen-year-old Donna, so alike with their red hair and freckles; Rickie, who is a brilliant student and very serious, although he is only ten; and little Raoul, just seven, with his Daddy's snub nose and blond curls. I don't know how much Don left—they lived very high on the hog. But the paper has offered Cindy a chance to continue Don's daily column. And her mother has come up from Florida to take over the house and take care of the children while Cindy works. It sounds like a good deal."

It wasn't. Cindy was in a state. And having her efficient, strong-willed mother around did nothing to increase her confidence. Years ago, Cindy had escaped her divorced mother's too-guiding hand and gone to Wisconsin to work on a newspaper, where she had met and married the glamorous Don. After leading a casual life with him and the children and doing occasional articles for the paper, Cindy was facing an alien world—and the demand that she live up to Don's image. She was unused to the pressures of daily deadlines. She told herself it was a blessing that her mother, who had been headmistress of a girls' school before she retired, was willing to step in and help her. Yet having her mother around made Cindy feel inadequate.

The problems started right after the service. Cindy had asked some of their friends to stop by the house. When Grandma saw her putting out ice and bottles, she was shocked. "I don't know what people will think. Having a cocktail party right after burying your husband."

"These people are our friends," Cindy protested. "They never came to our house without being offered a drink. Don would want it that way."

"Maybe," her mother said darkly, "Don would have lived longer if you hadn't been so free with the booze." She disappeared into the kitchen to fix a pot of coffee and sent the three children to the family room to watch TV and be out of the way.

In the days that followed, Grandma reorganized the house. Meals were served on time, and the casual snacking that had been the rule when the household revolved around Don's irregular hours was stopped. Grandma, noting that Raoul was a picky eater, instituted a "clean plate" policy for him; unless he finished his meat and vegetables, he would get no dessert. Cindy was too involved with her own pressing problems to complain. And when she got home, her mother was always ready with suggestions about how the column could be improved. Some of her ideas were good. But Cindy began to feel like the fourth child in the family.

The children were rebelling in their own way. Raoul was turning into a whiner, not at all like the lively, funny child he had been. Donna was increasingly impudent to her grandmother. And then Rickie, the dependable one, was expelled from school for smoking marijuana. Grandma decided he wasn't too old to be spanked and then locked him in his room. But he broke a window, crawled out on the roof, and ran away. The police finally found him and brought him home, but not before Cindy and her mother had a blazing row, which ended in Grandma packing up and going back to Florida.

Fortunately, she still had a home of her own, so the break was accomplished with a minimum of anguish. By the following Christmas, Cindy and the children were able to go down to Florida and enjoy visiting with Grandma, briefly, on her own terms. But beware of plunging into an arrangement with a widowed or divorced mother when your grief is fresh, because such plans may be hard to undo once you are committed.

Nature knew what she was doing when she limited the child-bearing age of women. Grandmothers, much as they love your children, do not have the stamina or elasticity to cope with them day in and day out. In addition, no mother can ever stop being a mother. No matter how old her child is, he or she is still her child. And the temptation to tell him what to do is seldom resisted. Between mother and daughter, the tie that binds can sometimes be painful.

Nancy Friday, in her book *My Mother, My Self*, says that no daughter ever lives up to her mother's ideal, her expectations. And when her daughter fails, the failure seems worse because to the mother, it becomes her own failure. When a girl marries, it becomes her biggest reunion with her mother because, according to Friday, "now we are all nice married ladies, like Mother." The second point of identification with Mother comes when a woman has her first child and mothering becomes so important sex takes on a secondary role. And the third is when her daughter is widowed and her mother feels it is her duty and obligation to step in and help. Which can mean taking over, because doesn't Mother Know Best?

She means no evil. Her intentions are the best. Once I interviewed the mother of an actress who told me: "Faith and I were always very close, although I tried not to be a typical stage mother. And when she was left a widow with two young children, I knew it was my duty to take over because her career was more important now than ever. It took me a long time to realize what a mistake that was. I was so strong and efficient she depended on me for everything. I thought I was protecting her, but I was wrong. Our relationship kept her from making friends her own age, from marrying. Now the children are growing up and I am not well, and when I die she will be so alone the idea frightens me."

When a young widow moves back home after her husband dies, she automatically becomes a child again in her parents' house. Marie, the mother of an eleven-month-old baby, moved back to her parents after her husband died of a brain tumor. She returned to her old job and her mother took care of the infant. But she came to a widow workshop group to say she had a problem. "I'm not ready to think of remarriage. But it is all Mom talks about— find a husband, find a father for that baby. One weekend Ted's boss invited me and the baby up to his camp. Ted and I had been there often and he was just being kind—he was not interested in me. We went and had a lovely time, but when my mother heard there were no other guests, she hit the ceiling. She used the word *immoral* and said nobody would marry me if I went on doing things like that. I told her there was nothing wrong between Ted's boss and me. Her answer was, 'But what will people think?' I said I didn't care, so long as I was comfortable with myself. And she replied, 'So long as you are under my roof, you accept my standards.' "

Marie eventually moved out to join forces with a divorced friend who had two young children. They shared costs of a baby-sitter. It wasn't an ideal situation but, as she said, "I am not a young woman any more. I have been married, and I am the mother of a daughter. I must maintain my own independence."

When you ask a widowed or divorced mother to move into your home with you, and give up her own, you are not only risking your own independence, you are incurring an obligation. You cannot turn her out if you decide it won't work or want to remarry. Unless a man is willing to take on a mother-in-law as well as your children in the package deal, you are trapped. It is fairer to everyone to make arrangements that are flexible and temporary. Sitters or students who thrive on change are safer than older relatives. Joining forces with another single mother or making a commune arrangement with other single parents may or may not work. But removing yourself from such a situation is far less painful than withdrawing from one in which you have an emotional obligation.

There will be times when your children will need a man to substitute for their father. Here a grandfather is a perfect answer. If your husband's parents live nearby, you and your children will benefit from making a special effort to let them figure importantly in your lives. Your husband's parents have their own grief because they have lost a child. They may be wary of you, fearing that you may remarry and take away their grandchildren. But keep this link open. Even if you remarry, there is nothing wrong with having a large extended family. And at every stage of development, children will need their father, and these are the people who can feed them the information they want. And on days when a father is conspicuously absent—Father's Day, father-and-son banquets and the like, baseball games to which children are admitted free if accompanied by a father—a grandparent makes an ideal substitute. Plan ahead for these occasions, and talk to your child in advance about them. Bear in mind that girls as well as boys need father substitutes. Sometimes you can use an uncle, the husband of a friend, or a neighbor with children who are near the age of yours. You may find a divorced man who misses his own kids will be glad to take yours on outings. But be wary of these arrangements. Wives, even ex-wives, do not always take kindly to having a widow's child or children added to the family. Just as your child gets fond of a substitute father, you might find him vanishing. Grandfathers are safer.

The first holiday alone can be devastating. Even if you share it with relatives or close friends, you and your children will be painfully aware of the absence of your husband. It may be easier to do something other than have a family dinner, go to a small ski resort or a dude ranch where a family atmosphere prevails. But if you prefer to continue family traditions, do not assign roles to children on these occasions that they aren't ready to fill. Rae Lindsay in her book *Alone and Surviving* tells about the first Thanksgiving after her husband died. A relative suggested that Rae's son, Sandy, sit at the head of the table in his father's place "since he is now the man of the house." Rae objected because Sandy was not the man of the house, he was a seven-year-old who had lost his father. Instead, she asked her father to sit at the head of the table. A year and a half afterward, when she was planning a family gathering in Easter, Sandy felt secure enough to ask his mother if he could sit at the head of the table.

Young children often seem ready for a father replacement before you are, or before any are available. Some can be very aggressive about seeking one. A Chicago widow found out that her six-year-old son was canvassing the neighborhood, asking every man he met to marry his mother. Some children will embarass a widow by demanding of every man who enters the house, "Are you going to be my new daddy?" A six-year-old girl I knew, after her father was killed in an accident, laid in wait for the postman and offered him the contents of her piggy bank if he would marry her mother.

Older children, however, may resent the idea of their mother's remarrying. They may even get upset if she simply goes to a meeting of Parents Without Partners (where she might meet men). Girls are often hostile, angry at a dating mother because they feel she is being unfaithful to the dead man. Adolescent boys may be jealous.

One attractive widow who was encountering problems with her teenage children when she started to date said, "It makes you wonder whether having such a good family relationship was so wonderful. I find that my divorced friends have far fewer problems with their kids." Actually, once children get used to the idea of a mother remarrying, those who have been devoted to a dead father will adjust to a replacement, or the idea of a replacement, better than those who have been in an insecure and unhappy family situation. Once a child has had a good and loving relationship with his father, he is predisposed toward investing love in a new and present figure.

"Marrying for the sake of the children" is never a good idea. Marrying because you cannot cope with a child who is difficult or delinquent is worse. A widowed friend of my husband ran into such a situation when he married a widow who was having a bad time with her twelve-year-old daughter. Sienna had gone to pieces when her father died. She refused to go back to school, developed all sorts of imaginary health problems, and would not go to sleep unless her mother shared her bed. Her mother, under the mistaken idea that all the girl needed was a firm hand, married Court. Immediately the girl ran away. When they found her and brought her back, she transferred her demands to Court, flirted with him, wanted to sit on his lap. When Court did not respond, she went into a depression, refused to bathe, disappeared for days at a time. Finally, Court had had all he could take. He told Sienna to shape up or get out. Sienna got out. She is now living in California in a commune, on drugs, and refuses to come home. Her mother is more frantic than ever, and her marriage to Court is on the rocks.

Delinquent behavior can start when a widow is so involved with her own grief that she is not aware of what is going on (and when others are reluctant to tell her). By the time she finds out, the problem may have reached crisis proportions. Even in a two-parent household, such behavior is not unknown and can cause much distress. When a widow is in no condition to take on additional burdens, drugs or rebellion can seem more than she is able to bear. She resents the child who is upsetting her. Or her anger can be directed at the husband who died and left her with "this monster."

Case histories show that the vast majority of boys who set fires comes from homes in which there have been recent changes, such as the loss of a parent. Troubles often start in small ways, with mood swings in the children, bed-wetting, then other antisocial behavior such as stealing, torturing animals, bullying younger children. Friends of mine found that whenever a certain child, whose father had died recently, came to visit their son, toys would be missing. They were reluctant to worry his grief-stricken mother but she, too, must have noticed his peculiar behavior because she sent him away to military school. There he was expelled for trying to burn down his dormitory.

Obviously, if less important cries for help are ignored, the child's devices to get attention become more and more outrageous. Sometimes psychiatric help is needed before the child is able to express what is really bothering him. Professionals urge early recognition of symptoms that indicate a child's need for attention and, if necessary, evaluation by a trained expert. Certainly, marrying in the hopes of bringing a firm male hand into the picture is not right for the child and definitely not fair to the man involved.

For parents who are suspect that a child may be turning to drugs, the Parents' League of New York, which gives programs on drugs for the information of parents, has these suggestions:

- Educate yourself. Read books and become knowledgeable. It is better to be informed than emotional.
- Learn the vocabulary of drugs. Children like to talk so that adults do not understand them.
- If you suspect your child has smoked marijuana, confront him or her directly. Don't be afraid to be wrong.
- Make your disapproval clearly known. Let them know you will not bend on this issue. Children will need ammunition to withstand peer pressure.
- Be suspicious if your child is suddenly ravenously hungry or if he sleeps more than usual. Marijuana can have these effects.
- Notice changes of personality, such as a normally quiet child becoming bubbly or an ebullient one becoming withdrawn.
- If it is clear that the child is smoking marijuana, discuss what is happening and what you can do to help him avoid the situation in the future.
- Explain that contrary to popular belief, marijuana does affect motor ability when driving a car.
- When your children are invited to parties, know who is

giving them and what supervision will be provided. Don't be afraid to forbid attendance at a party.

· Steer children into constructive activities that will use their energies such as sports or dancing.

· Tell children that, although the possession of small amounts of marijuana has been decriminalized, it is still not legal and any public use, display or distribution subjects them to arrest and a police record.

Sometimes second marriages based on mutual needs, and the needs of children, work out. But if you remarry for the sake of money or security or some other need, aside from affection and love, you will have three strikes against you. Happy marriages, marriages that are good for children, are invariably based on a strong bond between the parents, a bond that combines faith and trust and sexual love, a bond that can and should shut out the children on occasion.

You can't expect a man to accept your children as his, automatically. Nor will you automatically love his children as your own. So don't panic into remarrying for expediency, making a compromise that you both might regret and one which could do harm to your children. All marriages involve some concessions and compromises. But when you are in love, and your children recognize your happiness, compromises are easier because you are surrounded with laughter and hope.

You may not plan to remarry. Because you aren't actively hunting for a husband does not mean you should retire from the human race. You need friends, and friends should include men. And you need a social life apart from your children. And there is nothing which says that you have to sacrifice normal sexual appetites just because you are a single mother. However, how you manage your new social life depends a great deal upon what you are and how you feel about yourself and your children.

A widow who was deeply involved with a married man told me that her children became so devoted to him that they decided to break off their relationship because he could never leave his invalid wife, and he did not want to hurt the children more than he had. Another woman, after much soul-searching, decided to break off with a man who fascinated her because he simply did not like children. He tried to be polite with hers, but he obviously would never become emotionally involved. A friend, whose husband died when she was not yet thirty, never remarried because "I didn't want any man telling my children what to do." She had men friends, and occasional discreet affairs, but she wanted no man on a permanent basis because she intended to have full control. Now that her children are grown, she is marrying a man she has known for a long time.

You cannot think only of yourself when you are a mother. But you shouldn't think only of your children, either. In order to find your way back into the world of the living, you must keep yourself open for new friendships, new experiences. Children need outsiders as much as you do, the doorbell and telephone ringing. One woman whose father was killed when she was ten years old says, "I can still remember the evenings when the other fathers were coming home, and the other kids would be called in to wash up and brush their hair for Daddy. My brother and I would sit on the bottom step of the porch. We wouldn't say anything, just sit there feeling lonesome and terrible until my mother called us for dinner. She didn't work, most mothers didn't in those days if they had young children. I look on that period of my life as one long gray swamp. Nothing happened until Mother got a job in an art museum and suddenly we had new friends and gave parties and were living again."

A young widow told me, "One Saturday afternoon, the telephone rang. It was Jeff, a man from my office. He asked me what I was doing. I said I was baking brownies with my kids. There was a pause—he is a bachelor and although he knew I had kids we had never talked about them—and then he said, 'Well, some other time.' When I hung up, my six-year-old looked at me and said, 'Mom, you can't bake brownies with us all your life.' "

You can't hide much from young children who are so completely dependent on you. They can tell when you are let down and frustrated. The theory in the past was that when children aggressively seek a new daddy, it is because they want to be like everyone else, have both a father and mother. But now psychologists think that the persistence young children exhibit in hunting new daddies for their mother is more complex. One parent is gone; they want the other to be happy so she won't go away, too.

Bachelors can be gun-shy about children. I remember sitting with one at a wedding recently and admiring the girl he had just danced with. He told me, "Her husband died and left her with a two-year-old kid."

I said, "A kid who needs a father."

Greg shrugged. "The kid is okay, but I'm not sure about taking one on who isn't mine. With a divorcée, you get child support and the other guy is there. But with a widow, the kid is yours. Permanently. I don't know."

Later I happened to talk to the girl. She told me that after her husband died, she began seeing people from her old crowd, most of them singles. "But it isn't the same. Some of them are getting married. Others are living together. I'm no longer single. The baby is mine, we are a family. The other night Greg came over for dinner after we had all gone to the park. He played with Ginny while I fixed the food. When we got ready to eat I pulled her high chair up to the table and he said, 'Gee, don't we ever get any privacy?' I told him that was the way it was and the way it was going to be. He left right after dinner, and I guess I won't be seeing much of him anymore. It may not be easy finding someone who wants her as much as he does me, but that's the way it is."

Nancy, mother of two and a public relations woman, told me, "When Jack was alive, we would often stay down after work and eat dinner and go to a movie. I never felt guilty about it. But now if I have a date and don't go home, it's different. I feel guilty. I use the same sitter, the kids know her and she is good with them. But I have the feeling I am unfair when I have a night out. Maybe it will pass. But right now I simply don't enjoy myself and it must be obvious to the man, so I'm cooling it."

Matty, whose husband died of cancer, told me, "Jesse was ill for over a year. I had no sex during that time. After he died, a man I'd known for a long time in business asked me to go away for a weekend. I agreed. He didn't want anything but sex. Nor did I. But it didn't work because I kept thinking about how Jesse and I and the kids always had such fun on weekends. I didn't feel guilty about Jesse, I felt guilty about the kids. And do you know what happened? When I got home on Sunday night, the kids were glad to see me, but they kept telling me what fun they'd had with my folks, all the things they had done."

No matter how much you love your children, you can't expect them to fill all your emotional needs. Children cannot and should not replace male companionship. But how you go about this depends on you. Not your parents, not your in-laws, not whether your neighbors approve or don't. If you take guilt along with you on a date, nobody will have fun. But on the other hand, your kids won't have much fun with a lonely and frustrated mother. So what to do?

If you have young children, a night or a weekend away may be hard to arrange. So many single mothers settle for a succession of "uncles" who ostensibly sleep over on the couch. Kids are seldom fooled about where the uncles really spend the nights. But they are far more accepting and sophisticated about uncles, even a parade of uncles, than earlier generations were. Patty, a mother of three, widowed when she was thirty-two, has made a point of putting her children first, even when it comes to her job as manager of a small specialty shop. Her boss knows it, but Patty is such a super person he doesn't mind. Her customers are never surprised if the shop is closed with a sign, "Back in half an hour." They know it is some emergency with one of the children. Nor are they ever surprised to go into a fitting room and find one of Patty's children in the corner with a coloring book.

Patty likes men and they like her. She will often take a strange date home to have a drink while she fixes dinner for the kids. If she can't get a sitter, the stranger often stays on to take pot luck. And if he is there at breakfast time, the kids troop out to con him into making pancakes from a mix while Patty showers and dresses.

There was a period when the parade of uncles stopped and one man, Martin, became a regular. The major problem was his temper. He and Patty quarreled a lot. When Martin finally packed up and left, ten-year-old Billy asked his mother, "Why did you yell at him? You scared him away."

Patty thought carefully before she answered, "Martin was okay, but I decided I didn't want him around all the time. He made me mad often and so I yelled. It wasn't good, was it?"

Billy said, "It made us unhappy."

For a while there were no uncles. When Patty finally brought home Peter, the children seemed as nervous and anxious to please as Patty was. Finally they all relaxed. Peter was a splendid cook and made wonderful meals, a change from Patty's hamburgers and mixes. But he drank too much, and Patty decided to break off. After he was gone, Billy approached her, as the spokesman for the younger children. He said, "Mom, you didn't yell at Peter and make him mad, did you?"

"I hugged him and said no," Patty reported to me. "I just said he went away but we had parted friends. I realized that what bothered them was not the succession of men going through the house—they could take that—but seeing me angry, out of control. And if I do find someone I would like to marry, the kids may have taught me a good leson."

Children who are adolescents, or are approaching puberty, are not so permissive about uncles sleeping over. Teenage sexual impulses, as intense as they are, are extremely personal and private. The idea of a mother enjoying sex with a strange man can be terribly shocking. A teenage boy who sees himself as his mother's protector may be jealous of any man who tries to sleep with her. An adolescent girl may be even more punitive. She is about to realize her own autonomy and independence, her sexual role in life. The idea of a woman as old as her mother doing what she would like to do seems ridiculous and humiliating. Gerry, a widow I met at a widows' group in New Jersey, told us that her daughter, aged fourteen, would urge her to go to meetings of the local Parents Without Partners, but if she stayed out after eleven the girl would be waiting up angrily. Once she said to Gerry, "Who do you think you are? Some young chick on the make?"

Remarks like this can hurt unless you understand what motivates them. A widow who has her own advertising agency developed a steady relationship with a divorced man in her community. At first her two daughters, fourteen and sixteen, seemed glad her mother was dating. Marriage was never discussed, because the man was bogged down with alimony and child-care payments. But as Stafford spent more and more time around the house, sometimes staying over on Saturday night in the guest room, the girls began to act provocatively, flirting with him and making their appearance half-dressed or in thin nightgowns. Karen decided to end her relationship with Stafford because of the way her daughters were acting. On New Year's Eve, after she had gone several months without a date, she watched while the girls dressed for their parties. One of them looked up to ask, "What are you doing tonight, Mom?" Karen told her, "I'm going to stay home and wait for you." The girls left, but at midnight the oldest telephoned to ask if Karen was okay, saying, "I feel guilty thinking of you sitting there all alone."

The last thing Karen had wanted was to place a burden of guilt on her daughters and spoil their healthy return to the normalcy of fun and dates. The fault, she realized, had been hers. She should have insisted on more acceptable behavior from her daughters. She told me, "They were jealous, so they challenged me. I should never have allowed them to try to compete with me. The next time I'll be brighter."

When a widow begins dating, a teenage daughter can provide her own calculated roadblocks. Gael was just beginning to date again, and going out with quite a few men who were far from glamorous. Suddenly her daughter, Anne, who had adored her father, began to hang around the country club making passes at the tennis pro, a divorced man in his middle thirties. Gael tried to point out how impossible this relationship was, but Anne said, "It's no fun here with Daddy gone. As soon as Archie can find an apartment, I'm moving out."

Gael said, "You can't marry him. I forbid it." Anne grinned at her mother. "Who said anything about getting married? You're getting your sex, I'm going to have my share. That will make us even." Gael tried to explain that she wasn't interested in sex, she was simply trying to get used to being with men again, sharing male conversation. Anne's answer was, "Don't kid me. I wasn't born yesterday." Frantic, Gael decided to make a bargain with her daughter: she would stop dating if Anne would stop seeing Archie. Fortunately, before she made the mistake of cancelling out her beginning social life, Archie told Anne that he was going back to his wife and child. When Anne crept home, rejected and miserable, Gael hugged her daughter and said, "Do what I'm doing. Try going out with kids your own age. A lot of them may bore you. But look at them the way I do—at least they are giving you a social life. And maybe—as my own mother used to say when I started dating at your age—maybe one of them has a nice friend."

No one can lay down rules on the right and wrong way for a widow (or any single parent) to handle her sexual and social life. Some experts think that the casual attitude, the steady stream of uncles in the house, creates confusion and anxiety in children. Others believe that a mother's affairs should be kept secret until she can produce a man who might fit into the family picture. Widows in general tend to have fewer casual affairs than divorcées. A widow's respect for herself, her grief for her dead husband, make her more selective; she also is more aware that she is the only constant person in the lives of her children, so she must not do anything that might make them feel ashamed or abandoned. If this means waiting until your children are grown before you make a definite commitment, that is up to you. But if, like Patty, you are completely secure in your affection for your children and their confidence in you, you may feel you can expose them to a revolving door of uncles.

No matter which route you choose (though I hope you won't opt for the lonesome one), you will find that honesty, frankness, and a minimum of self-sacrifice will go a long way toward helping your children understand that their father is gone and cannot return, and that all of you are human beings, entitled to go on living and to form new attachments.

9

WORK—THE WIDOW'S SOLACE
AND SALVATION

Two weeks after my husband died, an editor for whom I had written many articles invited me to spend a winter weekend with her and her husband at their farm. It was cold and overcast, but I stayed outside with the dogs as much as I could because I sensed tension between my host and hostess. On Saturday night, when the darkness drove me indoors, I interrupted a quarrel. My editor friend emerged from the kitchen and handed me a drink. Then she said, "You don't know how lucky you are. You have a whole new life ahead of you; you are free to do anything you want."

I was shocked. Just when I was hurting so badly at having the ties broken that had bound me to my husband, being called lucky seemed like a sick joke. I was free, all right—so free I felt rootless, confused. Now I realize what she meant. Only after my husband died was I free to follow my career in the way that men, and single women, do. And as a result, for better or for worse, my work now is the single greatest source of satisfaction in my life.

Returning to the familiar routine of work going back to an office, can be a great help to a recent widow. Fanny Butcher, literary editor of the *Chicago Tribune*, went back to work a few days after her husband's funeral because of the pressure of deadlines. She was struggling with exhaustion when one of her colleagues told her, "You don't know how lucky you are, Fanny, to have something you can do, and do well, at this bad time. My mother went to pieces when my father died, because she felt no one needed her any more."

Today, when over half of all American mothers with preschool children work outside the home (usually because they need the money), returning to work after the death of a husband isn't a luxury or solace, it is a necessity. But when a woman has dropped out of the labor market to raise children, and has stayed at home afterward because it was what her husband wanted, she is faced with a double dilemma when she is widowed. She may have to settle, at least temporarily, for work that is neither well paid or interesting. Dr. Eli Ginzberg, chairman of the National Commission for Employment Policy—the man who is responsible for labor statistics—says, "A woman who drops out of the labor market for five to fifteen years is definitely handicapped." Sometimes he is quoted as saying "permanently handicapped."

Unlike the woman who toys with the idea of going back to work because her kids are grown and she feels bored, as a widow you are motivated by necessity. For emotional as well as economic reasons, you need work. You are scared, of course. And you are conscious that you are no longer a bright young kid ready to conquer the world. Still, you have advantages over the kids. A friend who returned to nursing after her husband died told me, "I find the patients relate to me much better than they do to the youngsters. I have had children, and aches and pains. I know what it is to be hurting."

Today, the best jobs for women are in fields where we didn't look in the old days—computer programming, engineering, accounting, banking, investment. If you were good at math in college or have since found yourself pushed by necessity into learning how to handle money and figures, don't discount this. The years you spent at home raising kids, running a household, managing a budget and a husband and doing volunteer work weren't wasted. You didn't go soft in the head, as some experts seem to think. You learned how to adapt, how to handle a crisis when the washing machine flooded or the john broke down, and to do it with a grin, if not a smile. You were your own boss, which required discipline. And all these qualities are of value when you return to the working world.

You may have missed a few brownie points by deciding to stay home and raise your children, but you learned a lot more about reality than you would have learned by sitting in an office. You are ready to cope; so don't let anyone, ever, discount your abilities. And never, never downgrade yourself.

Winston Churchill, who knew what it was to struggle, once said, "Success is never final. Failure is never fatal. The only thing that matters is courage." Patricia Neal, whose soaring career as an actress was interrupted by a series of near-fatal strokes, said when she accepted an award at Northwestern University: "None of us is perfect; none of us is without some disability or another . . . . Misfortunes come and go. They come to all of us in time and we simply have to cope with each one as it arrives. All through life, try not to be slung clear out of the saddle when the horse starts to buck. Stay put and ride it out."

Many of the women in the United States are descended from pioneer women who not only worked side by side with men, but devised ways to survive when the menfolk faltered. I had a grandmother who as a young girl set out from Canada and traveled through our Middle West making millinery to order, offering women those huge overdecorated hats they wore as "the latest fashions from New York and Paris," two cities she had never set foot in. She met the man she married in Tecumseh, Nebraska, and when he died before he was forty, she supported herself and her four children by running his brickyard.

Writing in *Savvy* (the women's magazine that advertises it doesn't tell women how to be secretaries, but how to hire secretaries), a professor from Ohio State named Albert Shapero says that through the ages women have overcome displacement (loss of a spouse by divorce or death) by displaying three qualities: desire for control over one's fate and belief that the control is within one's grasp; the feeling that "if he (or she) can do it, anybody can"; and the willingness to work long hard hours, take chances, and convince others to take chances on you.

Shapero concludes: "Women have always been entrepreneurs, overtly in some cultures, covertly in others. The widow lady on the frontier, like other displaced persons, had to make her way—and she did, whether it was by taking in boarders, washing, sewing, teaching school or running a whorehouse."

A friend who is a doctor told me that her father died when she and her brother were toddlers. He left her mother a house in Flushing, New York, a mortgage, and no money. She got a tenant, another widow with a small boy, who cared for the children during the day. Then her mother, who came from pioneer stock in Iowa, worked as a saleswoman in Macy's during the day and went to Columbia at night to study to be a librarian. She recalls, "Sometimes she had to take my brother and me with her. She would park us under the desk or table with coloring books. We'd fall asleep eventually. Then she'd wake us up for the subway ride home. It didn't hurt us. In fact, her courage motivated both of us to have careers. Yet when my husband died, leaving me with three small boys and a not very remunerative practice in Montana, what did I do? I ran home to Mother. She was still working, head of the local public library in Flushing. I expected her to take care of my children while I got a staff job in a New York hospital. But she refused; she said we could live with her, but it was up to me to work out my own problems. At first I was depressed. Then I got mad. I was determined to show her. It was the best thing that ever happened to me because it gave me confidence—if she could do it, so could I. I was turned down for a job by the hospital where I had trained. Instead of getting depressed and feeling worthless, I went home and mapped out a presentation, showing the specific work I had accomplished out in Montana, working with miners and their children. I went back to the hospital, insisted on another hearing and was hired."

A woman who is in charge of personnel for a department store told me that many of the women she interviews are recent widows or divorcées, women who have stayed home to raise children and now want to go back to work. "They are not dummies. They are competent women, the kind who held the household together. But," she says, "unlike the brash youngsters who dictate what they want, take it or leave it, they are so humble I could shake them. I have to literally make them tell me what they have done and accomplished, jobs like saving a school from bankruptcy by a series of fund-raising drives. Sometimes, if I have time, I can discover things like this. And sometimes I take a chance on a woman just because I know she can do a good job even if she doesn't. More often, I don't dare. Because a woman who is scared to death when she talks to me won't be able to speak up to a boss. Especially if the boss is younger, or—even scarier—both younger and a woman."

Let's take my friend Elena. She met her husband when she was a Spanish-speaking secretary in a big company and was sent to South America as a translator for the about-to-be-a-big-shot Harvard business school graduate. After they were married, he wanted her to stay home and devote herself to him, the house he bought in a fashionable section of Los Angeles and the children she promptly produced. Her pretty face and gentle manner were what first attracted him. But afterwards, he was disappointed that she wasn't more aggressive. They entertained a great deal, and behind scenes Elena was a competent and efficient manager. But she was shy with the colleagues he invited and even more reserved with the executives of the firm where she had once worked. Sometimes when the party was under way she would escape to the patio. One night I found her out there in tears. "I don't know what to say to those people. Russ gets annoyed with me. But I'm just no good at small talk."

Nor was she much good at the kind of volunteer work the wives of his colleagues did, fashion shows, charity bazaars. The only volunteer work she really enjoyed, she did secretly—going down to a settlement house in downtown Los Angeles and teaching the Mexican women and young girls who were new to this country English, so they could get jobs.

Russ died the day before his forty-fourth birthday, of a sudden heart attack. The two older boys were already in college and their daughter would be leaving to enter Barnard in the fall. Elena put aside Russ's insurance for their education. Then her lawyer suggested that, in order to keep busy, she ought to get a job. Elena protested, "But I can't do anything." His answer, "You were a secretary at his place when you married him. Why don't you go back and ask them for a job?"

It was a bad suggestion. But Elena made a worse mistake. She went to Russ's boss, whom she had entertained socially, to make the request. He was too embarrassed to turn her down himself, so he sent her to their personnel head, who asked Elena to take a typing test.

"I failed miserably," she told me later. "Partly, it was because I was rusty. Mainly, however, I was terribly nervous. The woman who gave me the test was kind. She suggested I might come back in a few days and repeat it. But I was too ashamed. And I just couldn't bring myself to go anyplace else, after that miserable failure. I was even too ashamed to call the lawyer and tell him. In fact, I sat home, pretending I had a cold, afraid to see anybody."

She was in the depths of depression when she had a call from the settlement house. One of the girls whom Elena had taught had been accused of stealing by her new employers and needed help. Would Elena try to find out what happened? Elena jumped at the chance to be of service, to be of value somewhere.

Today Elena is operating a thriving employment service. She has a cause, seeing that Mexican-American women are given fair treatment and adequate salaries. Where she couldn't fight for her own rights—although she is getting better at that, too—she could fight for other people. She has sold the big house and has moved into an apartment near her office. She no longer goes to the kind of parties where she has to escape to the patio. She has an assortment of new friends, many of them Spanish-speaking. And when she visits their houses, or entertains them at her apartment, she is in the middle of the action because she has so much to say. Most important, her children are delighted with her.

"Mom's a kick," her daughter told me recently. "I was teasing her about one of her new friends, a very nice guy who is plainly nuts about her. She looked me in the eye. 'Marry again? You must be out of your mind. Why should I tie myself down?' "

It's easy for a widow to make mistakes when she has been out of the job market for even a few years. Sometimes simple lack of confidence forces her into wrong moves. And sometimes desperation and panic push her into pitfalls she would have ordinarily avoided. Looking for a job is never easy, even when you are fresh out of college and full of your own importance. But there are certain things you can do to prepare yourself. And there are other things you should know, and guard against.

Listening in to conversations at career counseling sessions, the remark I heard most often was, "Don't count on friends to help you. You have to do it on your own."

In my opinion, friends aren't helpful, because they are approached in the wrong way and the demands made on them are either embarrassing or presumptuous. It is unfair to ask a friend for a job. It is unfair even to ask friends to send you to their contacts. It is not businesslike because it puts him or her on the spot; as a result, instead of getting what you want, you can lose a friend. But you *can* ask for advice. People love to give advice, and in the process they may offer to send you to acquaintances who might help, which is an entirely different matter. Also, when you ask for advice, have some ideas of your own. Get your head together and decide what you have to offer and what you think you would like. Then approach your friends with good questions.

Katherine Nash, a career counselor, has written a simple and useful book addressed to job-hunters, called *Get the Best of Yourself.* Her advice can be of particular value to a widow who lacks confidence. Nash believes that what she calls "fragmentation"—going after jobs aimlessly—is the curse of career building. "This is the age of specialization, when knowing who you are and what you can do will help you more than anything else."

She suggests that you sit down with a pad of paper and make lists of everything you accomplished while you were staying home. Don't generalize, be specific. Don't leave anything out. Your ability to organize children's parties may be a clue to your future. So may your handiness with tools. Or a knack of making over clothes. List your volunteer work. What jobs did you like and what ones bored you? Remember all the chores you did for the PTA, the charity drives you served on. Forget that you are a widow. Ask yourself what skills of yours are marketable. In Elena's case, it was not only her knowledge of Spanish. It was her experience as a housewife, someone who gave parties. She knew what prospective employers wanted, and her language skill was the bridge between someone who needed a service and someone who could provide it.

Nash also has a brilliant suggestion: that you ask yourself what single thing you have ever done that you are proudest of— whether it was winning a dance contest or persuading a friend not to kill herself. Your answer may be significant because it will point you toward an area in which you will be happy—and happiness is often the key to success. When you enjoy doing something, you are usually good at it. Sometimes very good. Bernard Slade made a living writing television scripts. Then he decided to take time off and do something for himself, something he really enjoyed. He wrote a play called *Same Time Next Year*, which was a smash hit and made a lot more money than his television scripts.

After you decide what you would really like to do, find out whether there are jobs available in that field. You have to be realistic. Times change and with it areas of employment. Computers have taken over many of the chores that used to be done by human beings; for that reason the computer field today offers limitless opportunities, if you incline in that direction. Nursing, which used to be in what the feminists refer to as the "pink collar ghetto," now has reached such importance, with salaries rising accordingly, that men are invading it in considerable numbers.

On the other hand, the economy has cast a pall over the travel agency business, once a favorite with women going back into the work force. There is hardly room for those who have had years of experience. Writing, I regret to say, is overcrowded with limited opportunities for all but a lucky few who write bestsellers.

In the next chapter you will find a job survey covering a variety of fields, some which offer a fast track, some in which the track is very slow. But money isn't everything. If you find a niche that you really love, money won't matter. A widowed friend who had always loved animals has a job acting as a receptionist in an animal clinic. The pay is peanuts, and she often takes a sick animal home over the weekend, which eats further into her already meager budget. But she is so absorbed in her clients, and so fond of her coworkers, that it doesn't matter. The animals don't care if her jeans are frayed, and neither do the doctors and attendants.

Whatever you settle on, find out everything you can about the field. Read trade magazines, especially the ones that have want ads. Get books out of the library. You will gain confidence from some kind of retraining. And, if you have your heart set on making the big time, there are a few facts of life for you to consider. Kate Rand Lloyd, editor of *Working Woman* magazine, says, "Until women are willing to be responsible for the bottom line, in dollars and cents, they will never make it to the top." Don't forget that your experience of running a home and managing a budget, of running fund-raising drives, of being on the board of your co-op or condominium, will give you an advantage over the young college graduate whose B.S. and educational credits may seem so formidable. You have worked with dollars and cents where they really mattered.

And don't apologize for your B.A. or your major in literature or music. Executive search firms at the moment are keen on the stereotype of the go-go managerial female type who, even in her dressing, apes the male executive. Writer Wilfred Sheed, speaking at Southampton College when he received an honorary doctor of laws degree, made a point that I feel is of major importance today for women in business:

> Usually the first little grey hairs of the mind don't begin to show for ten years or so (after graduation). At first, new jobs, marriages, relocations are ... stimulating enough. You don't need books or new ideas for a while. So you learn to live without them and you learn all too well. The world of work actually encourages this narrowness if you let it. Outside interests only slow you down in the rat race anyway. So the professional world becomes a kind of Franz Kafka mansion where the rooms get spiritually smaller and greyer the further up the stairs you go, and this is known as promotion. ... I should add I'm not talking about businessmen but about doctors, lawyers, the works. In every case, they claim that the pressure of work is walling them in. Yet in every field you're likely to find that the very best people do miraculously make time for books and the arts and it's the second raters who don't.

Practically no career today is off bounds for a woman. There is nothing frightening or formidable about a career as a CPA or a broker. You don't need to be a math wizard to be a banker or investment strategist. There are machines now who do all the figuring better and faster. Logic and a quick mind are far more important. And while we are talking about top management, if you have a college degree and are able to invest some time and money, consider getting a master's degree in business administration. Your husband's insurance might better be invested in your education now than saving it for your children's. Ten years ago less than 18,000 M.B.A.'s were granted. The latest figures show the number close to 50,000. But a woman with an M.B.A. is still a rarity in this new professional class. Some schools are very selective, turning down several applicants for each one they accept. Others reject very few. The difference, so far as I can find out, is that the more accessible ones have part-time teachers from the business world who are not always available for out-of-class conferences. This may not be proper academics but I'm not sure it is a bad thing to learn from people in the business field. Just to give you an idea of the kind of subjects you will take to earn an M.B.A., here is a list of subjects from a brochure recently sent to me from Pace, which has campuses in New York City and Pleasantville, N.Y.:

· Theories of Management
· Managerial Accounting
· Management Sciences
· The Soconomics of Managerial Decisions
· Macroeconomics: Policy and Applications
· Managerial Finance
· Managerial Marketing
· International Business Operations
· Environmental Aspects of Management
· Business Policy for Managers

An M.B.A. may not get you an immediate job, but it will open doors, and at school you may meet people in business who will be able to do more than open doors.

Once you have explored the first field of your choice, you may change your mind. Or you may decide not to go back to a field you left because—to be realistic about it—picking up where you left off is going to be difficult. Four years out, and perceptions change. As one recruiter puts it, "You had a perfect right to decide to stay home, but if you go back to the same organization that decision may affect your career." And the worst thing you can do is use your status as a widow as an opening wedge. People may feel sorry for you, but in some quirky way they will resist hiring you just because they feel sorry for you. They may rationalize this, saying, "She won't be up to the strain," or "She has too much on her mind." But the resistance will be there. Better far to go to an organization where your status as a widow will be regarded impersonally and of little or no importance. If the person who interviews you finds out you are a recent widow and offers sympathy, it must be accepted but quickly turned off with a businesslike, "Yes, it is hard but that is why I need a fulfilling job." Which brings us to the second trap.

Sometimes a kind friend, usually male, will feel sorry for a recent widow and offer her a job without really finding out whether she is qualified.

Of course such an offer is made with the best intentions. And if a job falls in your lap, you have to have a strong will to look a gift horse in the face. But taking a job without finding out whether you can do it can be a bad mistake on several counts. First, as I've pointed out in chapter 3, a recent widow is under stress. She is in no physical condition to take on challenges, especially when she's surrounded by strangers. Second, these strangers also may not be especially cooperative and friendly. She has been forced on them, and some may easily go out of their way to undermine her. And so—a very important third—when and if she fails, her confidence will be dealt a severe blow.

My friend Micky never seemed to lack confidence. She sailed in where angels feared to tread, winning tennis tournaments, running charity fashion shows, breaking masculine hearts right and left. She had been a successful model when she married Tim, a lawyer, and she helped him by being a marvelous hostess. Their parties were famous, thanks largely to Micky's energy and enthusiasm.

Tim died during open-heart surgery, after three bad heart attacks. He couldn't get insurance, and medical debts ate up his estate. Micky was broke, with two spoiled children to support in a fancy private school. Jack, Tim's best friend, came to her rescue. He was head of the local branch of a big insurance company and he felt Micky would make a wonderful saleswoman for them. He was wrong. Micky could do everything except sell. She couldn't even snare people she knew into signing up. Jack thought she would get over her nervousness, so he went along with her on interviews. But good salesmen—and saleswomen—are, I believe, born that way. Jack was convinced insurance was the best thing in the world for everybody and his enthusiasm was contagious. Watching him, Micky became increasingly less sure of herself. All the commissions she collected were due to Jack.

Two things happened. The other members of the staff began to make snide remarks about her and Jack. And the remarks got to Jack's wife. One night she telephoned Micky and accused her of having an affair with Jack.

Micky was horrified. The next day she quit. There was an embarrassing session in which Jack tried to give her a sum of money, thinly disguised as severance pay, and she refused. She told Jack she was so humiliated she never wanted to see him or his wife again.

On the way home, she realized that she hadn't eaten breakfast, and now it was long after lunch time. She stopped in a local restaurant for tea and toast. The manager himself served her; he said one of his waitresses had just quit and he was shorthanded. Micky asked him if she could have the job. They were both astonished. But the more he tried to argue her out of it, the more she liked the idea. The hours, from ten to three, were good because she could leave after the children went off to school and be home when they returned. The manager warned her that the work would be physically difficult, especially at first; she said she would welcome that. Then he asked, "What will your friends think? Half the local business people in town eat here, people who are your friends. Won't you be embarrassed?"

He hit closer than he had guessed. But Micky was still smarting from the false rumors. She decided she didn't care what people thought.

The first week she found being on her feet constantly and handling heavy trays was exhausting. It also hurt to see the expressions of surprise on the faces of her friends when they recognized her. But she made it a point not to show how she felt, and she went out of her way to give good service and be pleasant but not over-friendly. Her tips increased. She found herself looking forward to her job, mainly because her coworkers were so kind and helpful. Before long, they became like a second family, with their own jokes and gossip.

The only real problem was the children. They were ashamed to admit Micky was working as a waitress. One afternoon she overhear her son, little Timmy, denying to a friend that his mother "waited on table." Micky marched over and confronted the two boys.

"I'm earning an honest living. I'm a waitress and I'm not ashamed, because I am a good waitress. I used to be a model and I was a good model, but I'm too old to do that now. So this is the way I earn a living. And it is the way I'm able to send Timmy and his sister to an expensive private school. So I'm sorry if you are ashamed of me, Timmy, but your friend can go home and tell his mother it is true, Timmy's mother is a waitress."

It took a little while, but the children rallied. Not long ago, Micky heard Timmy telling his teacher, "Mom waits tables down at Caron's Restaurant. She gets good tips because she is a good waitress. And it's honest work, isn't it?"

Micky told the teacher afterwards, "I was so proud of him, I felt as though he had handed me a million dollars."

A job like Micky's can be a stopgap. It can also be an education, an introduction to a new world of people, people who become friends and support her for herself, not because they feel they ought to. Such work is physically demanding but, once she learns the ropes, it may be easier on her because she can function efficiently without worrying about competition or what her co-workers think of her performance. In other words, at a difficult time, it can be an oasis of peace, her strongest tie to reality. As a temporary solution, it is fine, it provides extra income, and it gives her a feeling of security. But a young widow, a widow in the thirty-to-mid-forty age range, should think of her future. She may remarry, she may not. Inflation looks as though it will go on forever, and the best hedge any person, man or woman, can have against inflation is a needed skill. Besides, work should be a challenge and an ego satisfaction. You feel better about yourself when you are doing something that is worthwhile.

"I'm not doing this job to fulfill myself. I'm doing it because I darned well need the money," is an answer I get from women who work as receptionists, clerks, saleswomen in department stores. Well, that is okay—for a while. But a woman who trains displaced homemakers, widows and divorcées, tells me that often women who have first decided on jobs that require small skills come back to her for retraining as electricians or plumbers, jobs that seemed utterly out of their orbit in the beginning. One woman who took training as a plumber told me everyone laughed at her, even her children. "But not after I brought home my first week's check. They were astonished. So, as a matter of fact, was I. I still am."

For the widow in her fifties or early sixties, the situation is different. Unless she has a really needed talent, and has worked at it, she may find the going rough. She is not eligible for Social Security and (according to life expectancy tables) still has a lot of years stretching ahead of her. One of the problems these women face is not that they are unemployable; there are plenty of fields in which they will function with more efficiency and human warmth than younger men and women. But it's that old bugaboo: age.

If you are working as a free lance, if you have your own business or your own franchise, your age is nobody's concern. You can lose a few pounds, have your face lifted, tint your hair and lie until the cows come home. But if you are asking someone to hire you, age is a concern. Legally, no interviewer is supposed to ask you your age. But they get around that by saying, "By the way, do you mind telling me how old you are?" Or they check the date you graduated; even if you got out of college when you were sweet sixteen, nobody is going to believe you. You can lie about your age, a   some women do. But doing this is also illegal, because it throws off pension calculations and messes up your Social Security records.

When somebody is trying to hire you, age becomes unimportant. It may never be mentioned until you sign on the dotted line. But when you need a job and are unsure of yourself, age can become your own bugaboo. Until you are more confident, temporary work can be the answer. Temporary agencies tell me that many handsome, well-groomed women of a certain age (as the French say) actually prefer temporary work because of the variety and the fact that they can work when they please. As a temporary worker, your age is never questioned. And sometimes if you function well, a temporary job can lead to an offer of permanent, full-time work.

There's an adage which we all learn (or should have learned) very early on: it is always better to have a job when you apply for one, no matter how dull your present work seems. However, just as a matter of making yourself more interesting to a new employer (and maybe to your old one) and keeping away from long personal telephone calls, upgrade yourself by learning everything about what you are doing, meanwhile asking questions about what others do. If your job is boring beyond belief, if you loathe your immediate superior, you may have to move on. But stick it out if you can and use the money to take classes or courses that will upgrade your skills. A session, or a seminar, with a career counselor is often a good way to help you direct your future realistically. You can't go wrong with a free course, but before you invest money, ask for references of past students, or find someone who has taken the course before you. There are literally hundreds of services and adult education groups, some sponsored by the government. (See pp. 259–263 for a partial listing.)

A good career counselor will help you assess your potentials and sometimes enable you to see your qualifications in a new light. Then you will have to make decisions on retraining. Sometimes you can take a night course while you are working on your Band-Aid job. In other cases—in the travel agency business, for example—you probably will have to start as an unpaid apprentice. A sister-in-law who did this in California reported that she trained under one of the toughest female travel agents in the business and really did slave labor. But it paid off because she learned enough to get a good job later with an agency. In other fields, if you wish to go out with the professionals and learn by watching, you may have to pay a small fee. And there is one other trick which has been used with success. If you have what the want ads call "gd. typing skills," there are small organizations that welcome re-entrants, and you can learn a lot about a business when you're typing. If, however, you haven't been doing your 60 words a minute for a long time, it is a wise idea to take a short refresher course so you won't fall apart when they give you the typing test. And remember, if you fail it because of nervousness, explain and ask for a second chance. Don't get discouraged; they are used to having this happen. And if you are sure you have selected the right field, and feel strongly enough to take a risk, going back to school full-time and getting a degree or enough training to qualify is less strenuous than working and taking courses at night. Going to school with younger people is not as tough as you may fear. Your motivation is probably stronger than theirs is. And it can be a real morale booster to discover that your grades are as good, or better.

The next step, after you have armed yourself with marketable skills, is to prepare your resumé. There is nothing mysterious about this, and, although many firms advertise that professionals can write you a better resumé, in the long run you know more about yourself and your abilities now than they do. (This is also an excellent way to learn the technique of selling yourself.) The resumé should be typed on an electric typewriter (a standard does a more impressive job than a portable), free of typographical and spelling errors, and should be photocopied, or (preferably) offset printed, on good-quality paper. Limit it to one page, if possible, using only one side of the paper. Make it easy to read and attractive in appearance. If you feel you need more than one page, go to a second page rather than crowd all your information together.

Your name and address should be at the top, together with a telephone number where you can be reached. If the telephone will be manned only at certain hours, indicate that, too. From there on, you can follow a personal approach or a formal approach. Two books that will be helpful are *Put Your Degree to Work*, by Marcia Fox and *Get the Best of Yourself*, by Katherine Nash. Nash, as I've already mentioned, is a career counselor. Fox is assistant dean in charge of placement at New York University's Graduate School of Public Administration and before that held a similar job at Ohio State University College of Law.

The formal, or traditional, resumé consists of the following entries:

1. A chronological listing of your education. It is usual to reverse the chronology, giving the most recent first and working back to college or perhaps high school, if you feel the high school is pertinent. Dates can be omitted.
2. Your job history, chronological or reverse. Dates also can be omitted, but it is advisable to list the number of years at a specific firm.
3. Listing of licenses or certificates obtained, such as real estate and professional clubs.
4. Your job objective: the kind of job for which you feel qualified, and your ultimate goals. This is optional.

The formal approach has one obvious drawback for a widow who is returning to work and has a gap in her time scheme. In the informal approach, instead of revealing where you have worked and when, you can list your skills, followed by places you learned or applied them. For example, a widow might write:

Public Relations: Directly after college, where I majored in public relations [*note that you don't need to say what kind of a degree you earned or whether you actually graduated*], I obtained a job with the Primus Advertising Agency in Chicago, where I handled publicity for a specialty dress shop, a manufacturer of hospital supplies, and a fabric house. Then I moved to the Fixit Press, where for two years I was in charge of promotion and publicity for their best-selling line of how-to books. I arranged author tours, national publicity. During the years I raised a family, I did volunteer promotion and fund-raising campaigns for the Wilmette Nursery School, the YWCA and Northwest Hospital.

Typing: Recently I took a six-week refresher course at the Chicago Managerial School and now type 50 words a minute. I have my own system of speed writing, developed in the course of my public relations work.

Music: I am a jazz enthusiast and play the piano. I wrote the words and lyrics for a musical comedy produced when I was an undergraduate at Wisconsin.

Athletics: I am a runner and a tennis player and keenly interested in football, baseball and ice hockey.

Note that she did not mention her age, her status as a widow, or the number of her children. Although she implies she is a fairly young women (tennis and jazz), she does not give actual years, nor does she say she dropped out to have a family. She does mention specific firms, where she went to college, where she took her typing refresher course. And she does not mention a job objective, although the information about her typing implies that she would be willing to start as a kind of girl Friday, not taking dictation per se but able to take notes in a meeting, etc.

Salaries should never be mentioned in any kind of resumé, nor references given. You might say, "References available upon request" although this is assumed anyway. And don't be afraid to list details such as the college play, or your interest in football. Someone might just read your resumé who is a sports bug or has a client who is mad for jazz.

Dave Lindorff, who writes the "Advice to the Job-Lorn" Column in the *Soho News* (New York) wrote this not long ago:

A few years ago, on the assumption that journalism is a writing job, I put together a resumé in essay form and got no replies. When my supply was exhausted, I typed up a shorter resumé in outline form— not because I thought there was anything wrong with the first version but because I was trying to cut my copying costs. Several months had passed, so I sent a number of the new version to the same old places and was quickly offered interviews.

What this suggests, besides the fact that most editors can't or won't read, is that a concise statement of your background and abilities is the best resumé. Particularly in times like these, when every employer is being bogged down in applications, you have to stand out with just a glance at the page.... And there are only two basic things every employer wants to know: your education and training, and your job experience.

All the experts suggest that, instead of sending out a resumé cold, you should include a brief cover letter addressed, if possible, to a specific person. (If you aren't sure of that person's name or how to spell it, call and ask the switchboard operator.) Mention the position you want and how you came to select this particular company. Never talk about your problems, simply ask for an interview and again give a telephone number where you can be reached, mentioning the business hours when you, or someone who can take a message, will be at that number. If this is not possible, explain you are working but will call at the end of the week for an appointment. Be sure your name and address are also on the covering letter. And finally a bit of advice from Nash: "Don't whine, insult, brag, lie or con. Be upbeat but honest." In conclusion, thank the person to whom the letter is being sent, for their "consideration." Or, if this turns you off (as it did one woman, who asked "would a man say that?"), skip it. But don't be shy about calling up a place a week or so afterward, if they don't call you, to ask for an appointment. Your resumé may have been lost. Anyway, it is harder to say no on the telephone than to send a form letter or ignore you completely.

When you go for your job interview, dress simply and comfortably. You don't need to buy anything new or have your hair done. As a matter of fact, trying to dress up will only make you more uneasy. I would recommend that you don't choose a pantsuit for your first appearance. Much as they are worn in offices, sometimes the person who is interviewing you may be put off by what he or she might consider as too-casual attire.

Don't plan more than two interviews in any given day. You don't want to risk being late—a black mark even if you have to wait— and you want to be as fresh as possible.

Don't talk too much; make a point of listening and listening carefully. This may be hard when you are nervous, but you must be prepared when you are asked a question to answer intelligently and clearly.

Don't be afraid to ask questions. Not about salary, heaven forbid, but about what the job involves.

And be aware that questions which sound sympathetic may be tricky. For example, asking "Are your kids sick a lot, like mine?" may be a way of finding out if you will need time off, or feel you will. Be polite. But answer, "No, thank goodness, they are usually healthy. Besides, if they need anything, my mother is always available."

And finally, don't overstay your welcome. When conversation drags, or you feel uncomfortable, get up, hold out your hand, and thank the person who interviewed you. If the response is warm, and you feel you have made a good impression, it is not a bad idea to follow up with a brief personal note.

For a final example, take Mary Ellen Gordon, a late bloomer who found out that her husband hàd terminal cancer. She conquered her fear and lack of experience so successfully that she was featured in a special education section of the *New York Times.*

She went to college but never bothered to get a degree because she expected to marry and have children. Which she did contentedly and busily—she produced eight children—until at the age of forty-nine she learned that her husband had cancer.

"I was very afraid; I had no confidence and I was not at all sophisticated. I didn't know what to get into. I just knew I would have to get a job. But I felt very old and I didn't know if I would be hired."

While her husband was still alive, Gordon took a seminar for adults who wanted to retrain themselves for careers. Although the theater was her great love, she decided to become a respiratory therapist because it was a more practical choice. She went back to school at night while her husband was ill and earned a degree. By then she had met so many people in that field that she had no problem finding a job.

After her husband died, she discovered there was enough money to go back to college and take a degree. She chose communications as her major. When she graduated. she put into practice a technique she had been taught in the career seminar. She called everyone she could think of who had contacts in the communications field and asked how she could get a job. She found out she would have to train as an unpaid intern, but she took a gamble because she had enough money to support herself and her children for two years. After that, if she didn't get a job in her chosen field, she could always go back and work as a therapist. In just one year, she landed a job with a company that made TV commercials.

She offers this advice to other widows: "Act. Walk out of the house and go to school, or to an employment agency, or to a counseling service, or whatever. It's the most difficult thing in the world because of fear. But in action the momentum carries you through and it gets easier. Don't just fantasize, do it!"

10

WHERE THE JOBS ARE— AND AREN'T

The statistics quoted here about job markets in selected categories are based on data supplied by the U.S. Bureau of Labor. The opinions are mine.

Accounting: In the last decade, jobs in the accounting markets rose from 25.3 percent to 30.2 percent. "There's more need for financial and tax analysts than I've seen in twenty years," says Taft employment agency president Peter Gay. He says that the brokerage houses pared back so much in the sixties that even in a sluggish economy there will be jobs.

Fancy salaries go only to the top performers, but the title CPA— Certified Public Accountant—(required for a career in public practice but also commanding a premium on the industrial side) promises not only financial security but sometimes a lot better than that. And woman accountants since the early seventies have been easier to place than men. In a survey of applicants for over one hundred accounting jobs paying between $15,000 and $50,000, it was found that women were chosen over men three times out of four. If you enjoy management of money, as well as making money, this may be your field. However, Phyllis Palmer, mother of four and a senior accountant in the firm of Deloitte, Haskins and Sells in Orlando, Florida, warns, "Some women can't cope with the hours and the pressure. My husband says I've got it in my blood and that's true. Anyone who's in public accounting to stay has got it in their blood or they wouldn't be there."

Advertising: Once a glamour field, and an economic haven for people who wanted to write the great American novel, advertising is now a very fast track indeed. The rewards are big, but so are the pitfalls. When accounts are lost, heads roll. And being clever and able to turn out catchy phrases helps, but it is not enough. You need enough business sense to know what will work and what won't. I'd say beware.

Architecture: The percentage of women entering architecture has not matched the rising numbers of those entering law, medicine, and business. Yet the U.S. Department of Labor's Occupational Handbook lists architecture among those careers with the greatest opportunities. The key, according to Lynne Meyer Gay, an architectural consultant with her own private practice in Cambridge, Mass., is specialization. The field is expanding in complexity and technocracy and includes such specialties as industrial development, real estate, environmental and computer architecture, researcher, building programmer, construction manager and preservationist. Thus, if you have cherished a desire to go into this field, today a B.S. is just as acceptable as a B.A. degree in fine arts. A Colorado architect with her own firm, who hires only women, had been a fine arts major at the University of Colorado and later took architectural courses from the Extension Center in Denver, meanwhile working for architects. In Texas, the University of Houston offers a three-year master's program for people who have a bachelor's degree in "related" subjects. A Texan who decided to take this course after her husband died said, "I didn't want to be one of those widows who later in life say with regret that they always wanted to be something but never got around to it."

Art Management: The study of fine arts is an indulgence. Many an artist earns his living as a carpenter or a schoolteacher.

Commercial art is more remunerative, but the really good jobs and high salaries are for the few. Actors and actresses have driven taxis and waited tables in order to eat; for anyone returning to the job market, a career on the stage is chancy indeed. If you are willing to start in small ways, perhaps perform in showcase productions, because you feel you have to prove yourself, go ahead. However, there is an alternative for widows with artistic skills who don't want—and can't afford—to go it the hard way. With businesses and corporations becoming more interested in art, a new field has opened: art management. For someone with a talent or keen interest in the arts, art management—doing the office chores, keeping books, raising funds, planning tours—provides vicarious pleasure as well as the excitement of rubbing shoulders with creative people. Art Management programs are offered at many universities including: American University, Washington, D.C.; Brooklyn College, New York; Drexel University, Philadelphia; the University of Indiana; New York University; Rollins College, Winter Park, Florida; the University of Cincinnati; the University of Wisconsin; the University of Utah; the State University at Binghamton, New York.

Broadcasting: If you really feel you want a career in broadcasting more than anything else, and know in your heart you could make good, the trick is to start in a small way, get your foot in the door at your local station, no matter how lowly the position. Mary Miller, manager of KCBY-TV in Coos Bay, Oregon, warns anyone with such aspirations not to let academic careers and expectations keep her from taking an obscure job in order to learn the ropes. She said her own broadcast career started as a secretary where she kept her eyes and ears open and was ready to jump in as soon as there was an opening. The trick is to start small, learn quickly, and be willing to relocate quickly and move on, increasing responsibilities and station size with each move.

Banking: During the past decade, the percentage of female bank officials has almost doubled. One way to break into this field is to start as a teller (growth expected in this field in the next decade, 21.3 percent) and then take courses at night at a university or at the local branch of the American Institute of Banking.

Banking is one job where automation is creating more jobs than it is destroying. Knowledge of computers is going to be essential for anyone applying for a job in the near future, and it will be helpful today. At present the banking industry employs about a million Americans; it is estimated that by the end of the 1980s this figure will have doubled. And the jobs will be more interesting, as machines take over the duller tasks, with opportunities opening in corporate planning, public relations, and marketing. Edward G. Nelson, president of the Tennessee Valley Bancorp, says what he looks for in new recruits is "a broad liberal-arts education spiked with small doses of accounting and law, and some proficiency in a foreign language." He adds, "Formal education should teach a person how to think. Let us take care of teaching him banking."

More and more women customers prefer to take their banking problems to other women, finding them more patient and cooperative than men. A young man I know who was recently promoted to vice-president of a bank said that some of his colleagues were not very happy when a woman was promoted over their heads. They were scornful when one day, in the midst of difficult negotiations with a stubborn client, she burst into tears. The next day, they discovered that several men in the bank had tried to negotiate with this particular client, and had had no luck. The woman had succeeded—and the burst of tears had done it.

Boutiques: Ten years ago, when rents were cheap and you didn't need fancy fixtures, you could open a store for between $5,000 and $10,000. Today, according to Howard Partman, who teaches a course on how to open and run a boutique at New York's Parsons School, to open a 10,000-square-foot store, you need a minimum of $200,000. You have to be a professional and know exactly what you are doing; just a liking for fashion and clothes isn't enough. Retailing training is important, so try taking a saleswoman's job for a paid learning experience. Partman also recommends specializing; a successful shop on New York's West Side offers only suits—and a few dresses—for working women. As for going into a partnership with someone else, he warns, "Make sure it's someone with the same taste you have."

Chemistry: At the college level, students are finding out that they can earn salaries of $19,000 and more with a B.S. in chemical engineering. And women are in such demand that, with good grades, they can earn around $21,000. If you have a B.S. degree with a major in chemistry, or in biology with the traditional one-year course in organic chemistry, you are eligible for a short retraining chemistry course run during the summer at Mt. Holyoke College, sponsored by the General Electric Foundation. Age has little to do with eligibility, but you must have been out of college at least since 1978. The students live on campus for two weeks in the summer (day care is available for children), spend three hours in the morning at lectures and four hours in the afternoon in the laboratory using the latest equipment such as the nuclear magnetic resonance spectrometer.

Computers: "Anything computer-related appears to be mush-rooming," according to Charles Prince, who runs an executive-search firm. "The industry is so capable of spinning off new jobs and new concepts, it's become the most recessionproof resilient field." And Steven Joffe, manager of the New York office of Source EDP Inc., a nationwide employment agency specializing in computer personnel, says, "There are five times as many jobs available as there are people looking for them."

Computer programmers are the professionals who write the instructions that govern a computer's operations; analysts are the higher-paid specialists who define and design the specifications that the programmers follow.

Computer schools that attract students through advertising have been criticized on the ground that graduates do not qualify for jobs, but instead often must take entry-level jobs at companies and go through training programs again. Often companies prefer to select candidates with regular college degrees and take them through the training programs, hoping they will have the potential to move up to managerial positions. This is because some companies have complained that new graduates from the computer schools know how to feed the computer but lack the maturity of judgment needed to debug programs. In any case, it is better to pay a high fee for a reputable course than succumb to the blandishments and promises of big jobs advertised by others. Beware of schools that follow up your request with telephone calls or cards indicating that a "personal interview" has been scheduled for you. One Manhattan school was fined $15,000 by the Federal Trade Commission because the school assured prospective students that its job placement rate was 95 percent, whereas it was 46 to 64 percent. Still, this is an excellent field to explore. The labor forecast tells us the boom is likely to continue over the next ten years, so that jobs will be plentiful in areas ranging from computer programming to computer sales.

Direct Mail: Because of the number of working wives in the labor force, the rising cost of gasoline and the use of credit cards, armchair shopping has become a big business. Direct-mail careers range from the copywriters who create the letters and catalogs to artists, layout experts, market analysts and office personnel who fill orders and do the paperwork. In addition, some small organizations without retail outlets have grown enormously just through sending out catalogs. The Direct Mail Marketing Association, with headquarters at 6 East 42nd Street, New York, N.Y., offers courses in many cities across the country and also keeps lists of more than thirty colleges and universities that include courses in their curriculum.

Electronics: The electronics field is another boom area that is wide open for women, offering jobs in everything from repair to engineering, according to Dr. Robert Allen, chairman of the accreditation commission of the National Association of Trade and Technical Schools. He says, "Women often have better manual dexterity than men, because of smaller hands." He also adds that electronics is a clean business, unlike auto repair, and it does not involve heavy work since the trend is toward ever more miniaturization. Robert F. Stevens, an official of the association, reports that women electronics specialists have an easy time finding jobs and schools are actively seeking them. In choosing a school, however, make sure it has state approval and is accredited by the National Association of Trade and Technical Schools. It also helps to talk with personnel managers of technically oriented companies, who sometimes have their own training program.

Engineering: An engineer is a person who puts science and mathematics to practical use in industry, directing anything from the design and production of plastics to chocolate making. It used to be a predominantly male field, but the lure of money and industry's increased willingness to hire women makes this an interesting new field for ambitious women. Although on the average women still make less money than men, the pay is good. Teaching pays less than industry, but Helen Grenga, professor of metalurgy at Georgia Tech's School of Chemical Engineering, teaches twelve months a year, does no consulting work and makes $33,000, just three years after receiving tenure. (The median pay for engineers is between $10,000 and $45,000 but goes to "over $50,000" when they rise to managerial or supervisory functions.) Surveys show that companies are hiring 5 percent more engineers and "looking five years down the road in plans, we are going to need these people so we better get them on board," according to the Endicott Report prepared by Frank Endicott, retired director of placement and emeritus professor of education at Northwestern University.

Fashion: Looking from the outside in, I would say this is a rough world where instinct and intuition must go hand in hand with knowledge about cash flow, fabrics, shipping, manufacturers, and employee relations. Just loving clothes isn't enough. You have to be willing to work long hours and take punishment. Let me mention two examples.

Libby was petite and lovely, with a beautiful figure and a real flair for clothes. Her husband used to call her "Doll." When he died, she naturally wanted to go into some kind of fashion work. As a starter, she took a job in a good store in Los Angeles. It was also a finisher. In the first place, she was awkward at making out sales checks, and never improved. In the second, she grew to hate the customers. She quit, had her face lifted and remarried.

Now take Janet. Janet was also a kind of doll wife, adored by her husband and two children. When her husband died, Janet tried to get a job in one of the Seventh Avenue dress houses. No luck; she had neither designing nor selling experience. But one designer took pity on her and sent her to a public relations firm that specialized in fashion. Janet started at the lowest rung of the ladder, going for coffee, doing errands, wrapping bundles. She was thirty-nine, no spring chicken, but she gritted her teeth and kept going. One day the office manager, a strong, tough woman, came in on a Sunday and found Janet on her hands and knees shampooing the carpet in the reception room. She was intrigued enough to stop and chat. The white rug was soiled, and Janet on her own had decided to clean it.

Janet today is on her own, free-lancing, organizing and announcing fashion shows for the very designers who wouldn't hire her. To prepare for this, she left the PR outfit and got a selling job in a big department store. Surviving that, she moved into public relations at a specialty shop (a job she heard about through her ex-boss). There she learned how to run fashion shows, hire models, and placate the press. She went through some lean years, but now she is on top. I might add that she is also married, not to a man in the business. But he is so enchanted with her that he sits up with her the night before a show helping her and takes time off from his own law practice when he can to attend her shows.

Franchises: For the past two decades, franchise businesses have been one of the fastest growing segments of the economy. A good franchise operation gives you a chance to be your own boss in a business that has a name already established in the field. It will provide training on how to run the franchise successfully. Some will supply everything you need to open your doors, and even help you get the necessary credit.

But there are traps in franchises, and potential buyers should first do some in-depth market research. Drive around; when you see an operation belonging to the franchise you're interested in, go in and talk with the owners. They will probably be glad to advise you, as you won't be in competition with them. They may also be dissatisfied and be willing to air their grievances. Three key questions: Did the company give you good backing? Did you get everything you were promised? Is your profit as much as they said it would be?

The Federal Trade Commission ruled as of October, 1979, that franchise organizations doing business across state lines must make a full financial disclosure to prospective investors. Ask for one of these and study it carefully. And don't query or make visits to franchises on lists provided by the company; the names of dissatisfied franchises may have been omitted deliberately.

One franchise company advertising in the financial pages of newspapers also has these suggestions: Does the franchisor have a Servicemark filed with the U.S. Patent Office to protect your investment from being copied? And a Trademark filed to protect products sold through your store? Does the franchisor provide an assigned and protected trade area definition to prevent another store from being sold in your market before your store has achieved maximum capacity? Who are the franchisor's principals? What are their backgrounds and experience in franchise operations and in national sales and marketing? And what are the franchisor's long-term plans and attitudes toward this business? The franchisee relationship? The profitability of your shop? And his overall attitude toward development, product offerings, marketing assistance, and the future growth of your business?

There is no such thing as a sure deal. But there is a difference between good and bad investments. Talk to a certified public accountant, discuss it with a tax lawyer, see your local banker. And never sign anything unless you have legal advice.

Free-Lancing: As a free-lancer, working on my own time (without lunch today because I am rushed) in my own office in my own apartment, I can say that free-lancing has its advantages—and disadvantages.

In the first place, you must have discipline. You must go to work every day at a specified time and quit only after a certain time.

Don't spend your business hours chatting on the telephone to friends. Don't go out to lunch except on business (or occasionally with a glamorous man). And don't, if you are going to have your business contacts call on you, have your office in the bedroom. If you don't have a spare room, put it in the living room.

Speaking from my own experience, I can warn you that the IRS will want to see your office and perhaps measure it, if you take a percentage off your rent as a tax deduction. Here, according to a tax court decision, is the formula as of 1980: It is necessary to figure the size of the office in square feet and also how much time the free-lancer spends in it. In a case under contest, the taxpayer had an outside job but also worked self-employed at home transcribing legal documents and preparing tax returns. She figured her office space took up half the apartment so she tried to deduct half her rent as a business expense. The IRS conceded the space but, as she used the office only six hours a day, they cut the deduction to one-eighth of the monthly rent because she used it only one-fourth of the twenty-four-hour day. The tax court was more liberal. Because the taxpayer worked forty hours a week outside and went to night school, and had to spend some time sleeping, they allowed her the deduction of one-fourth the rent.

Gloomy economic conditions can be especially hard on free-lancers, because even under normal conditions it is a feast-or-famine proposition. (I once explained my meager wardrobe this way: "When I have a lot of work, I'm too busy to buy clothes and when I don't, I'm too scared.") The sad fact is that in a period when companies are cutting back, free-lancers are the first to go. And if you are self-employed, you have nothing to fall back on but your own savings. You can't qualify for unemployment insurance.

Also, beware the company who tries to hire you full-time on what they call a free-lance–contractor relationship. Actually, they may be just trying to get out of paying into the Social Security fund and the state's unemployment fund. If, for example, you have to do everything the staff people do, come to work at regular hours, working a regular shift, you are probably really an employee. So if you are let go, apply for benefits. Your case may have to go for a hearing, but that costs nothing but your time.

Government: According to a survey, 15 percent of the American work force is now employed by the government. And the trend toward increased employment of women in state and local government may keep pace despite economies and cutbacks. If you are interested in a foreign assignment, be aware that the government is having difficulty finding enough recruits who speak foreign languages. It is especially favorable for you if you can list on your job application blank that you speak or read Russian, Japanese, Chinese, Arabic, or Portuguese. Large adult education centers and community colleges have courses in foreign languages. And if you have your eye on one of the jobs in a man's field, listen to Nancy Kasselbaum, senator from Kansas, and Sally Angela Shelton, the U.S. Ambassador to Barbados. Both are divorced, and both agree that their jobs would be difficult if they had husbands.

Kasselbaum, who is credited with having run as a candidate, not as a woman, was helped by having come from a political family (her father was Alf Landon) but she said after the election, "I can honestly say that if I were still married, I would not be going to the U.S. Senate."

As for Ambassador Shelton, who in addition to her job in Barbados represents the United States on seven other islands, she says, "I recently was asked what I do in my spare time—meaning whom do I date—I replied that I didn't have any. This is literally a seven-day-a-week job." She also says that at her age (thirty-five), she finds independence very agreeable. She can pick up and fly out of the country without consulting anyone. She is her own boss. Once, she says, a man described her as being "overly directive"— which "is another way of saying 'bossy.' I am convinced that if I were a man it would have never come up." Her background was Southern Methodist University in Dallas, graduated Phi Beta Kappa from the University of Missouri, Master's Degree in international relations from Johns Hopkins, Fulbright scholar in Paris. For six years, beginning in 1971, she was legislative assistant for foreign policy to Senator Lloyd M. Benson, Jr., Democrat of Texas. Then she went on to the State Department.

Out of 150 United States Ambassadors, less than 10 percent are women. But in the eastern Caribbean, Shelton's bailiwick, her second in command is a woman and the commander of the U.S. Naval facility in Anguilla is a women.

Obviously politics is a man's world. How can more women move into it? Kasselbaum says, "Don't feel intimidated. Analyze your electoral base. Know where your strengths are to draw on." Kasselbaum is not aggressive. She says, "I don't have to be aggressive to be strong." And as the ERA movement moves on, which it will despite setbacks, one of her "big concerns" is for the women in politics who feel threatened by having to be aggressive. To be a success, you have to be assertive, but that doesn't mean you have to scream and pound the table. A lawyer whose family has been in politics "from way back" and is thinking of running for office herself, told me, "The best courtroom lawyers have always been the quiet ones, the ones you sometimes had to strain to listen, not the shouters. Politicians should be heard, of course, but the rabble-rousers are on their way out, I believe. Political speeches are made more and more on television, and television is certainly not a shouter's medium. Quiet forcefulness is infinitely more effective."

Ronnie Eldridge, manager of community and government affairs for the Port Authority of New York and New Jersey, says, "Politics is all of life. Every relationship in which power is used is a political relationship. If I sit down to dinner with my kids and they want something, that's a political exchange." Some women don't feel comfortable with power but, according to Mrs. Eldridge, "It's not that women don't know how to play games. Some don't understand that games are being played. We're naive. We're not brought up to pay attention to the same signs of power as men and we're hampered because we don't understand them."

As for going into politics, the hardest thing for a woman to do is ask for money, according to Carol Bellamy, president of the City Council of New York. But all in all, Bellamy feels things are changing; women are more concerned about politics today, and are willing to arm themselves with practical information about how the system works. "You learn the system and then you can make changes," suggested a health care activist at a meeting on

"Political Power for Women" held at The New School, New York. A lawyer at the same meeting added, "I think women now are less ambivalent about power. I think they've become more calculating, in the ways men are, about their careers. Women are smartening up a whole lot."

Hortitherapists: Scientists have discovered what a lot of women have long known, that working in a garden or even with plants on a window sill, gives a great psychological lift. Now several universities, among them Clemson, South Carolina, the University of Maryland, Kansas State University, and Michigan State, are offering hortitherapy programs. Dr. Taze L. Senn, who heads the Clemson horticulture department, defines hortitherapy as "the use of the arts and skills of horticulture to help people help themselves." Hortitherapists work for governmental units like prisons, medical organizations, centers for the handicapped and the aged. Courses in psychology and special education courses are useful as a background, but the main requirement for anyone entering the field—which Clemson University says is fine for people reentering the job market—is a Bachelor of Science degree. Clemson-trained hortitherapists with master's degrees have been placed in jobs paying $12,000 to $16,000 a year, and Senn feels the future is bright, especially for women. He recalls one graduate of his program who had been a chemistry teacher. Now she works in a school for the mentally retarded.

Husband's Business Takeover: Sylvia S. was married to a successful manufacturer of handbags. They had a big house in the suburbs of New York City, and two active children; Sylvia was also a championship golfer, which took care of her spare time. When her husband discovered he had cancer, they thought of selling the business and spending his remaining years in a warmer climate. But exploratory surgery left no doubt that the disease had progressed to the point where he had only a few months left. He stayed at home, and she sat by his bed while he taught her the business. "It was painful," she says today. "At first I thought I couldn't do it, I only pretended to listen to him because it gave him something to occupy him. Then I began to get interested.

Now I realize the business is my salvation. I've sold the house, given most of the contents away to charity, and bought a condominium near the office. Last year we did the best business in our history. And I love it. I didn't know what I was missing, playing golf all those years."

Evelyn B. says, "For thirty-eight years, I was a suburban mommy." When her husband died suddenly, "I felt a responsibility to the people who had worked for him, some for thirty or forty years. I went to the office the day after the funeral and told them their jobs were secure." Then, against the advice of her accountant, who thought she couldn't work from nine to five every day, Mrs. B. moved into her husband's office.

"I've seen too many women who just didn't know what to do with themselves after their husbands died. You feel so vulnerable." She found that the new responsibilities helped her adjust to her loss. "But then I realized I was in a position of power, and the feeling there was something I could control was wonderful. There's a tremendous seduction in making money. I'm not just a suburban lady any more."

Beatrice Fitzgibbon, director of the Women's Economic Development Corporation, which offers free counseling and assistance to women entrepreneurs, says, "We used to get only women who had started their own businesses. Now we're getting widows, almost all of whom have been advised by their husband's counselors not to keep the business—and all of whom decided to do it anyway. Some of them had husbands who didn't want them to bother their pretty little heads; then there were others whose husbands had deliberately let them in on what was happening. For them it was a lot easier."

Olive Ann Beech, who recently sold the $615 million Beech Aircraft Company, was chief executive from 1950, when her husband died. Even before taking over the top job, Mrs. Beech showed her mettle when her husband lay in a coma in a hospital while fourteen top executives attempted to take control of the company. She discharged them all and he came out of the hospital, where a few weeks earlier she had given birth to their second daughter, to regain the corporate reins. In 1953, after her husband's death, another attempt was made to get control and Mrs. Beech fired the men and then went on to run the company. She is now seventy-six and is believed to have been very much involved in the decision to sell Beech, the second largest manufacturer of planes for general aircraft.

Another widow I met took over her husband's trucking business. Still another runs her husband's locksmith and automotive lock supplies business. Like all women who tackle traditionally male-oriented businesses, they've had to be tough. The widow who took over the locksmith business told me, "Some accounts felt they could take advantage of a woman and not pay. I sued them and won."

Lawyers and accountants, once they realize a widow is serious, are often able to give her a crash course in money management and business administration. Other women take entrepreneur programs, such as those run by the American Development Corporation. Joyce Robichaux, who took over the Baldwin Ice Cream Company in Chicago when her husband died, enrolled in a federally funded program for small business owners. She says, "I used to be Joe Robichaux's wife. Now I'm Joyce Robichaux, and it's a good feeling."

Law: A law degree is often a great help if you go into another business, such as business management or banking. So, if you happen to have dropped out to have a family, you don't necessarily have to go back into law, although the women lawyers who specialize in advising women are doing well. However, in the decade which is coming up, the Labor Department says that both U.S. coasts will be overstocked with legal professionals, whereas the need for women lawyers in small towns and suburbs will be up an approximate 18.9 percent.

Librarians: A woman employed as a broker by one of the big firms tells me that she started out as a librarian in a museum after taking a course of Library Science at a prestigious university. "I wasted ten years until I saw the light." Library work has long been considered one of the typical ladylike professions for literate women. Feminists scorn it as a pink-collar ghetto field, offering low salaries, small opportunities for advancement, long hours and tedious customers. One indication of how the field is regarded is the fact that few men have bothered with it. Today 85 percent of librarians are women, and many of them are looking for jobs in industry because opportunities are shrinking with the cutbacks in our economy. But if you keep your eyes on the fast track, there are opportunities in industry for trained librarians, and the pay is commensurate with other employees, at least until you reach the managerial level.

Managerial Jobs: Once you have a job in the field of your choice, begin thinking about advancement. The market today is alive with all kinds of courses teaching women how to get ahead, from noon-hour sessions that cost $5 to weekend seminars that run up to $500. Some companies will foot the bill for these courses, and others even hire consultants to run counseling sessions for the staff.

However, before you are ready for this, there are certain things to think about. At a Chicago career conference, the following points were made: Get as much experience as possible and remain flexible. Don't be afraid to change jobs if a better offer comes along. Never take a job without checking out the boss; if you don't get along with each other, you'll never advance. Don't get personally involved with people in your office. Develop a distance between your professional and personal self.

I hesitated a bit at the admonition not to get involved with people in your office. I made some of my best friends when I was on a magazine staff. But Jerald Jellison, Ph.D., a University of California psychology professor who holds power management seminars for women sponsored by the college's continuing education department, says, "The first concern of every good business person is the success of the business. That means making money. You're obliged to hire the best person for the job, not your friend. The world of work is not a world of friendship." He also warns that self-disclosure, giving someone the intimate details of your life, gives him or her enormous power over you. That can come back to haunt you.

If you adopted one kind of attitude when you were on a lower level, making friends and being a key figure in the gossip sessions, you may find yourself resented when you are promoted. In a complaint session at a big company, one of the gripes heard consistently was about women supervisors; "They get promoted and it's like we were talking a different language." And in *Having It All*, a career guide by Joyce Gabriel and Bettye Baldwin, the authors comment: "It's good to remember that having a high-level job doesn't necessarily make you a better person. You risk losing more than your friends if you lose who you are as a person in the process of becoming a bigwig." In other words, by being nice but not too palsy, you can bridge the gap between yourself and old colleagues better after a promotion than if you got too close to them. You want people to like you but, as one expert put it, "Remember you're not there to win a popularity contest, this is no camp where you become best friends with your bunk mate the first night."

A few other tips from the seminars:

- It's okay to let people know you are ambitious. You can't be passive or invisible and expect recognition. It's even okay to be aggressive. Other women may resent you, but men won't.
- Learn how to delegate. If you are given a big job, don't show what a martyr you are by staying at the office until the cleaning woman arrives. Ask for help. That is what men executives do. And one top executive (male) of a big company told me, "There's only one thing that worries me about my women executives. They are hesitant about passing on work. They feel they can do it better themselves. That's wrong."
- Beware of sex. Marlene Saunders, correspondent and producer at CBS, says, "Affairs happen all the time. I think people can handle it." At a big department store, where hours were long and pressures intense, there were a lot of intramural love affairs, mainly, admitted one of the participants, "because we didn't have time to go outside to find romance." But going to bed with your boss in order to sleep your way up is frowned on. The vice-president (female) of a big advertising agency told me, "The thing you as a woman have to

always remember, that if you start something with a man who is your boss, you can't say no again without losing your job. You also make yourself suspect with other executives. And in spite of all our freedom, if any affair gets too hot and management or the stockholders think it is bad for business, who gets fired? The woman."

· The women's professional organizations, the so-called "female networks," can be of enormous help not only because of the seminars they hold, but because of the contacts. And don't just join. Volunteer, be active and visible. In Women in Communications, a national organization that includes college students as well as working women in the field, I have found that the visible women are the ones who either have, or are aiming at, top jobs. For example, Jo-Ann Huff Albers, past president of Women in Communications, now is executive editor of the *Kentucky Enquirer*. From the time she joined the *Cincinnati Enquirer* until she was appointed to her present job, she never lost sight of her goal, despite what she refers to as many "sticky wickets." Her advice includes the following useful points:

· Take a general accounting course.
· Judge yourself by your own standards, not the standards of people around you.
· Don't be afraid to admit you don't know something. Pick the brains of the best people you can find.
· When you present a problem to someone, always offer a possible solution.
· Resolve that you will succeed.

Nursing: In the past, the dropout rate for nurses was high. The most common complaints were not low pay and inconvenient hours, but politics, red tape, fragmented patient care and arrogant doctors. Today, the picture is changing.

The acute shortage of nurses has caused hospitals in many cities to offer bounties ranging from $100 to $1000 for registered nurses. Because of the increasing specialization in nursing, the hospice concept and the new responsibility put on nurses (who are assuming roles once the domain of doctors), this field is no longer in the "pink ghetto" class. Salaries are increasing and working conditions are improving, sometimes as the result of protests such as strikes. In fact, more men are now entering the field. Nursing education has shifted markedly from hospital-school training to bachelor's degrees at four-year colleges; some nurses, with an additional eighteen months of training, are becoming nurse-practitioners, nurse-anesthetists and nurse-midwives. Dr. Alvin F. Poussiant, Assistant Dean of Harvard Medical School, says that he foresees a lot of opportunities in the health field for women, as well as in related professions such as social work, laboratory work, physical therapy, and the like, offering good pay and interesting challenges.

Photography: In addition to an artist's eye, photography requires considerable manual dexterity and, depending on where you decide to work, physical stamina. But it is one field in which you can continue to improve your skills wherever you are, even if you take time off for raising a family. One widow I know taught photography in a museum before her children were born. When the youngest was four, she tried to return to the field but found there were no museum openings. Meanwhile, at home, she had been taking pictures of her children and those of her neighbors. Her husband died of cancer when the youngest child was three. She tried to get a magazine job, but was told her samples were "too arty." One of her neighbors suggested that she might make a specialty of photographing children and children's parties, starting with the birthday party the neighbor was giving for her eight-year-old son. Sally soon found herself not only photographing children and their parties, but teaching a course for children interested in photography. And she's had a one-man show in a small gallery recently which brought in more business.

   A good way to learn practical photography is to start as a darkroom assistant. Once you have mastered the technical skills, there are many fascinating workshops available run by well-known photographers, trips to Alaska, Santa Cruz, Africa, France,

Greece, or nearby beauty spots. Many of these are sponsored by colleges, so contact the one nearest you for information.

If you are thinking of starting out on your own in a studio or free-lancing, here are some tips from Morgan Luciana Danner, a successful free-lance photographer and writer:

- Just because you can take beautiful pictures doesn't mean you will succeed as a full-time professional photographer. You must specialize in one field—architectural photography, action photography, biological photography, photojournalism. For one thing, you can offer expertise. For another, a specialty enables you to establish proper contacts who will call you when they need a particular skill.
- Have a portfolio that shows your skills. If you have been published, include page proofs or tear sheets.
- Choose a location that puts you near your specialty—hospitals if you are going to be a biological specialists, suburbs if you are going to specialize in child photography.
- Be sure you have the right equipment for your specialty. Professionals are sure to spot you as an amateur if you turn up with the wrong cameras or not enough lenses.
- Be sure you are in good health. Unless you can afford to hire someone to carry your equipment, photography equipment can be heavy and can create back problems. Also, if you plan to do photojournalism, this may require both agility and stamina—and long hours.
- If you don't feel completely secure in your chosen specialty, formal schools are available all over the country. Eastman Kodak has a list of such courses, available free by writing them at Rochester, New York, 14650, Department 412–L.

Public Relations: This is an enormous growth field for some women, if you have the right kind of personality. There is hardly a public figure or an organization that does not have its own PR man or woman—and sometimes a large staff with carpeting on the floor and roses on the desks of the decorative secretaries. Once upon a time you had to have a newspaper background to get a PR job; the well-paid and highly respected Anthony De Lorenzo, who retired as vice-president in charge of public relations at General Motors to open his own agency, was hired when he was working for the Associated Press. But today public relations is a far cry from the job a newspaper man used to take to increase his take-home pay. It is an industry, and to succeed in it you need determination, perserverence, a knowledge of what newspapers and magazines want (you have to do an enormous amount of careful reading and research) plus the kind of charm that will excuse your pushiness. It's not all three-hour lunches and cocktail dates, although an astute company is willing to lay out a certain amount of expense account money if the targets are right. It is hard, sometimes humiliating, work. But if you are good, it pays. Sometimes you can latch on to important figures where your only chore will be to say "no" tactfully.

Although many of our best public relations people never took any kind of formal training, about thirty colleges now have public relations courses. Your local library will probably have a number of titles on public relations for initial exploration and study. And if you can afford $50—or are a student taking a public relations course, in which case the cost is only $12.50—there is a book published by the Public Relations Society of America called *Your Personal Guidebook—To Help You Chart a More Successful Career in Public Relations*.

Real Estate: Time was when real estate was the widow's haven. And in some areas, a smart persistent woman who knows her properties and has a keen way of assessing clients, can still make money. A pamphlet published for widows by the American Association of Retired Persons, tells of one widowed architect who found it impractical to update her training to function at a full professional level, so she got a job selling real estate. She was so useful her boss took her in as a partner. The lull in real estate may be temporary and regional, so in our changing economy there still may be a good chance to make big commissions on expensive properties if you enjoy selling, like people, and have good contacts. A New Jersey agent, a woman who has been in business for thirty-three years and intends to stick with it, says, "If a widow comes to me and says she needs money right now to live, I advise her to take a job with a regular salary. But if she says she has enough to live on, and she is under forty, and a go-getter, I figure she may make it. Nobody knows what is going to happen, and people still need to live someplace."

Secretaries: In 1911, a woman named Katherine Gibbs hocked her family jewels to start a training program in Providence, Long Island for women in what had been the virtually all-male occupation: secretary. The company now has seven branches. Lynn Savage, who recently resigned from the First Woman's Bank in New York to become president and chief executive officer at Gibbs, says, "Women reentering the work force represent the fastest-growing part of the market. I think it's critical that they have the training to do that."

A shortage has developed in secretarial services; one executive blamed this on the fact that "with so many women getting four-year degrees and finding executive positions, there's no one to fill the jobs." Consequently, employment agencies and the National Secretaries Association are launching a program to encourage dropouts to reenter the office world. With the proper training—or retraining—prospects are excellent today, and the mature woman is welcomed by many firms. Richard Ross, who heads Mature Temps, a New York agency that specializes in placing people in temporary jobs, says, "One bank reported to me that these workers were more reliable and more productive than younger employees. The result was that it lowered the cost."

Temporary secretaries earn from three dollars to eight dollars an hour; the average salary for an executive secretary is $12,342 a year and the members of Seraphic Secretaries, an organization of women who work for top executives in corporations, earn salaries as much as $30,000 to $35,000 and wield enormous influence. Even a beginner can earn $150 a week. Consequently, it is a field that is now being invaded by men again.

But times have changed in the last ten years, and secretaries should be aware of the need for retraining, or at least brushing up on skills. Here are some of the things to be noted, according to the National Secretaries Association:

- Despite the prevalence of dictating machines, shorthand is a great plus. (Jobs that require it can command $1,200 to $2,400 more than the going rate.) The bigger executives often prefer dictating to a live secretary rather than to a machine. For one thing, she is handier and, if she is clever, helpful at untangling awkward thoughts. For another, it gives the executive a feeling of having wishes catered to efficiently and personally. Yet many younger secretaries just haven't had the patience or ambition to go beyond speedwriting, which will not be enough if you really aspire to a big-time secretarial role.
- The copy machine has replaced messy carbons.
- Electric typewriters today are far better than they were even five or ten years ago, but you might need retraining, especially to learn the special features they offer. Some magically permit all sorts of changes, retype the corrected page on their own and store the old copy in case it should be referred to again.
- The influence of the women's movement has tended to eliminate the practice of sending secretaries out on personal errands, and otherwise turning them into "go-fers." But I feel part of the credit belongs to the shortage of good secretaries and the necessity of the boss behaving well if he or she wants to keep one.

Selling: "Clerking" in a department store, as the term once had it, was low on the rungs of the pink-collar ghetto. Even today, seven out of ten retail salespeople are women. But today, women have begun to land the better paying jobs in industry, selling steel, farm equipment and the like. Being out on the road isn't easy for a woman alone with young children, and some companies wouldn't hire one, but Mrs. K., who now is president of a marketing corporation, believes it is the quick way to good money and managerial positions. She had her mother, also a widow who had recently retired, come and stay with her two boys, ten and eight, during the week when she was on the road. She kept in touch with a telephone call to them at the same time each night "to touch base and hear about their day," and she made a point of trying to be back on Thursday night so that her mother could go to her own apartment and she would have the weekend alone with her boys. "I paid for her apartment, so that she never would feel she didn't have her own home." And it worked out, for now she no longer travels, but hires other women who do, and her mother drops in during the day for a quick visit with Mrs. K.'s full-time housekeeper and a chat with the boys, if they happen to be home.

Of course "being on the road" is not always glamorous. It means nights in impersonal Howard Johnson rooms that all look alike, lunching on greasy hamburgers and weak coffee and sometimes driving miles in the rain without a sale. You need a sense of adventure and the kind of built-in enthusiasm for making a sale that characterizes good salespeople. One woman I met at a women's career seminar told me, "My dad was a salesman—so was my brother. When I had my kids, I was the best saleswoman the church bazaar ever had, they always made me chairman. After my husband died, I tried working in an office. It bored me stiff. Now I have a job out on the road, and my kids don't mind either—I'm so much happier and better tempered."

Jean Young, who was Chairperson of the International Year of the Child, suggests that traveling mothers try to take their child or children (one at a time) along on business trips when it can be arranged. "Just the idea of the child knowing what the parent is doing can help him handle things better when you are away." Sometimes her seven-year-old goes along with her when she travels; customers often invite him to meet their children and stay with them during the day when she is occupied. She thinks that letters, even more than phone calls, are essential, "because the child realizes this requires special effort on your part." And be very cautious of bringing gifts home every time you go away. "It isn't healthy for the child or the parent."

Older children can be given responsibility for certain tasks. A fifteen-year-old boy was put in charge of preparing vegetables and salads, while his twelve-year-old sister had responsibility for setting the table and helping the housekeeper wash up. Their widowed mother felt they should be "excused" on weekends when she was home and the housekeeper was off. But her son told her, "Mom, having to do these things has made us feel we're

helping you. What I'd really like when you are home is to have
Cathy do the vegetables—I'll supervise—and have you teach me
how to cook."

Starting Your Own Business: Jerry Brown of California said not
long ago, "A hundred years ago, everybody worked. The children
worked. The men and women all worked. The postwar commodity
boom was founded on your housewives sitting in the suburbs . . .
directing consumption . . . while the man went out and did his
job. But that's over with now and we're back in another industrial
revolution where everybody works all the time to make a go of it."
    Perhaps not everybody works yet, but certainly a widow and her
children are back in the days of the Industrial Revolution.
Beatrice Fitzpatrick, chief executive officer of the American
Women's Economic Development Corporation, says, "The next
great group of entrepreneurs is going to be women." An entrepreneur, as defined by one of the country's oldest business-
oriented schools, Babson College of Boston, is "the originator or
principal mover of an enterprise. Such individuals are characterized by a willingness to take risks and to invest money in the
development of a service or product."
    You can start very small, in your own home, if you have a good
idea. One mother with two handicapped children started a
company that designs and sells clothes for handicapped children,
and now she and her co-entrepreneur operate a mail order
business that hires thirty-five seamstresses, mostly other mothers.
Or you can invest in a restaurant, a health food bar, a small
boutique, a gourmet food service. Babson College's Dr. John
Hornaday warns, "What is needed is energy, self-confidence,
willingness to take risks, the need to achieve, persistence, re-
sourcefulness," plus "enough time to do all the things needed,
cover all the fronts." He adds that the successful person who starts
her own interest has been doing similar things all her life, from
running a lemonade stand as a little girl to designing dresses or
hair styles for her peers as a teenager, "and getting a fair price for
her services, too."
    Herman Goodman, president of the Franklin Corporation, one

of the oldest of the small business investment companies formed under the Government's Small Business Administration, agrees that the successful small business person is born, not made. "It's a combination of guts, instinct and judgment of people." He also recommends certain basic courses: management, marketing, accounting, business law, and corporation finance. "I think special attention should be paid to the bankruptcy law," Mr. Goodman said. There is a high bankruptcy rate among new businesses, he noted.

That's the bad news. The good news is that all over the country, courageous women have started their own small businesses and are succeeding. And many others have found that they can market special skills right from their own homes. A Long Island photographer, who had dropped out of a successful magazine career to have children, could not resume it after her husband died because she had to care for her nine-year-old boy, David, who had rheumatic fever. One of her skills was refinishing furniture. She advertised in the local newspaper and transformed her basement into a workshop. Her older son took the station wagon and picked up and delivered for her. Now she is doing so well that when he goes to college, she is planning to hire a local handyman to drive the station wagon and help in the workshop.

Then there is the widow in Evanston, Illinois, who went back to work as a saleswoman after her husband died, and ran into the usual problems of a working wife—preparing meals when she got home late, giving up entertaining because she was too tired, and not being there when the kids had an emergency. Her solution: she opened a Best Friend Catering Service. She prepares dinners for working wives and delivers them at specified hours. She works as a cateress at parties, taking care of the hostess's children as well as washing the dishes. And as a special plus, she is available to shop, or transport the children, or run children's parties, at $10 per hour. She has had to hire other widows to help her. Last Hallowe'en, she cleared over $500. She ran two children's parties, supervised a costume contest at a local store, and spent two hours personally finishing an elaborate space machine costume for a ten-year-old boy whose lawyer mother was detained in court.

Two women in the resort area of Nantucket who were working as waitresses to make needed money, got together and started a small cottage industry, Nantucket Designs for Children, producing handmade children's clothes, crib quilts and handwoven blankets. They use workers who have seasonal summer jobs but are not busy in winter, who can work in their own homes. First they sold the clothes in local shops, but now they have outlets as far away as Boston.

A business, such as the one started by my photographer friend, can begin in a small way. But once it starts to grow, you need an attorney's advice on zoning and other legal aspects; an accountant to watch your tax position; and a friendly banker to help you with additional financing. Nor does it hurt to register with the U.S. Small Business Administration in its PASS (procurement automated source system) program. This program is designed to improve government contract or subcontract opportunities for small businesses by listing them in a computerized system used by more than 300 procurement centers of the federal government and 60 prime contractors around the country. This service is offered free if you are a minority member or a woman and own a business. The address where you can obtain forms is listed under career directories at the end of this book. (See p. 262.)

Teaching: As we move into the 1980s, experts predict a 16.6 percent increase in demand for elementary public school teachers. Many public school teachers are dissatisfied with low salaries and the lack of encouragement for good performance. In addition, women seldom are promoted to jobs with authority; although 67 percent of the nation's teachers are women, only 7 percent of principals are female, according to a survey of the National Association of Secondary School Principals. For a widow who has had experience teaching, especially in fields where there are shortages, such as science, mathematics, and industrial arts, this means that her path will be smoothed if she wishes to return to work. A friend who was close to sixty when her husband died had worked occasionally as a substitute in the suburban public school system where she lived. She tried to be hired full-time but for budgetary reasons was turned down; but during the past six months she has worked nearly four days a week and is not dissatisfied with the arrangement.

There will also be predicted shortages in the fields of educating the handicapped, in adult education, preschool, and kindergarten. However, in higher education the keen competition for jobs that exists today is not expected to abate. Graduates with doctorate degrees are still having a rough time in the job mart. Teachers are retiring later, and people who took "temporary" jobs teaching are fearful of moving out into the job market. However, here again, the knowledge of computing will open doors. According to Lawrence Cremin, President of Teacher's College at Columbia University, "If you know computing, you'll get snapped up."

Travel Agencies: The fact that you love to travel doesn't qualify you for a job in a travel agency. There is a lot of paperwork involved, and even registered agents find that in the computer age they need refresher courses. Also, before you get to the free trips, you will have to spend many hours in the office doing dull chores. I know of one perfectly reputable agency where the owner insisted that his employees get in early or stay late to vacuum and clean up the office. Even the agents with long experience were not excluded. Again, as I've noted, when the economy falters, this is a business that can be badly hurt.

Volunteer Work: Very often a volunteer job will give you a chance to test your skills and give you a clue as to what you might look for in a paying job. I heard of one widow who became so acutely aware of the need for better patient-staff communication at the big metropolitan hospital where her husband was admitted that she volunteered to work in the social service department. Without credentials, she simply went around the hospital talking to sick people, finding out their complaints, and then conveying them to the staff. Her tact was enormous, and so was her need to be of service.

After her husband died, she decided to train as a social worker and asked the head of the social service department for advice. As a result, while she is going to school, the hospital is now paying her to work part-time, doing the same kind of work she did as a volunteer. She believes that she can eventually find full-time work in this or a similar job.

You won't get rich doing volunteer work. In fact, it may cost you money. The allowable reimbursement rate for business mileage on cars per mile is about double the rate for volunteer workers who use their cars. But if you need a bridge between the reality of the working world and your status as a widow, there is a tremendous need for volunteer work; it does bring you out into the mainstream, and it is good for the ego. Even if you feel depressed, getting out and meeting people, making new contacts, raises your morale. And if and when you decide to get a full-time job, you can certainly ask the professionals for recommendations and clues as to where to look. Be sure, also, that when you are looking for a job, the professionals know you will need time off for job interviews.

Agencies are well aware that they lose a lot of volunteers because they don't treat them professionally and with respect, as they do the regular staff. Some today are even offering "contracts" that are renewable after a certain period, and which can be used in applying for jobs. In Marin County, California, volunteers were placed on a contract basis and encouraged to select the field in which they would work—everything from career counseling for jailed inmates to creating libraries, coordinating programs, and doing legal research. The result was that the program attracted not only the traditional volunteers—retired and financially secure men and women—but a number of job reentry people. They felt that the period of professionalized volunteer service allowed them to build confidence and served as a testing ground to see if they would like to continue the type of work for which they had volunteered.

Writing: I just found out that "Mary's Little Lamb" was written by a forty-two-year-old widow some 150 years ago. When her husband died just two weeks before the birth of her fifth child, Sarah Hale turned to writing to make a living for herself and her children. "I had qualms," she said, "about entering a profession restricted almost entirely to men." Nevertheless, she did and went on to become editor of the magazine *Godey's Lady's Book*. For women with equal stamina and courage, I am sure there is a market in publishing today. But for the faint of heart, the field of writing books and magazine articles has fallen on evil days, with too many aspirants chasing too few outlets. According to a recent survey made of the members of the international writers' association PEN, the median income of writers was $4,700 with 68 percent earning under $10,000 and 9 percent earning nothing. Most of them had other jobs, with teaching the usual choice. Unless you have a burning need to write, or an idea for a novel that will outsell *Princess Daisy*, I would say forget it.

Breaking into the newspaper business on a small newspaper is the best route for the reentries these days. But salaries aren't great, and opportunities for advancement on the big dailies are rarer still for women.

Zoo Work: With the increased interest in animals and environment conservation, there has come a wave of people interested in working in zoos. Here again, the opportunities are slim, and the financial rewards small. But if you are willing to work as a volunteer, and have a background in zoology, you might just be in the right place at the right moment. An accounting course or even an M.B.A. wouldn't hurt—zoos need to keep books, too. And you might even decide to become a veterinarian. There are opportunities to make money in this field, and women are welcome.

11

THIS IS THE FIRST DAY OF
THE REST OF YOUR LIFE

It was a cold Saturday morning, with splatters of rain that threatened to turn into wet snow. But about thirty women had paid their five dollars each and were waiting for Lynn Caine, author of *Widow*, a bestselling book of a few years back, to arrive at the midtown YWCA to chair a widows' meeting. As I waited with them, this is what I heard:

"After a year, I expected a miracle. Some kind of magic. But nothing happened."

"Sometimes I think the second year is worse."

"Everybody expects you to be okay. So when people ask me how I feel, I say fine. They wouldn't believe how I really feel."

"I worked like hell to reshape my life after Bart died. I was proud because people kept saying how great I was, what a good adjustment I'd made. But after the anniversary of his death, I just fell apart."

"The other night I hit bottom. It struck me that, in spite of being the star of the family, the big achiever, I depended on him more than I ever realized."

And when Caine, a tiny woman with a pale childlike face and huge warm dark eyes, arrived, clutching a carton of hot coffee, she said, "My book *Widow* came out a little over a year after my husband died. I should have been happy. It got great reviews, and my publisher was so pleased he gave me a champagne breakfast in

Boston, a big party. But I cried all the way back on the shuttle because my husband wasn't here to share my triumph."

The shock of widowhood has been described as an "explosion that sends you rocketing off into space." All the experts—therapists, money men, lawyers, family counselors—have one piece of advice for new widows, which I have repeated many times over in this book: make no major decisions for a year. But after that year is over, the widow is supposed to be able to return to orbit, to dry her tears, say "Good-bye, my love," and take up her new life. I'm afraid it isn't that simple. Miracles are few and far between. Even after the confusion and the panic and the frantic efforts to cope that go with accepting the fact that death is final, there is often a letdown, a feeling that nothing is worth the effort, and a nagging depression that my friend Doria described to me in a poem:

I've got the dark brown tooled-leather blues
I live in a house without any views
I'm the kind of a woman you can always refuse
Just a poor little widow with tooled-leather blues.

Depression is no fun. Like my friend Doria, you try to laugh at yourself in public and cry in private, in the johns of ladies' rooms or behind locked bedroom doors. As time drones on, the loneliness, the anxiety, the helplessness and the boredom seem worse because you can't share them with anyone else. You know better than to appeal to friends, they've had it. Forget the children— they aren't there to be leaned on. And forget doctors, too, unless you can afford the astronomical prices an analyst will charge to listen to you once or twice a week for an hour. Even then you sometimes feel you aren't getting your money's worth. As one widow put it, "My shrink makes me feel I'm boring him."

So what's the answer?

First, you have to accept the fact—and it *is* a fact—that after a year, the worst is over. You have been thrust into a new situation, and any change is painful. But you have survived. Your life may never be the same, but it is life. You will have relapses—try to remind yourself that you weren't always happy in a marriage that now, in terms of retrospect, seems so good—but the quality of your relapses is different. You are no longer stunned; problems can, if you make the effort, be taken singly and reduced to proportions you can manage. You can't change what has happened to you, but you can learn from it, and agonizing over what is past is only self-defeating.

Keep the new friends you have made as well as the old. Reach out to them, and your children and relatives, but don't turn into a professional taker. Keep going to groups—self-help groups, widows' and widowers' groups, Parents Without Partners, bereavement groups—as long as you find them of value. But be aware that these are crutches. Eventually you must discard them and stand on your own feet. Clinging to misery can also become a way of dependence.

You may daydream about remarriage. But remarriage is not a way of escaping or making your problems go away. Besides, if you are frantic, you have a slim chance of attracting any man, except one with worse problems and hang-ups than you have. And be realistic. Government statistics say that if a widow is forty-five or older, her chance of remarriage is about 12 percent. And if you are under forty-five, your chances of finding a man diminish by the number of young children you have. So don't think of marriage as a way of dragging yourself up out of the slough of despond.

Second rule: You must face the fact that you have to depend on yourself because there isn't anyone else. But don't expect too much of yourself just because everyone else does. Try, but if you fail, failure is not fatal. We all fail. There is no point in being overwhelmed by guilt or discouragement. Pick yourself up and try again, and make your goal not quite as high.

There is a traditional ceremony in the Jewish religion, the unveiling of the monument. This takes place a year after death, and symbolizes the "end of the chapter but not the end of the book." Your life as a mourner is finished. You have completed what psychologists call your "grief work." But your life has not ended. It is time to enter the next chapter.

The old religious ways of handling death were designed to give a mourner a chance to discharge his grief. Rabbi Jack Riemer, the editor of *Jewish Reflections on Death*, writes:

> Judaism is realistic. It knows that death is part of each man's life, and it knows that self-deception is no good. So in the Bible the patriarchs face up to the fact of death with simple honesty. "Behold I am now about to go in the way of all the earth," says David to his son, "Behold I am now about to die," says Joseph to his brothers. It is as simple, as painful, and as undeniable as that.
>
> This realism about death and about the need to know it and prepare for it all the days of one's life is a motif that can be traced all the way through the tradition. So, for example, on the Day of Atonement the tradition bids a person don the kittel, the plain white linen garment that is at once both the symbol of freedom and status and also the shroud that he will wear at the end of his days. It is a humbling and a chastening thing to wear one's shroud once a year.

The older religious ways gave mourners a chance to pour out their anguish. In the Jewish religion, at the cemetery, as part of the burial service, the family performed the act of keriah, tearing of the clothes in anguish. And for the next seven days of shivah, the period of concentrated mourning, torn garments were worn, food was prepared by friends and neighbors, errands run and telephones manned by people outside the family.

Today, however, memorial services have replaced funerals; and sometimes, at the request of the dead person, there is no service at all. Swift cremation is preferred as hygenic, modern, and sensible. Widows no longer wear dark colors, and among Catholics the traditional black band of mourning on men's suit jackets is seldom seen today. In our attempts to cope with death intellectually, in our death courses and our euthenasia societies, we have deprived those who mourn of the emotional outlet offered by the old conventions.

One Sunday night, at a widows' and widowers' club, I saw a classic illustration of this modern dilemma. Before the regular session, the therapist was holding a meeting with some newcomers, newly bereaved. Each new widow was encouraged to tell a little about herself and her feelings. There were tears. But there was a bit of laughter, too, when one young woman described the painful fiasco of her first date, a disaster with which we could all identify.

We were interrupted by a knock on the door. A woman entered, handsome, beautifully groomed, her eyes hidden by dark glasses. Our laughter stopped when she said, "I can't believe I am in the right group. My husband has been dead a year and I am still crying. I came here tonight because I have a problem I can't talk about to anybody else."

Refusing to sit down, leaning against the door, she told her story. The family was Jewish but not religious. But her husband, Josh, had liked the old traditions, so he had held unveilings for both of his parents. Now Josh had been dead nearly a year and his widow—let's call her Kim—felt she wanted to have an unveiling for him.

She took off her dark glasses. Her eyes were puffy from crying. "I asked my younger son, Dick, what he thought. He wanted to turn the whole thing into a big party, with drinks and food. I was shocked; the last thing in the world I wanted was that. I am a private person. I have never let anyone, even my sons, see me cry. Dick said then, 'In that case, Mom, count me out.'"

She dabbed at her eyes with an immaculate handkerchief and put on her dark glasses again. "My older son was worse. He said Dad had never been religious and that it would be hypocrisy for us to have an unveiling. He told me he wouldn't come and neither would his wife. I didn't know what to do. I couldn't sleep all night. Finally I decided to come to this meeting and ask if anyone could suggest something."

The young widow who had been describing her blind date asked, "Why do you want an unveiling? For your husband's sake or yours?"

Kim didn't know. She admitted she was fumbling toward something she didn't understand. Finally she decided it was for her sake, a way of saying good-bye. The therapist encouraged her to go ahead with the ceremony whether her sons came or not because it was something concrete and positive she could do, a decision made on her own, a step forward in her move toward independence.

Now, sitting with Lynn Caine in the YWCA on a blustery Saturday morning, I thought back to that discussion with Kim and wondered whether her sons had come to the unveiling. For we were talking about the strange business of having to carry on without help from anyone else. As sleet pounded on the windows, somebody came up with the term "spiritual discipline."

I jotted it down as she went on to describe what she meant: "Sometimes when I wake up I wish I hadn't, because I am afraid this is just going to be another lousy day. Particularly if it's a weekend and I don't have to get up and go to work. The temptation to lie there, crawl back under the covers, just wallow in my misery. But then I tell myself that I have this day, it is a gift, I must use it to some purpose." She looked around shyly at the rest of us. "What I mean is, it's a way of not letting go."

A friend who became a widow before I did—a brilliant vice-president of a prestigious advertising agency—once said to me, "This is the first day of the rest of your life."

I was startled to hear such a corny sentiment coming from my sophisticated friend. I couldn't even find it in Barlett's *Familiar Quotations*. But the more I thought about it, the more I began to realize its value. This is the principle upon which Alcoholics Anonymous was founded. And the logic of taking one day at a time, one hour at a time, is as sound for widows as it is for alcoholics. If you can take one day at a time, as a gift to use and use well, you can get through it. But you can't remain passive and expect things to get better by themselves. You must make something of that day, do something concrete, even if it is only cleaning out a closet or baking a cake.

Third, you must accept the fact that leaning is a tough habit to break. Long after your husband is dead, you may find yourself facing a situation and wondering what your husband would have thought. But he isn't here and you are, and today is today. Dead men tell no tales and give no advice.

Wives today think they are liberated, standing on their own feet. But how many of them really are? They may be independent financially, but they depend on husbands as the emotional center of their lives. And sometimes when their husbands die, they shift the emotional center to their children, a move that invites pain, more pain, and disappointment. Watch a wife stand up and accept an award or some kind of honor: invariably she thanks her husband or her children for their "understanding." Men rarely do that—except for the first-time author who in his acknowledgments thanks the little woman for her patience or her typing. This only points out how unprepared women are really to stand up alone.

After my husband died, a couple we had known well—our best friends, in fact—continued to invite me for weekends. I was grateful, but I did not enjoy those weekends. After some soul-searching, I figured out why: they were so damned close, so intimate, so tied up with each other I couldn't stand it. I was jealous. Gradually we drifted apart. When the wife did call me, it was when she was in town for lunch, and that was less painful for me with just the two of us, but painful enough because she talked about her husband so much.

One Friday, halfway through our chef's salads, she glanced at her watch and threw down her napkin. "I must run. If I miss the two o'clock train, Steve will be frantic. You know how dependent we are on each other."

I knew. I also felt a pang, a big, sick-making pang. Then I watched her leave, and suddenly a light bulb flashed over my head like something out of an old Rube Goldberg cartoon.

Being dependent on someone else is wonderful and easy, like sitting in a warm bath. But too much dependence is enervating. For what happens when you lose that person? You collapse. You fall apart like Humpty Dumpty and it is no fun putting the pieces together again. Men become dependent, too. Even in the kind of marriage where responsibilities are shared, a man seldom realizes how much he counts on his wife until she is no longer there. Sometimes when a man has been married for several years, it is more difficult for him to adjust than it is for a woman under similar circumstances. But, simply because in our society women alone outnumber men alone, the struggle to make a new social life is far less difficult for men. A man may even find the demands on his time unwelcome and a little startling, denying him the solitude he needs to resolve his grief. But he never feels like a "fifth wheel."

In the beginning, there is the need to replace the dead husband. This happens to divorcées, too. I shall never forget the one who told me she was looking for a man just like her ex-husband but "without his faults." The trap for widows is that when grief is fresh you tend to forget that the dead man had any faults. My grandmother, widowed when she was not yet forty, used to say wryly when she heard a recent widow idealizing her dead husband, "There are no bastards in cemeteries." A marriage entered into when a widow is in this frame of mind has to be doomed. Nobody can or should replace a lost love or a dead child, for the so-called replacement has to live up to impossible standards.

However, I believe I can guarantee you this: Once you have become a whole independent person and are able to see your dead husband both with affection and perspective, your chances of having a good second marriage are excellent. First, you are more mature. You recognize that when two people live together, there will be conflicts, differences of opinion, and compromises. There is nothing wrong with making compromises, so long as you both make your share.

Second, once you learn to be independent and to stand on your own, another light bulb tends to go on. You find out that the best possible way to keep friends and lovers is to take them as they are, give them space, not try to change them.

This viewpoint—one marked by objectivity, not subjectivity— can come only with maturity (and sometimes does not develop even then). A cousin of mine, a navy captain, went back to a college reunion the year after his wife died. There he met again one of his old neighbors, also widowed. He invited her down to Washington for a weekend and made arrangements to meet her plane and take her to the hotel. At the last minute, he was called into an important meeting and had to send an aide to the airport. The aide got things mixed up and met the wrong plane.

Tee Dee (who is now happily married to my cousin) told me later, "At first I was angry. I thought, what kind of a man is this, not turning up so early in his courtship? If I had been twenty years younger, I would have turned around and gone home. But then I thought, maybe something unavoidable has come up, I'll check in at the hotel and wait for his call." She did, and soon Bill arrived, mortified and apologetic.

Taking people as they are, without nagging or making demands, is also a great way to deal with your children as they grow up. A widow I know, a beautiful woman of Italian background, had always been possessive about her children but became even more so after her husband died. During one weekend when I visited her, I saw her alienate her fifteen-year-old daughter by criticizing the way she had set the table, and drive her son into a wild-eyed fury by complaining about the way he was dressed to go to a party. So far as he was concerned, he was wearing exactly what his peers would wear, jeans and a T-shirt. But finally, to make peace, he went up and changed into a shirt and slacks. When he came downstairs he said to her, "Mom, you're both a sadist and a masochist." His mother then burst into tears. She had worked hard, planning what she had hoped would be a pleasant weekend, and now she had spoiled it, not only for her children but for her guests.

Giving stepchildren space, especially if they are teenagers, can also work. A friend, widowed when she was not yet thirty, did not remarry until she was almost fifty. By that time, her children were grown and out of the house but her new husband moved in with his daughter, a teenager who resented his remarriage. The girl sulked all day, but when her father came home she threw herself in his arms and spent the evening trying to monopolize him. One night when I was there, she went so far as to sit on his lap all during the cocktail hour.

I wondered how long Leslie would be able to take it. But she simply ignored the situation. She gave orders to the housekeeper that Sally's room was to be left as it was, which was a mess, and she said nothing when Sally cut classes and did not go to school. She also left instructions that the housekeeper was not to fix Sally's meals during the day. There was always plenty of food in the refrigerator, but Sally usually went around the corner to the fast food restaurant. Then one day, just before Leslie was to go to Europe on a buying trip, the housekeeper fell and broke her hip. Leslie decided to go anyway, leaving Sally and Daddy to cope.

When she returned, she found herself welcomed with everything but a brass band. The maids they had hired had all walked out. His sister had come for a week and given up. A filthy house and a refrigerator stocked with decaying food greeted Leslie. She shrugged and registered at a hotel. When she dropped by the following Saturday to pick up some of her winter clothes, she found that Daddy and Sally had managed to clean up the house and throw out the decaying food. Sally had made coffee—it was terrible coffee, but Leslie took a cup and sat down at the kitchen table with the girl. And Sally told her, "Daddy and I made a list of employment agencies. But we don't seem to be any good at interviewing people. Would you help us?"

Leslie told me later, "I didn't want to be a mother to Sally. I didn't even like her. But we've made an adjustment now. She is back in school and really trying. I will never be her mother and I don't intend to try. But on my birthday she sent me a card which really touched me. It said, 'I think you're the only pebble on the beach.' "

Stepchildren can, in their own Machiavellian way, cast a pall on the best second marriages. It is difficult enough if there is a real live mother in the background. It can be worse if the mother is dead; ghosts are very rough competition. Everything is easier for the widow if she can go on living in her own home, where she and her children feel they belong. But even this can cause complications. A widow named Emily had lived for many years in a big, old house in Connecticut. After her husband died, her children begged her not to sell and she didn't. The two boys left home and the girl, Nan, was in college when Emily met an artist, a widower with grown children. He sold his own house before they were married and moved in with her. There was no problem about room. But one weekend his married daughter and her husband and baby visited them, and for convenience Emily put the baby in Nan's room. Of course that was the weekend Nan came home unexpectedly. There were tears and resentment, and Nan blamed her new stepfather.

But it can be much more difficult when you move into a house where your new husband lived with his wife before her death. My friend Mimi, a TV writer, lived a footloose life after her foreign correspondent husband was killed on assignment. When she met Ted, a CPA from Boston, she had a pad on the West Side of New York in a theatrical neighborhood, while he had a charming old saltbox in a fashionable Boston suburb. She and Ted fell desperately in love. One weekend when he was down in New York visiting her, he persuaded her to go to City Hall with him and get married. I went with them and for a wedding present I gave her a glamorous blue dressing gown, knowing that she was moving into a house that was completely equipped.

They decided to honeymoon up in his house before she came back to quit her job and close her apartment. She took a few things in an overnight bag, including the robe I had given her. The first morning, after Ted had gone to work, the doorbell rang and Mimi opened the door to Ted's proper Bostonian cleaning woman. Mimi was wearing the robe I had given her, and her beautiful red hair was streaming down her back. The cleaning woman eyed her and asked, "And who might you be, my dear?"

The confusion was cleared up, and the cleaning woman became Mimi's devoted friend. But meanwhile Mimi had the difficult task of living in another woman's house, replacing her possessions and taste with her own. "Alice is a gentle ghost," Mimi wrote me, "but still a ghost. Ted told me to go ahead and make any changes I liked. But one morning when I served breakfast on some pottery plates I had found, he looked up in surprise and asked what had happened to the breakfast set—Alice's breakfast set. We had quite a row, during which I told him I didn't like living in another woman's house. It was then I realized that he was so used to everything there, even without Alice, that it never had occurred to him that I might not be happy slipping into her shoes."

It's been said many times that you cannot know another person until you have lived with him or her. In our present society, the living-together arrangement has helped some young people avoid the trap of an unworkable marriage. They have found out, before the legal knot was tied, that they weren't suited to each other. This casual type of trial marriage makes even more sense with mature people, but unfortunately it can be complicated by the attitude of children and relatives. Even the most liberated children tend to get a bit uptight when they find a widowed parent moving in with someone of the opposite sex; or worse still, inviting a stranger to move in with her, in the case of a widow I know. The couple, both writers, both used to living alone and set in their own ways, rented a vacation house together. The children on both sides raised so many objections the couple told them they were married. The vacation house worked so well they decided to take it on a year-round basis. At the end of two years, they decided to buy it. And, in order to make arrangements less complicated, they also decided they had better get married. One night, pretending they were going away on separate business trips, they sneaked off and made it legal.

Once you get used to being independent, on your own, life can be both exciting and fulfilling, whether or not you have a husband or lover. But it does take some adjusting, learning to breathe the rarified air of freedom.

In an unexpectedly long-running and popular little off-Broadway show called A Coupla White Chicks Sitting Around Talking, one theme that stood out was the challenge of being free, not dependent on anyone, not forced to follow old rules or conform to other people's notions of how to behave. What emerged from it all was the confusion people feel without rules. In the show, the provocative question was asked: "Now that I realize I don't have to do what I was always told to do, what am I going to do?"

Many married couples go through life pretending to be something they aren't in order to conform, make a place for themselves in a conventional society. Of course it's a phony way to live, but many of them don't even know they are being phony. Then, when tragedy forces a widow into a new situation, the shock, combined with grief, can be shattering. She may feel as though she were stepping off into outer space. She resents the challenges, the difficult decisions, the terrifying knowledge that she is on her own, that whatever she does and whatever she becomes is up to her.

During my marriage, I had two people on whom to lean, my literary agent and my husband, both of whom were interested in my career. I took out-of-town assignments, traveled a lot of crazy roads, but at night I always called my husband long distance, checking in. And when I wrote a magazine article or a short story, or a book, I had my agent to tell me whether or not it would sell, and talk money with editors and publishers.

My agent died a few years before my husband did. I lost the security of one man but still had another. When my husband died, I suggested to my new agent, a woman who did not encourage dependence, that I write a book called *Women Alone*. Having always been a woman alone, she thought it was a good idea and she sold it. To do the research and also to help me find out what I was going to do on my own, I did a swing around the country talking to widows, divorcées, and women who had never married. I had some chilling moments.

Once, in the suburbs of Detroit, I went to a party in a bar after a singles meeting. An oaf began feeling my legs under the table. When we got up to dance, he pushed against me and suggested we cross the border into Canada and spend the night in a pal's apartment in Windsor. I escaped to the ladies' room and stood looking at myself in the mirror asking, "What am I doing here? Is this going to be the story of my life now?"

Another night, I went to a group of so-called university graduate singles, held in the apartment of a man someplace in outer Los Angeles. I went with the woman who had organized the group and who brought tea and buns, to which we all contributed a dollar. For entertainment, our host read from the Bible, the Book of Job. Except for him, we were all female. When the tea was finished, our peerless leader, in whose car I had arrived, stayed on to help our host wash the teacups, or whatever. The other women scurried off to their cars, leaving me without transportation in a city that lives on wheels. I didn't have the nerve to return to the man's apartment and call a cab for fear I might interrupt something cosier than dishwashing. I stood on the corner wondering what I was going to do when a cab passed on the other side of the boulevard. Making a U-turn, the driver called out, "Lady, you shouldn't be standing there alone in this neighborhood. Can I drop you someplace?"

In that book, I came to the conclusion, "Happiness is not a goal. Self-respect is." Today I disown it. I can't define happiness. I suspect it means different things to everyone. But I do know that, through self-knowledge, it is possible to be alone and happy. One of the happiest women I know has never married but has had three important commitments in her life. Now for twelve years she has lived alone with her plants, her animals (two cats and a dog), her music, and an insatiable curiosity about everything that she satisfies in a house crammed with books and magazines and newspapers. She told me her secret: "A sense of humor and complete selfishness." In her lexicon, being selfish means doing what you want to do. And what is wrong with that? I have another friend who is so happy when she is engrossed on a project like making out her income tax, or helping settle an estate, that she shuts off her telephone and doesn't go out or see anybody for days on end. "Why do people think that's terrible?" she asked me. I told her I didn't.

I should confess that at one time I might have been less understanding. In my second year alone, when I was putting into practice what I had learned researching *Women Alone*, I was pretty frantic. I traveled, I gave big cocktail parties, I collected new friends the way kids collect baseball cards. If I faced a weekend alone I cried wolf to everyone I could think of. If I found I had to spend it by myself, I would strap myself to the typewriter chair and work until I was too tired to think. Or cry. When I went to *A Coupla White Chicks*, I saw myself when one of the characters said, "Boy, it's really hard work being happy."

Now that I am less frantic, I have learned to cherish my privacy. I don't mind going to a movie alone if the spirit moves me, and sometime a free evening with a good book is more fun than going to a party. I watch television less, I've discovered, than most married couples. Maybe it is because I don't need noise to cover up lack of communication between me and my dog. I have fewer friends I see regularly than I did when I was first alone and they are, I confess, more important. If even one dropped away, I would feel the loss acutely. I have put down new roots. But I trust that if it should be necessary to change and move on, I would be capable of doing that without panic.

Loneliness, or acute alienation, is said to be the great American malaise today. Certainly life styles are changing. Census figures tell the story: 42 percent of the population, one out of five households, consists of one person. Fewer people were married in the seventies than in any previous decade of this century. In 1974, the marriage rate for those under forty-five was as low as it had been at the end of the 1929 Depression. And a report released by demographers at Massachusetts Institute of Technology and Harvard University estimates that by 1990, the number of households containing unattached individuals—those who have never been married, have divorced, or are widowed—will nearly equal the number of households with married couples. Of course, pendulums may swing back, but the authors of this study warn against any public policy that "clings to the romantic idea of an American family life as it was expressed during the immediate postwar period when people married quickly and had large families."

The woman living alone should no longer be an object of pity, or feel sorry for herself. Susan Isaacs, who had a lively and successful first novel, *Compromising Positions*, writes that novels of the eighties are concentrating more and more on the woman who is self-reliant. These women may "live with men, work with them, adore them or despise them, but they do not need them to survive," she says. But fiction is not real life, and kind friends still think of a woman alone as underprivileged. Columnist John Leonard, a wise and witty man, wrote in the *New York Times* about a horde—"A wall of human flesh"—of unattached females he and his wife had invited to meet an artist, temporarily eligible, who then turned up at the Leonards' party with a sex kitten on his arm. Leonard deplored the taste of men who do not appreciate charming, intelligent women and the "waste" of these women.

Frankly, I do not consider myself wasted, simply because I did not remarry. Indeed, when I see some women who did, just for the sake of companionship, I count myself lucky. I would have enjoyed growing old with my husband as a companion, because as time went on we shared more and more things and became closer. I didn't mind waiting on him when he was ill and helpless and increasingly difficult, because I loved him so much. But to marry without deep affection and sexual rapport and excitement is, I believe, a mistake at any age.

You cannot count on another person, ever, to supply your

happiness, whether it is a husband, lover, or child. You have to bring your own joy with you into any relationship or situation, as my most popular single woman friend says.

Very few people can get along completely alone. But some need other people more than others, depending upon your own personal sense of security. In *Women and Anxiety*, Helen DeRosis says that the degree to which you can live alone and not reach out to others depends upon your "sense of strength and the effectiveness of your woman-power." It is often lovely to feel close to someone else but, according to DeRosis, this is not an "inviolable imperative." And it is secondary to what she calls "self-ownership," that you have times when you can be alone without feeling deprived.

Actress Liv Ullman, who has portrayed many women alone and who in private life lives alone with her teenage daughter, told a *New York Times* reporter, "There are many women who put their arms and legs around a man . . . and the moment you let go, she'll fall on the floor. The man who carries you around, even if he does it for the rest of his life, is not going to be happy and is not going to make you happy. We must come to love with the gift of our own selves, our own interests—something that fulfills us outside this man. . . . There is fear in every love, and in every hello there is fear of good-bye. . . . Live with it, and not in spite of it. And don't think your fear—of loneliness, or rejection—is exclusive, because everyone has part of it. The important thing is to trust in yourself."

None of this means that you have to go through life with a cold heart. In order to live, you must be vulnerable. You can't protect yourself from hurt, from rejection, from loving and perhaps losing again. A friend who remarried wrote me a long sad letter the other day saying, "Clint has moved out and is living with a thirty-two-year-old girl, a copywriter from his office. What is worse, he has told everyone. I wish I'd never met him. How wise you were to have kept your independence and not remarried."

It wasn't fear or wisdom that kept me unmarried. It was chance. And I'm not smug about it, or sure that I won't change my mind sometime. The important thing to learn, whether you are alone or not, is to be secure enough in yourself so that rejection is not devastating—if and when it happens—and loneliness is not something to complain about or fear. The poet May Sarton, a woman who lives alone but does not reject friendship or love, quotes Charles E. Oustakas on loneliness: "I began to see loneliness as neither good or bad, but as a point of awareness of the self, a beginning which initiates totally new sensitivities and awareness, and which results in bringing a person deeply in touch with his own existence and . . . with others in a fundamental sense."

Once in a while I hear one of my women-alone friends say, "I am so set in my ways, I doubt I could ever marry anyone." To my way of thinking, settling down into independence is as bad as living a phony life. Change keeps you alive, interesting, and interested. Old habits can become bad habits. The same old job, the same old beau, may be safe, but what is happening to you?

If you want to live your life to the fullest, you must be prepared to accept moves and new ideas, no matter where they lead you. Emotional security is better than too much worry about physical security. Don't be a fool, of course. Take reasonable precautions. But I've found that those who walk through life with a purposeful stride and shoulders back get into less trouble than the worrywarts who are fearful and show it.

Your first forays into dating are inevitably embarrassing, awkward, and ego-deflating. Even the man who seemed so nice at the widow and widower rap session may turn out to be pretty awful out of context. But don't give up and sit home, although that is easier. Taking chances, meeting the men your friends produce, is a way to learn how to handle yourself when someone you like comes along. A widow who got a job in a travel agency told me, "I gritted my teeth and went out with a lot of jerks. I kept reminding myself that you can't expect every man to be a prize, but most of them have something to offer. And you're just going out on a date. You don't have to marry him. There was one man I remember who could talk only on one subject: ice hockey. I stopped going out with him when I learned more than I wanted to know about the game. Then a really attractive man came out of left field and asked me to a hockey game; he was really impressed with how much I knew."

Traditionally, men are used to making their own decisions. The women's movement is demanding the same rights for us. So take them. When widowhood has dropped instant freedom into your lap, it may be difficult to realize that you have the right to say yes or no, or to make the first approach if a man seems interesting. Look as good as you can because that will make you feel better. Don't do things that make you uncomfortable; you have to be yourself and like yourself. You don't need to telephone a man if that's not your style, but you can drop him a casual note that includes a not-too-urgent invitation. If you don't want to go to bed with a man, you can say no. You don't have to explain why, but you don't have to make a big deal out of it, either. You can't win approval by pretending to be something you aren't. Once you are in charge of yourself, you won't be defensive. You won't try so hard to please, nor will you reject with a heavy hand. Just being yourself is a rare and attractive quality; people will reach out to you because you're fun.

Don't be afraid to make up your mind to remarry if that is really what you want. It isn't easy to put such a decision into practice. But you can't sit home waiting for Prince Charming to ride up to your door in a white Jag. A Washington lawyer went about it in a way that I envy; but then she was always a fighter, having battled her way up to become a lawyer, and a member of a prestigious firm. She was thirty-nine when her husband and ten-year-old son were killed together in a car accident. After a year of being so devastated that she almost gave up, she decided that she must remarry and try to have another child; otherwise she would not have the courage to live.

Chris was not beautiful, but my husband used to say that she was "the prettiest homely girl" he ever knew. Which meant she had personality and charm. She did her research. She found out her statistical chances of remarrying. So she set about finding a man fast. She told her family and a few close friends what she wanted. She tried singles' affairs. ("In a town like Washington, they were loaded with young government workers and a handful of pimply young men.") She began going out of town to meetings, college reunions, trips arranged by the Bar Association. By chance, on a flight to London, the man sitting next to her was an accountant from Boston, a widower who talked to her about his concern over his sixteen-year-old daughter. The girl was due to go to Radcliffe the next fall, but she had decided to drop out and stay home and take care of her father. "I can't let her do that, but she insists she must."

I had given Chris my book *Women Alone*, which she had read, dutifully. One bit of advice I gave in it—advice that is still valid—was "If you meet a widower you like, move in fast before he finds out where to take his laundry." Chris moved in fast. She saw a lot of the man in London and invited him and his daughter down to Washington the week after she returned. Pamela, the daughter, was a young beauty. Chris had no difficulty finding dates for the girl, and she had a wonderful time. Then, as Pam and her father waited in the airport for the plane to take them back to Boston, Pam said to Chris, "I've had such a good time. I'd like to live in Washington."

Chris said, "I have lots of room. You can move in with me. And bring your father, too."

Later, Chris told me, "There were difficult times, of course. I gave Pam her own room and let her fix it up and she came down from Radcliffe a lot. Sometimes she spent so much time with her father that I began to feel like an outsider in my own house. When I was three months pregnant and didn't have to worry about miscarrying, we told Pam. I was afraid she'd be jealous, but she was darling. Now she is seeing more of her own friends and not leaning so much on her father. Maybe that is because of the baby, but I like to think her pulling away is normal: she is simply making a life of her own."

Taking on children of another marriage, particularly teenage children, can be difficult. There have been a number of books written about dealing with the problem, and there are special organizations and groups of stepparents who meet to discuss ways of dealing with the wicked stepchildren. The high rate of divorce has been behind this surge of attention to the problem. And if a widow remarries a divorced man, she may find herself plunged into conflict with the real mother of the child, or children.

However, she has one advantage, if she has worked through her own grief. She knows what it is to mourn a loss. And the loss of a parent can be as real and painful to a child of divorce as to a child who has lost a parent through death. You cannot take the place of a mother, even if the child is very young. But you can care for a young child. And you can be a friend to older children. The important thing, as I've said before, is honesty. Children, especially unhappy children, can spot phoniness a mile off.

Not all relationships need lead to marriage, living together, or sexual involvement. As a single woman, some of my most rewarding friendships are with unattached men. For both men and women, the sixties and seventies were times of readjustment. Promiscuity was considered a sign of our new freedom. This decade may have its inflationary and employment problems, but going to bed with strangers is no longer considered necessary in order to create a free and independent life style. Janice Haraya, writing in *Boston Magazine* about her own generation, says, "Today the new intimacy has taken hold. Among college students, dating around is out. Commitment to one person is in.... But perhaps the most compelling evidence of the thaw between the sexes exists in the vastly increased number of nonsexual male-female friendships. The door to these friendships, bolted in the past, has been opened by coed dorms, affirmative action programs, and other institutions that allow men and women access to each other's turf. Now that the door is ajar the sexes are mapping a new geography of friendship."

There are men who prefer freedom, who dislike being tied down. One of them quoted a remark of Alexander Korda's to me the other night: "All women are different, but all wives are the same." There are also men who have never married because they have low sex drives. They enjoy the company of women but they shun commitment, social or sexual. These men make interesting companions, they can be counted on as escorts when you need one, and they can be also counted on for holidays and weekends. They provide variety. For example, you may go bowling or play tennis with X, enjoy movies with Y, and have Z on the back burner when you need to produce a presentable and intelligent date for a party. As a rule of thumb, if you want a long-term relationship, sex does not play a part. A long-term sexual arrangement, unless the man is married and cannot or will not divorce his wife, is almost impossible to sustain without resentment on one side or the other. Maybe it shouldn't be so but I fear that is the nature of men and women.

In a companion-friendship relation, you function as equals. Sometimes he picks up the check, sometimes it is your turn. On occasion, you may do more than your part, and on other occasions, he will. Keeping track of obligations is childish and giving pleasure is a way of making you like yourself. The only problem— and it can be a problem—is to let yourself bog down in a relationship that has become a burden. Jo Foxworth, author of a delightful book called *Boss Lady*, once told a group of women, "It's tough to get out of a warm bed, even if you've grown to hate the person who's in there with you." This is true of every phase of life, male-female relationships, love affairs, jobs, how and where you live. Don't get into a rut. Or if you are in one, take steps to pull yourself out.

Among the freedoms offered in this decade is the attitude toward homosexual relationships. Once upon a time *lesbian* was a dirty word, like *pansy* or *faggot*. I remember that when I was first widowed my doctor (male) said to me, "Don't become a fag hag." He was referring rather gracelessly to the kind of woman alone who collects a coterie of male homosexuals around her. He scared the hell out of me. But since then, I have discovered that male homosexuals can be amusing companions and good friends, useful in emergencies. And I have also numbered among my friends women who are lesbians. We have grown both wiser and more understanding about sexual preferences.

Perhaps the shortage of kind and understanding men has caused women to turn to each other. Or perhaps lesbian women now dare being honest about their preferences, as do homosexual men. At any rate—and thank heaven for it—we are shedding the old shibboleths. We are able to accept people for what they are. No longer do we need to be phony.

Which brings up a problem that the woman alone may face in her relationships with men: impotence.

Throughout the ages, women have faked orgasms, sometimes to please husbands and lovers, sometimes just to get them out of bed and on their way. That is why it is so difficult for some women to be compassionate about impotency in a man. This is especially true when a man has been passionate and demanding and then cannot function. The result for him is not only frustration but humiliation.

A young man who went through a devastating divorce told me recently in a burst of frankness, "I can take it if a woman refuses to go to bed with me. That is her business. But it really hurts if she has gone to bed with me once and then refuses."

Illness and physical weakness affect potency in some men, but not in others. A doctor who was a young intern when John Barrymore was hospitalized in the last year of his life told me, "He had women—dozens of them. It was disgusting. No, as a doctor, I should say it was amazing." Alcoholism can affect potency. But so can dependence, the feeling that the wife is no longer a sex object, but has turned into a mother and a nurse. This happened to a woman I know. Her husband was sick for three years before he became terminally ill. He depended on her for everything. He began calling her "Mama." Their sex life diminished, then stopped. After he died, she found out he had been going to bed regularly with his secretary, almost up to the time he went into the hospital to die.

Sometimes when a man has nursed a dying wife or has lived with an incapacitated woman over a period of years, he has sexual problems. Beginning again may be hampered by guilt or the fear that he will not function. If you are interested in a man and find him sympathetic, patience and understanding will work wonders. But, for your own sake, do not marry a man hoping to cure him or with the understanding that there will be no sex. It may work sometimes, but I have heard of too many unhappy endings. In one case, a woman agreed to a companionate marriage with a man she had met in bridge tournaments. She died of a heart attack not long afterward, and her son told me that the man not only insisted on trying to have sex but blamed her for his inability to function. He also devised ways of punishing her, refusing to let her see old friends, shutting off the telephone. He was obviously a neurotic, and she should have known this before she married him, but she didn't. In another case I knew about, an intelligent and financially stable man who had never married was avid in his pursuit of a delightful widow. She had difficulty getting him to bed and his performance was poor. But she married him, hoping that it would improve. It didn't. He wasn't homosexual, but simply had low libido. They are still married—but barely. She has her affairs; he tolerates them, then punishes her with sarcasm. She freezes dinner tables with remarks like this one (directed at her husband after he had discussed her current lover in unflattering terms): "Actually, I think John is jealous of my men. It would solve everything if he could only take my rejects to bed. But he is so conventional."

It is expecially horrid because these two were once pleasant people.

In the column John Leonard wrote about lonely and unappreciated single women, he commented on the fact that many of them "settle" for affairs with married men. I don't quibble with his choice of the word "settle." When a woman falls in love with a married man who has been both tender and attentive, she would always prefer having him free. For a while—especially for the man involved—there is a certain amount of added excitement in intrigue and secret meetings. But then come the lonely long weekends and holidays when he has to be with his wife and family.

These married men are a far cry from the lechers and opportunists who dash in to take widows to bed before the neighbors' casseroles are washed and returned. These married men aren't jerks. They are kind, considerate, mature, and usually very, very good in bed. They do not push or rush you. They bring charming gifts and take you out to romantic dinners with delicious food. They are fun. And they know how to make a woman feel loved and cherished.

These men aren't always glamorous or rich. But they are responsible. They aren't the ones who fled into divorce during the dangerous forties, the age when men begin to look around for younger and juicier flesh. They were busy carving careers and supporting expensive families. Maybe their marriages weren't as good as they had hoped. But they stuck it out. So here they are now, in their fifties and early sixties—a period which without any real evidence has been tabbed as the male menopause—and eager for a real emotional involvement. Many are vaguely unhappy, wondering if what they accomplished, with so much effort, was really worth it. Sometimes their wives are women who have plunged into careers and poured their attention and enthusiasm into work instead of the men they married. Other wives have stayed home but buried themselves in civic or social work, have become pillars of the community. These wives aren't what you might call fulfilled, either. They resent the fact that their husbands are too busy working to be adequate husbands or fathers. But they do take their presence for granted. They are part of the scenery.

These husbands have, as a rule, tried one-night stands and casual affairs and found them wanting. What they need is understanding, along with love and passion, brains and intelligence mixed with sensitivity and humor. And there you are, with all of that to offer, plus vulnerability. "I didn't expect all fun and games," one deeply involved woman told me. "But I decided with my eyes open, that whatever happened would be worth it. Because I fell in love."

Until women's liberation, most widows were either too cautious or too frightened of public censure to have an affair with a married man. Those who did kept their shameful secret carefully concealed. But today the single woman—divorced, never married, or widowed—has come out of the closet. In print, on television, they tell about their love affairs with married men, giving all the details except his name. They don't offer excuses. They feel no shame. When asked about the wives of these men, they shrug. "Why should I worry about her? She had her chance and blew it. Besides, she has the important times, the holidays, the weekends. He wouldn't be involved with me if she had cared enough to keep him."

Don't knock romance. Or being in love. But the trick is to know where you stand and where you are going. High romance cannot go on forever. In a good marriage, it is replaced by mutual interests, affection and understanding. If not such a good marriage, boredom and bickering and resentment seep in. And in an affair, there will come the time when passion and recklessness must give way to caution, nervousness, and fear of being found out. Even when a marriage offers little except security and the affection of children and grandchildren, there will come a time when these things matter enormously.

If, before they do, he divorces his wife and settles for marriage with his love, he may bring such a load of guilt and regret to the second marriage that the pain and triumph aren't worth it. Unless he was wise enough to see exactly what he was letting himself in for, you may be in for a worse time than the wife he discarded.

I have a strong conviction that only one kind of woman can manage a love affair with a married man without being hurt. This is the woman who values her own personal liberty more than anything else. She cannot be badly hurt because she really doesn't want a man around full time. She enjoys the sex, the attention, the friendship and male conversation, but she has no interest in having him full-time. She has other priorities. She has her work, her career, her independence, and her privacy. "There may come a time when I will regret not having remarried," one such woman told me, "but I don't think so. Anyway, why sacrifice my freedom for a future that is a mystery?"

No matter how smart or balanced or beautiful or mature or rich you are, you can't control your life completely. Accidents happen. Tragedies. And miracles. All you can do is accept what you have. And do the best you can about it.

The secret of learning how to cope and control your life really isn't complicated. It is simply to get acquainted with who you really are beneath the superficial level, to explore your hidden desires, your impulses (libidinous and otherwise), and your fantasies. This doesn't mean that once you know yourself, you have carte blanche to go out and indulge your wildest notions. Far from it. It means that recognizing what you really like may clear up those tensions and nameless anxieties that bog you down.

In connection with this exploration, I attended some workshops given by Helen DeRosis, author of *Women and Anxiety*. Along with her private practice as an analyst, Dr. DeRosis gives popular and well-attended workshops on dealing with anxiety and depression, and is founder and president of Depressives Anonymous, a national nonprofit organization.

Most of the people who come to her clinics are women—not, I

like to think, because women are more troubled than men, but because women are more willing to seek help, less ashamed to admit problems.

Her workshop technique is to ask a volunteer from the group to stand up and put into words the reason she needs help, her problem. Then we, the audience, are invited to participate. First, to ask questions that will clarify exactly what the problem is. Then, once we have determined that, to make suggestions on how it can be solved. DeRosis doesn't lecture, but she guides our comments and suggestions so that often we are shown that the original problem may be more—or less—complicated than it seemed.

For example: A widow whom I shall call Sherill, a television actress, said she was having a difficult time with her twenty-year-old daughter. The girl had been fifteen when her father died and had taken his loss very hard. But she seemed to be all right until recently.

"Now," her mother said, "she is going out with an impossible man."

A girl in the audience who appeared to be about the daughter's age asked defensively, "What do you mean when you say *impossible?*"

Sherill answered, "I'll tell you two things about him. He is neither single nor solvent."

Sherill was a very attractive woman, tiny, with a halo of short blond hair. A perceptive audience member asked her, "Is the daughter resentful of your dates?"

Sherill smiled. "I don't go out that much, except with old friends. I have a career that's very demanding and I was very much in love with my husband. I haven't found anybody who measures up to him."

"How long has she known this man?" "Have you tried to forbid her seeing him?" "Do you think he will get a divorce?" The questions came fast. And, as Sherill answered, it became clear that, although the man said he couldn't get a divorce, the girl was willing to take him on those terms. And the arguments with her mother only made her more and more defiant about spending time with him.

Finally Sherill said, "We can't even have a simple discussion about something in the newspaper now without it turning into a battle." She looked at Dr. DeRosis and added, "We were such a happy family when her father was alive. We did everything together. Now—"

DeRosis summed up: "Sherill, your husband is dead. That is a fact which can't be changed. And if a child can't have two parents, one is perfectly capable of functioning. But you must make the home situation less tense. She knows how you feel about this man, so stop talking about him. Avoid showing disapproval when she goes to see him. You can't stop her, so don't fight a losing battle. He knows how to make her feel comfortable, so of course she goes to him when the home situation is tense. Right now she is so wound up she isn't ready to meet other men. But try ignoring the situation and see what happens. Sometimes an affair like this dies a natural death, and out of it she will learn not to make the same mistake again. But don't enter into a competition that you can't win."

At the next workshop, I happened to be behind Sherill waiting for the elevator. I asked her about her daughter. Her face lighted up. "Everything is much better. Just doing something about it instead of worrying has helped. I guess I'm less tense, which makes her less defensive."

Writing down a problem, putting it in front of you in black and white, helps you concentrate on the essentials instead of spending sleepless nights crowded with worries and regrets and wishful thinking. And sometimes the things we think we are worrying about aren't the real problem. One woman who stood up in front of the workshop seemed familiar. She had a pretty round face and bright red hair, but she was overweight and the short-waisted print dress with a full skirt only emphasized this. I wondered where our paths had crossed when she said, "I'm forty-six. My husband has been dead three years, I would like to remarry. But I can't get interested in men my own age. I like them in their thirties."

Suddenly, I remembered. This same woman, dressed differently but again in an unsuitably youthful outfit, had attended a widows' group where I had been present and stated her problem about liking only younger men.

We hadn't been able to help her, or at least satisfy her. We had discussed going out with younger men and found nothing very wrong about that. One woman suggested that sometimes a young man was attracted by older women because they were mother figures. I had come up with a quotation from May Sarton: "Whatever people I take into my life I take because they challenge me and I challenge them at the deepest level. Such relationships are rarely serene but they are nourishing."

Then Jackie had further confused us by saying, "I prefer younger men. But they don't challenge me that much. All they are interested in is bed."

Dr. DeRosis didn't give her workshop a chance to fumble around with Jackie's problem. Instead, she said crisply, "Jackie, what you are really worried about is growing old." And while the shock settled down on the rest of us, DeRosis added:

"Worry about age is fear of the unknown. But why waste time fighting or fearing the inevitable? Every decade is the prime of your life if you make it so."

In her workshops, DeRosis gave us homework. We were to do the following: 1) Select a single troublesome issue that causes you to feel anxious or that creates tension, guilt, anger, depression, or conflict; 2) Choose one possible solution to deal with the issue. (My aside: don't worry about alternatives. Just pick one possible solution that you might live with.); 3) Put it in action (DeRosis warned that unless you implement a decision, it becomes just an intellectual exercise and futile.); 4) Evaluate the result of this action in terms of losses or gains. (Then if you think it hasn't worked, go on to another alternative. When asked what to do if both solutions seems unsatisfactory, DeRosis advised, "Pick the lesser of two evils. Then try to find a third or fourth alternative.")

I had just returned from the workshop on Monday night when I had a telephone call from an old friend in Minneapolis.

Kate's husband, an airplane pilot, had been killed in a crash when her children were toddlers. Kate apprenticed herself to an interior decorator and now has her own shop and an attractive house in the suburbs. She never remarried, because "I didn't want anyone else telling my children what to do." Now the boy is in college and the daughter is working in New York. For two years,

Kate has been seeing one man exclusively. He has been divorced twice, with children from both marriages. Kate has traveled with him to Europe and the Orient. She has spent weekends on his boat. From the beginning he told her he would never remarry because he wanted all the money he has made—and he is quite a rich man—to go to his children.

Now he is terminally ill. He has sold his apartment and his boat. From the hospital he went into a nursing home where he is very unhappy. He has tried to persuade Kate to let him move into her house, promising to bring a full-time nurse. Kate is torn.

"I'm still crazy about him. But I know he will be an invalid. There will be no more trips and probably no sex. Even his children won't take the responsibility. And one of his ex-wives called me to say, 'Don't expect a dime out of that bastard. You're a fool if you take him in.'"

I tried to argue her out of it. So, I found out, had her daughter. I told her that he would get more demanding and difficult, as most invalids do, and, since this man was difficult enough to start with, she would be saddling herself with a real problem. When Kate remained doubtful, I suggested she sit down and write out all the pros and cons. I hoped that would convince her. Instead, she decided to let him move in with her. She read her reasons aloud to me:

First, he has offered to hire a full-time housekeeper. With competent help, I will be even more free than I was before, when I had to visit him at the nursing home. I can come and go as I wish, and even travel.

Second, I will be able to live well, with his contribution to the household. The burden of his care will be on other people, and I will have his company, which I enjoy.

Third, I have discussed the arrangement with my closest neighbors and they agree I am doing the right thing, even though I am not married. I know that when he dies, I will be lonesome, but I'd be more lonesome now if I left him to die in a nursing home.

Fourth, I admit I resent his not being willing to marry me, not so much for the money—although I could use that—as for the idea. But I knew that from the beginning. It was okay then. So it has to be okay now. I decided I had to live with what is today.

I still think Kate is wrong, but it is her decision. I know she isn't being a martyr, nor is she too concerned about what her children and I think. She knows we will love her anyway. In order to live with yourself comfortably, you must like what you see. And I don't think Kate would have liked herself if she had let down a dying man whose company she enjoyed when he was well. Gloria Steinem, the key pin of the women's movement, has said, "Self hatred in women is the most dangerous thing. You have to wait until (women) have enough confidence to be generous to other women." And, let me add, to men.

Kate wrote me that before he moved in, he insisted that they sign a living-together arrangement. "At first I was insulted because I thought he didn't trust me not to sue his estate after he died. But then I decided if he was going to be businesslike, so would I. I specified exactly what he would supply—the nurses, the housekeeper, and the living expenses, including maintenance and repairs. I also insisted that when the end was near, he would let me move him back to the hospital where his children would take charge. No sex was mentioned. I figured that was because he didn't think he was capable. I learned later he did this because an agreement is more likely to be held up in court if it is drawn along purely financial and practical lines, just like any business agreement. I wish in your book you would tell widows to insist on a living-together agreement if they move in with a man, or he moves in with them, no matter how much they trust him. But leave out sex."

Happiness really means rapport with yourself first, and then with others. It means the ability to give on your own terms, and accept on these same terms. Being responsible only to yourself means you can be more honest, and basic honesty is the most rewarding and exciting thing in the world.

As an example, I give you Anne Morrow Lindbergh, who has had her share of tragedies and rewards, glamor and horror. Ten years ago, at the suggestion of her publisher, she took on what she now refers to as a "job"—editing the publication of her diaries and letters covering her life and that of her celebrated husband during the period 1922 to 1947. Her husband died in 1974. The last two volumes were published without his participation. In the introduction to the last volume, *War Within and Without*, which covers the controversial years 1939 to 1944, when Lindbergh was widely criticized as an anti-Semite and pro-Nazi, Anne Morrow Lindbergh writes: "It [the book] is, I realize, more personal, more open and more vulnerable and, because of this, ultimately more honest than any of the preceding volumes. . . . I can see and admit my own mistakes, and those of my husband." And toward the end of the book she says, "How hard it is to have the interdependence of marriage and yet be strong in oneself alone."

Appendix

A

BIBLIOGRAPHY

GRIEF AND WIDOWS

Caine, Lynn. *Widow*. New York: William Morrow, 1974.

Colgrove, Melba; Bloomfield, Harold H.; and McWilliams, Peter. *How to Survive the Loss of a Love; Fifty-Eight Things to Do When There is Nothing to Be Done*. New York: Lion Press (distributed by Simon & Schuster), 1976.

Flach, Frederic F. *The Secret Strength of Depression*. Philadelphia: Lippincott, 1974.

Gorer, Geoffrey. *Death, Grief, and Mourning*. Garden City, NY: Doubleday, Anchor Press, 1967.

Gould, Lois. *Such Good Friends* (fiction). New York: Random House, 1970.

Kliman, Ann S. *Crisis; Psychological First Aid for Recovery and Growth*. New York: Holt, Rinehart and Winston, 1978.

Lerner, Gerda. *A Death of One's Own*. New York: Simon & Schuster, 1978.

Lewis, C. S. *A Grief Observed*. New York: The Seabury Press, 1963.

Liebman, Joshua Loth. *Peace of Mind*. New York: Simon & Schuster, 1946.

Linzer, Norman, ed. *Understanding Bereavement and Grief*. New York: KTAV Publishing House/Yeshiva University Press, 1977.

Lopata, Helena Znaniecki. *Women as Widows*. New York: Elsevier North-Holland, 1979.

Morris, Sarah. *Coping with Crisis*. Chicago: Chicago Review Press, 1978.

————. *Grief and How to Live with It*. New York: Grosset & Dunlap, 1972.

Parkes, Colin Murray. *Bereavement; Studies of Grief in Adult Life*. New York: International Universities Press, 1972.

Potthoff, Harvey H. *Loneliness: Understanding and Dealing with It*. Nashville: Abington, 1976.

Riemer, Jack, comp. *Jewish Reflections on Death*. New York: Schocken Books, 1974.

Ryan, Kathryn Morgan, and Ryan, Cornelius. *A Private Battle*. New York: Simon & Schuster, 1979.

Sarton, May. *Journal of a Solitude*. New York: W. W. Norton, 1973.

Schoenberg, Bernard; Carr, Arthur C.; Peretz, David; and Kutscher, Austin H., eds. *Loss and Grief: Psychological Management in Medical Practice*. New York: Columbia University Press, 1970.

Taves, Isabella. *Love Must Not Be Wasted*. New York: Crowell, 1974.

Pamphlets

On Being Alone, National Retired Teachers Association (NTRA), American Association of Retired Persons (AARP), and Action for Independent Maturity (AIM) Guide for Widowed Persons. Free from 1909 K Street NW, Washington, DC 20049.

Your Widowedhood Retirement Guide, free from AARP, 1909 K Street NW, Washington, DC 20049.

CHILDREN AND GRIEF

Bernstein, Joanne E. *Books to Help Children Cope with Separation and Loss*. New York: R. R. Bowker Co., 1977.

Feifel, Herman, ed. *The Meaning of Death*, New York: Blakiston Division, McGraw-Hill, 1959.

Furman, Erna. *A Child's Parent Dies. Studies in Childhood Bereavement*. New Haven: Yale University Press, 1974.

Grollman, Earl A., ed. *Explaining Death to Children*. Boston: Beacon Press, 1967.

_____. *Talking about Death; A Dialogue between Parent and Child*. Boston, Beacon Press, 1970.

LeShan, Eda. *Learning to Say Good-by When a Parent Dies*. New York: Macmillan, 1980.

Pincus, Lily. *Death and the Family; The Importance of Mourning*. New York: Pantheon Books, 1974.

Rudolph, Marguerita. *Should the Children Know? Encounters with Death in the Lives of Children*. New York: Schocken Books, 1978.

FOR CHILDREN

Bernstein, Joanne E., and Gullo, Stephen V. *When People Die*. New York: Dutton, 1977.

Hurd, Edith Thacher. *The Black Dog Who Went into the Woods* (fiction, ages 5 to 9). New York: Harper & Row, 1979.

Kantrowitz, Mildred. *When Violet Died*. New York: Parents Magazine Press/Scholastic Book Services, 1973.

Klein, Stanley. *The Final Mystery*. Garden City, NY: Doubleday, 1974.

Mann, Peggy. *There are Two Kinds of Terrible*. Boston: Little, Brown, 1977.

Pringle, Laurence. *Death Is Natural*. New York: Scholastic Book Services, 1977.

Viorst, Judith. *The Tenth Good Thing about Barney* (picture book, ages 5 to 7). New York: Atheneum, 1979.

Zim, Herbert Spencer and Bleeker, Sonia. *Life and Death*. New York, Morrow, 1970.

SINGLE PARENTING

Brazelton, T. Berry. *Toddlers and Parents: A Declaration of Independence*. New York: Delacorte Press/S. Lawrence, 1974.

Cadwallader, Sharon, *Sharing in the Kitchen: A Cookbook for Single Parents and Children*. New York: McGraw-Hill, 1979.

Curtis, Jean. *Working Mothers*. Garden City, N.Y.: Doubleday, 1976.

Friday, Nancy. *My Mother/My Self: The Daughter's Search for Identity*. New York: Delacorte Press, 1977.

Glickman, Beatrice Marden, and Springer, Nesha Bass. *Who Cares for the Baby? Choices in Child Care*. New York: Schocken Books, 1978.

Greenleaf, Barbara Kay, with Lewis A. Schaffer. *Help: A Handbook for Working Mothers*. New York: Crowell, 1978.

Hope, Karol, and Young, Nancy, eds. *Momma: The Sourcebook for Single Mothers*. New York: New American Library/Plume, 1978.

Jones, Eve. *Raising Your Child in a Fatherless Home*. New York: Macmillan, 1963.

Klein, Carole. *The Single Parent Experience*. New York: Walker, 1973.

Lindsay, Rae. *Alone and Surviving*. New York: Walker, 1977.

REMARRIAGE, LIVING TOGETHER ARRANGEMENTS, STEPCHILDREN

Ashley, Paul Pritchard. *Oh Promise Me . . . but Put it in Writing: Living Arrangements without, before, during and after Marriage*. New York: McGraw-Hill, 1978.

Berman, Claire. *Making It as a Stepparent—New Roles—New Rules*. Garden City, NY: Doubleday, 1980.

Bernard, Jessie. *Remarriage: A Case Study of Marriage*. New York: Russell & Russell, 1971.

Clair, Bernard, and Daniele, Anthony. *Love Pact: the Layman's Legal Guide to Living Together Arrangements*. New York: Grove Press, 1980.

Flach, Frederic F. *A New Marriage, A New Life*. New York: McGraw-Hill, 1978.

Hite, Shere. *The Hite Report: A Nationwide Study of Female Sexuality*. New York: Macmillan, 1976.

Kreis, Bernadine. *To Love Again: An Answer to Loneliness*. New York: The Seabury Press, 1975.

Lowe, Patricia Tracy. *The Cruel Stepmother*. Englewood Cliffs, NJ: Prentice-Hall, 1970.

Roosevelt, Ruth, and Lofas, Jeannette. *Living in Step*. New York: Stein & Day, 1976.

Siefert, Anne. *His, Mine, and Ours*. New York: Macmillan, 1980.

Thayer, Nancy. *Stepping* (fiction). Garden City, NY: Doubleday, 1980.

Updike, John. *Marry Me* (fiction). New York: Knopf, 1976.

SELF-HELP

Barbach, Lonnie Garfield. *For Yourself: The Fulfillment of Female Sexuality.* Garden City, NY: Doubleday, 1975.

Bequaert, Lucia H. *Single Women Alone & Together.* Boston: Beacon Press, 1976.

Brown, Gabrielle. *The New Celibacy.* New York: McGraw-Hill, 1980.

Caine, Lynn. *Lifelines.* Garden City, NY: Doubleday, 1978.

DeRosis, Helen A. *Women and Anxiety: A Step-by-step Program to Overcome Your Anxieties.* New York: Delacorte Press, 1979.

DeRosis, Helen A., and Pellegrino, Victoria Y. *The Book of Hope; How Women Can Overcome Depression.* New York: Macmillan, 1976.

Evans, Glen. *The Family Circle Guide to Self-Help.* New York: Ballantine, 1979.

Flach, Frederic F. *Choices: Coping Creatively with Personal Change.* Philadelphia: Lippincott, 1977.

Greening, Tom, and Hobson, Dick. *Instant Relief: The Encyclopedia of Self-Help.* New York: Seaview Books/Simon & Schuster, 1979.

Harris, Janet. *The Prime of Ms. America: The American Woman at Forty.* New York: Putnam, 1975.

Lindbergh, Anne Morrow. *War Within and Without: Diaries and Letters of Anne Morrow Lindbergh, 1939–1944.* New York: Harcourt Brace Jovanovich, 1980.

Potok, Andrew. *Ordinary Daylight: Portrait of an Artist Going Blind.* New York: Holt, Rinehart & Winston, 1980.

Scarf, Maggie. *Unfinished Business: Pressure Points in the Lives of Women.* Garden City, NY: Doubleday, 1980.

Taves, Isabella. *Women Alone.* New York: Funk & Wagnalls, 1968.

Wydro, Kenneth. *Flying Solo: The New Art of Living Single.* New York: Berkley Pub. Corp., 1978.

DIET, HEALTH, AND STRESS

Bach, Lydia. *Awake! Aware! Alive! Exercises for a Vital Body*. New York: Random House, 1973.

Benson, Herbert. *The Relaxation Response*. New York: William Morrow, 1975.

Boutelle, Jane & Baker, Samm Sinclair. *Jane Boutelle's Lifetime Fitness for Women*. New York: Simon & Schuster, 1978.

Brown, Barbara B. *Stress and the Art of Biofeedback*. New York: Harper & Row, 1977.

Carrington, Patricia. *Freedom in Meditation*. Garden City, NY: Doubleday, Anchor Press, 1977.

Corriere, Richard & Hart, Joseph. *Psychological Fitness; Twenty-One Days to Feeling Good*. New York: Harcourt Brace Jovanovich, 1979.

Lowen, Alexander. *Bioenergetics*. New York: Coward, McCann & Geoghegan, 1975.

LeShan, Lawrence L. *How to Meditate; A Guide to Self-discovery*. Boston: Little, Brown, 1974.

Mayer, Jean. *A Diet for Living*. New York: McKay, 1975.

Selye, Hans. *Stress Without Distress*. Philadelphia: Lippincott, 1974.

Spino, Mike. *Beyond Jogging; The Innerspace of Running*. Berkeley, CA: Medallion Books, 1976.

Pamphlets

Aesthetic Cosmetic Surgery, single copies free, American Medical Association, Dept. OP 208, P.O. Box 821, Monroe, WI 53566.

After the Diet . . . Then What?, $1, Campbell Soup Co., Box 8717, Clinton, IA 52736

How to Select a Cosmetic Facial Surgeon, single copies free, American Academy of Facial, Plastic and Reconstructive Surgery, 70 West Hubbard St., Chicago, IL 60610.

Stress, free, P.O. Box 4458, Grand Central Station, New York, NY 10017.

Stress and Your Health, free, Metropolitan Life Insurance, 1 Madison Ave. New York, NY 10016.

MONEY AND INVESTING

Blodgett, Richard E. *The New York Times Book of Money*. Rev. and updated ed. New York: Quadrangle, 1976.

Brown, Robert N. *The Rights of Older People*. New York: Avon, 1979.

Dreman, David N. *Psychology and the Stock Market: Investment Strategy beyond Random Walk*. New York: Amacom, 1977.

Galbraith, John Kenneth & Salinger, Nicole. *Almost Everyone's Guide to Economics*. Boston: Houghton Mifflin, 1978.

Goldberg, Herb, and Lewis, Robert T. *Money Madness; The Psychology of Saving, Spending, Loving and Hating Money*. New York: Morrow, 1978.

Newman, Joseph, dir. ed., *Teach Your Wife How to Be a Widow*. Washington, DC: US News & World Report, 1977.

Porter, Sylvia Field. *Sylvia Porter's New Money Book for the 80's*. Garden City, NY: Doubleday, 1979.

Quinn, Jane Bryant. *Everyone's Money Book*. New York: Delacorte Press, 1979.

Strassels, Paul. *All You Need to Know About the IRS*. New York: Random House, 1980.

Tobias, Andrew P. *The Only Investment Guide You'll Ever Need*. New York: Harcourt Brace Jovanovich, 1978.

Tuccille, Jerome. *Everything the Beginner Needs to Know to Invest Shrewdly*. New Rochelle, NY: Arlington House, 1978.

Williams, John M. *A Woman's Guide to Successful Investing*. Garden City, NY: Doubleday, 1975.

Pamphlets

Budgets: Planning with Your Beneficiaries, free, Educational & Community Services, American Council of Life Insurance, 1850 K Street, Washington, DC 20006.

Borrowing Basics for Women, free, Citibank, 399 Park Ave., New York, NY 10043.

Home Buyers Information Package, free. Katherine O'Leary, Division of Products, Dissemination and Transfer, HUD, Washington, DC 20410.

Investor's Information Kit, free, New York Stock Exchange, P.O. Box 252, Dept. M. New York, NY 10005.

Social Security: The following booklets may be obtained free at your local Social Security office: *A Woman's Guide to Social Security; Your Social Security; Social Security Checks for Students 18 to 22; The Advantages of Social Security; Women and Social Security.*

The Credit Handbook for Women, free from American Express, Box 929, New York, NY 10010.

Women: *To Your Credit,* free from Commercial Credit, Baltimore, MD 20202.

Magazines and Newspapers
Business Week
Dollar $ense, distributed by E.F. Baumer & Co., 41 Shatto Place, Los Angeles, CA 90020, to member banks in 21 cities and offered without charge to customers.
Forbes
Money Magazine
US News & World Report
Wall Street Journal

Job Hunting and Careers

Bird, Caroline. *Enterprising Women.* New York: W.W. Norton, 1976.

Bolles, Richard Nelson. *What Color Is Your Parachute? A Practical Guide for Job-Hunters & Career Changers.* Berkeley, CA: Ten Speed Press, 1972.

The Catalyst Staff. *Marketing Yourself: The Catalyst Women's Guide to Successful Resumés and Interviews.* New York: Putnam, 1980.

————. *What to Do with the Rest of Your Life: The Catalyst Career Guide for Women in the 80s.* New York: Simon & Schuster, 1980.

Fox, Marcia. *Put Your Degree to Work: A Career-planning and Job-hunting Guide for the New Professional.* New York: W.W. Norton, 1979.

Foxworth, Jo. *Boss Lady; An Executive Woman Talks about Making It*. New York: Crowell, 1978.

Gabriel, Joyce, and Baldwin, Bettye. *Having It All*. New York: M. Evans, 1980.

Harragan, Betty. *Games Mother Never Taught You: Corporate Gamesmanship for Women*. New York: Rawson Associates, 1977.

Hennig, Margaret, and Jardim, Anne. *The Managerial Woman*. Garden City, NY: Doubleday, Anchor Press, 1977.

Higginson, Margaret V., and Quick, Thomas L. *The Ambitious Woman's Guide to a Successful Career*. New York: Amacom, 1975.

Hunt, Ruth. *Job Tests for Women; How to Identify Your Skills and Work Needs so You Can Get the Job That Is Perfect for You*. New York: Ace, 1980.

Kellogg, Mary Alice. *Fast Track; The Superachievers and How They Make It to Early Success, Status and Power*. New York: McGraw-Hill, 1978.

King, David, and Levine, Karen. *The Best Way in the World for a Woman to Make Money: The Founder of Careers for Women Tells How to Get In and Move Up Through Executive Sales*. New York: Rawson Associates, 1979.

Korda, Michael. *Success! How Every Man and Woman Can Achieve It*. New York: Random House, 1977.

Nash, Katherine. *Get the Best of Yourself; How to Find Your Success Pattern and Make it Work for You*. New York: Grosset & Dunlap, 1976.

Pamphlets

A Woman's Guide to Apprenticeship, free, enclose self-addressed label. US Department of Labor, Women's Bureau, Washington, DC 20210.

A Working Woman's Guide to Her Job Rights, single copies $1.60. US Department of Labor, Superintendent of Documents, US Government Printing Office, Washington DC 20402.

Career Opportunities for You in Life Insurance, free, American Council of Life Insurance, 1850 K St. NW, Washington, DC 200006.

Careers Working with Animals, $5.95, Humane Society, 2100 L St. NW, Washington, DC 20037.

Job-Finding Techniques for Mature Women, Women's Department, US Department of Labor, Superintendent of Documents, US Government Printing Office, Washington, DC 20402.

Reaching Out, a description of Women's Educational Equity Act Program, free, WEAP Dissemination Center, 55 Chapel St., Newton, MA 02060.

The Job Outlook in Brief, free, enclose self-addressed label, Women's Bureau, US Department of Labor, Washington, DC 20210.

Toward Matching Personal and Job Characteristics, free, enclose self-addressed label, US Department of Labor, Washington, DC 20210.

Newspaper Columns and Magazines

"Advice to the Job-Lorn," every week in the *Soho News*, by Dave Lindorff. Soho Weekly News, 514 Broadway, New York, NY 10012.

"Careers," appears Wednesday in the *New York Times*, by Elizabeth M. Fowler.

New Directions for Women, listing employment news and training opportunities, quarterly, $3 a year, Box 27, Dover, NJ 07801.

Savvy, the magazine for executive women, monthly, 111 Eight Ave. New York, NY 10011.

Working Woman, monthly, 600 Madison Ave., New York, NY 10022.

Appendix

B

OTHER RESOURCES

WIDOW AND BEREAVEMENT PROGRAMS

As a result of the self-help and mutual-help movement, many one-of-a-kind groups for widows and widowers have sprung up all over the country. Some of the grass roots clubs are among the best. They meet in local restaurants, spaces donated by local mental health organizations, business offices after hours, hospitals, funeral homes. Social workers can steer you toward one near you, or look for meeting announcements in local newspapers. Hotlines such as the ones run by FISH (a national nondemonimational service organized through local churches in which volunteers act as "brothers" to those who need help), by the Shanti Project in California (415–524–4370) and by various Community Health Centers also have lists of such organizations. Or you can get in touch with the national and regional offices listed below for names and addresses of clubs near you. For $2, the nationwide Widowed Persons Service will send you their extensive listing of local WPS and other related groups in the United States and Canada.

NATIONAL GROUPS

COPO (Catholic One Parent Organization). Contact the Family Life Division of your local Catholic Archdioces, Apostate Division.

National Hospice Organization, 1750 Old Meadow Road, Bethesda, MD 20014.

Society of Military Widows, P.O. Box 1714, La Mesa, CA 92041.
THEOS (They Help Each Other Spiritually) Suite 106, Penn
Hills, Mall Office Bldg. Pittsburgh, PA 15235.
Widowed Persons Service NRTA-AARP, 1909 K Street NW,
Washington, DC 20049.

REGIONAL GROUPS

Coordinating Council of Widowed Services, Southeastern Michi-
gan, Inc., 17300 Haggerty Road, Livonia, MI 48152.
Grief Education Institute, P.O. Box 623, Englewood, CO 80001.
NAIM, Catholic club for the widowed. US Catholic Conference,
Family Life Division, 721 N. La Salle Dr., Chicago, IL 60610.
Northwest Conference for the Widowed (Washington, Oregon,
Idaho, California), 2321 West 15th Ave., Kennewick, WA
99336.
St. Claire's Hospital Community Center, Pocono Road, Denville,
NJ 07834.
TLA (To Live Again) chapters in Pennsylvania and Delaware.
P.O. Box 103, West Chester, PA 19380.
University of Wisconsin–Madison Center for Health Sciences,
Phyllis Carey, Bereavement, 600 Highland Ave., Madison, WI
53792.

SPECIALIZED GROUPS

Cancer Care, One Park Avenue, New York, NY 10016.
Grief Counseling for Survivors of Sudden Death, P.O. Box 179,
Walnut Crest, CA 94596.
Survivors (of suicide victims) 27060 Cedar Rd. #108, Beachwood,
OH 44122.
Young Widows and Widowers of Westchester, Jewish Community
Services, 172 South Broadway, White Plains, NY 10605.

SINGLE-PARENT PROGRAMS

Momma, c/o Jean Towsend, 200 East 4th St., Santa Ana, CA
92705.

Parents Without Partners. Check your local telephone book or write the national headquarters, 7910 Woodmount Ave., Bethesda, MD 20014.

The Single Parent Resource Center, 3896 24th St., San Francisco, CA 94114.

TEEN-AGE SERVICES

Big Brother or Big Sister. Check your local telephone book or write Surburban Station, Philadelphia, PA 19103.

Teen-Age Hot Lines. See your telephone book or consult a mental health center near you.

PROGRAMS FOR ALCOHOLISM AND OBESITY

Alcoholics Anonymous. Look in your local telephone book.

Association of Drink Watchers International, P.O. Box 179, Haverstown, NY 10927.

Overeaters Anonymous. Check your local telephone book or write to them at World Service Office, 2190 190th St., Torrance, CA 90504.

Responsible Drinkers, P.O. Box 1062, Burlingame, CA 94010.

FOR CHILDREN UNDER TEN

Barr-Harris Center for the Study of Separation & Loss During Childhood, 180 N. Michigan Ave., Chicago, IL 60710. Direct services to families with young children, community education and consultation service.

CAREER COUNSELING AND SEMINARS

American Women's Economic Development Corp., free training for women starting their own businesses. 1270 Ave. of the Americas, New York, NY 10020.

Business and Professional Women's Foundation, administers career funding and scholarship programs for women over 30. 2012 Massachusetts Ave. NW, Washington, DC 20036.

Catalyst, a nonprofit organization, sponsors a national network of 190 Career Resource Centers and will make referrals to career counseling and continuing education programs across the country. Write them at 14 East 60 St., New York, NY 10017.

Chemistry Instrumentation, a two-week program funded by General Electric Foundation, Mt. Holyoke College, South Hadley, MA 01075.

Clairol Loving Care Scholarship Program awards grants up to $1000 to women over 30 who are studying on the undergraduate or master's level in professional schools for vocational training. The program funds both full- and part-time education and grant money can be used for tuition as well as child care, transportation, books, etc. Clairol Loving Care Scholarship Program, 245 Park Ave., New York, NY 10022.

Council for Career Planning, a nonprofit organization, gives individual counseling to women with college degrees. Fees vary; all sessions under $100 for three one-hour sessions. 310 Madison Ave., New York, NY 10017.

Counseling Women, six-week workshop for women reentering the job market, given spring, fall, and winter, $150. 14 East 60th St., New York, NY 10022.

Direct Marketing Association offers courses in cities across the country and also will supply lists of individuals offering direct mail courses. Fees vary. 6 East 42nd St., New York, NY 10016.

Displaced Homemakers Network, funded through CETA (Comprehensive Educational Training Act) by the Department of Labor, offers supportive counseling and seminars aimed at quick employment for women who have not worked for several years. Preference is given to women in need of paid employment. For the most recent national listing of centers, projects, and programs providing services, send $1 for the *Displaced Homemaker Program Directory* to Displaced Homemakers Network, Inc. 755 8th St. NW, Washington, DC 20001.

Hunter College, Center for Lifelong Learning. Seminars for women with college degrees and family responsibilities. Ten weeks, $225. 695 Park Ave., New York, NY 10021.

The Institute for the Study of Women in Transition explores alternatives for single women in careers, finance, politics. 5 Market St., Portsmouth, NH 03810.

Katherine Nash Associates. Individual counseling, $50 an hour. 251 Central Park West, New York, NY 10024.

Mid-Career Counseling Center, SUNY. Seminars on career development and vocational counseling. Seminars, $40. Individual counseling, $40 for two sessions. Stony Brook, Long Island, NY 11794.

North Country Connections. Workshops and seminars on career development and vocational counseling. Box 2201, Oceanside, CA 92054.

Univance Career Centers (see your local telephone book) offer career counseling in Los Angeles, Sacramento, and San Francisco, CA.

Vistas for Women. Workshops in career planning, $55. Individual counseling on a sliding scale from $3 to $40. YMCA, 515 North Street, White Plains, NY 10605.

Voluntary Education Program, run by the Defense Department, offers free aptitude testing, career guidance and training in over 200 fields for service men and women. These courses are given at virtually every military base at sea, and even at missile silos.

Wider Opportunities for Women Work Center trains economically disadvantaged women for careers as carpenters, electricians, service technicians. 1649 K St. NW, Washington, DC 20006.

Womanspace. The School of General Studies at Columbia University directs an eight-month career internship project which matches participants with employers in a wide variety of fields. Write Career Internship Project, 306 Lewisohn Hall, School of General Studies, Columbia University, New York, NY 10027.

Women in Information Processing, national network for women in the field of computers, word procession, offers career counseling, resumé guidance, a scholarship program, newsletter and publications. Charter membership, $40, student membership, $25. 1000 Connecticut Ave. NW, Washington, DC 20036.

Women's Information Service, (WISE) offers free job counseling, 38 Main St. Hanover, NH 03755.

Women's Resource Center, funded by a Ford Foundation grant, helps mature Michigan women find new careers. 226 Bostwick NE, Grand Rapids, MI 48603.

DIRECTORIES

Directory of Personal Image Consultants. Listing consultants in seventy-five cities and thirty-four states who deal with public speaking, workshops in self-esteem, etc. At your library or $17.50 from the Editorial Services Co. 1140 Ave. of the Americas, New York, NY 10036.

Financial Aid: Where to Get It, How to Use It. Business and Professional Women's Foundation, 2012 Massachusetts Ave. NW, Washington, DC 20036, $1 plus self-addressed stamped envelope.

Internship Programs for Women (1980) provides information on many internships, $3 from National Society for Internships and Experimental Education, 1735 U St. NW, Washington, DC 20006.

Jobs in the Arts and Art Administration lists national sources for career counseling and job placement and referral in the arts, $1. The Center for Arts Information, 625 Broadway, New York, NY 10012.

The National Association of Women Business Owners supplies information for women starting their own businesses. 2000 P Street NW, Washington, DC 20036.

The National Center for Educational Brokering lists employment counseling services for women in its directory. 405 Oak St., Syracuse, NY 13203.

U.S. Small Business Administration (PASS Program), 1441 L Street, Washington, DC 20416.

Wider Opportunities for Women, Inc. lists employment counseling organizations for women, 1649 K Street NW, Washington, DC 20006.

A Woman's Guide to Career Preparation: Scholarships, Grants, and Loans. Career guidance, sources of financial aid and alternative methods of education, $5.95. Ann J. Jawin, Garden City, NY: Doubleday, 1979.

The Women's Educational Equity Communications Network offers Resource Roundup #5, "Expanding the Options of Older Women" and Top Sheet #1, "Are You a Displaced Homemaker?" Send a stamped self-addressed envelope to WEECN, Far West Lab, 1855 Folsom St., San Francisco, CA 94103.

Women's Networks: The Complete Guide to Getting a Better Job, Advancing Your Career and Feeling Great As a Woman Through Networking. Discussion and state-by-state lising of varied networks. By Carol Klein, New York, Lippincott and Crowell, 1980, $5.95.

INDEX